The Illustrated
Pirate Diaries

Copyright © 2008 Marshall Editions
A Marshall Edition
Conceived, edited, and designed by Marshall Editions
The Old Brewery
6 Blundell Street
London N7 9BH

HarperCollins books may be purchased for educational, business, or sales promotional use. For
information please write to: Special Markets Department, HarperCollins Publishers, 10 East
53rd Street, New York, NY 10022.

FIRST EDITION
Library of Congress Cataloging-in-Publication has been applied for.
ISBN: 978-0-06-158448-0

08 09 10 11   10 9 8 7 6 5 4 3 2 1

Printed in bound in China by SNP Leefung Printers Ltd

Publisher: Richard Green
Art Director: Ivo Marloh
Managing Editor: Paul Docherty
Project Editor: Amy Head
Design: Two Associates
Picture research: Veneta Bullen
Indexer: Lynn Bresler
Production: Nikki Ingram

The Illustrated
Pirate Diaries

A Remarkable Eyewitness Account of
Captain Morgan and the Buccaneers

ALEXANDER EXQUEMELIN

TERRY BREVERTON, CONSULTING EDITOR

Collins

An Imprint of HarperCollinsPublishers

Left: This map by Willem Blau of the Caribbean islands (c.1650) includes Cuba, Hispaniola, Jamaica, and the coastline of central America.

CONTENTS

EDITOR'S PREFACE

⁓

A GENERAL

HISTORY

OF THE

Robberies and Murders

Of the moſt notorious

PYRATES,

AND ALSO

Their *Policies, Diſcipline* and *Government,*

From their firſt RISE and SETTLEMENT in the Iſland
of *Providence,* in 1717, to the preſent Year 1724.

WITH

The remarkable ACTIONS and ADVENTURES of the two Female Pyrates, *Mary Read* and *Anne Bonny.*

To which is prefix'd

An ACCOUNT of the famous Captain *Avery* and his Com
panions; with the Manner of his Death in *England.*

The Whole digeſted into the following CHAPTERS;

Chap. I. Of Captain *Avery.*   VIII. Of Captain *England.*
 II. The Riſe of Pyrates.   IX. Of Captain *Davis.*
 III. Of Captain *Martel.*   X. Of Captain *Roberts.*
 IV. Of Captain *Bonnet.*   XI. Of Captain *Worley.*
 V. Of Captain *Thatch.*   XII. Of Captain *Lowther.*
 VI. Of Captain *Vane.*   XIII. Of Captain *Low.*
 VII. Of Captain *Rackam.*   XIV. Of Captain *Evans.*
And their ſeveral Crews.

To which is added,

A ſhort ABSTRACT of the Statute and Civil Law, in.
Relation to PYRACY.

By Captain CHARLES JOHNSON.

LONDON, Printed for *Ch. Rivington* at the *Bible* and *Crown* in St.
Paul's Church-Yard, J. Lacy at the *Ship* near the *Temple-Gate,* and
J. Stone next the *Crown* Coffee-houſe the back of *Greys-Inn,* 1724.

Title-page of the First Edition, 1724

This wonderful partial biography by Exquemelin is our main source for information on the buccaneers and pirates of the 17th century. Four decades later, Daniel Defoe (under the pseudonym of Captain Charles Johnson) gave us his remarkable *A General History of the Robberies and Murder of the Most Notorious Pyrates* in 1724. Defoe's book was taken from various sources, including trial transcripts; for example, that of the crew of Black Bart Roberts, the greatest pirate trial in history. Exquemelin's account inspired early novelists like Defoe to begin writing pirate fiction and resulted in hundreds of imitations—they even paraphrased his descriptions. To Exquemelin's book, more than any other, we owe our stereotypes of pirate characters and actions. According to Edward Cox, "This work became the inspiration of a vast number of novels, plays, imaginary voyages, and doubtless inspired many an adventurous spirit to turn sea-rover... It has well been called the classic of buccaneering books."

These two books of Exquemelin and Defoe (Johnson) not only recorded factual (and some fictional) events, but also stimulated perpetual interest in their protagonists. The difference is that Exquemelin actually sailed with the buccaneers, under Captain Henry Morgan, Rock the Brazilian, and others—he witnessed the events first hand. However, even today we are unsure of Exquemelin's origins. He has been variously described as Flemish, Dutch, Breton, and a French Huguenot; most often as a Dutchman. Despite this, it seems that he was born in Honfleur, France, in 1646 and died around 1707. The first edition of his book was principally entitled *De Americaensche Zee-Roovers* and published in 1678 in Amsterdam in Dutch, although the original manuscript was probably in French. This was followed by a 1679 German edition, printed in Nuremburg and called *Americanische Seerauber,* and the 1681 Spanish edition, *Los Piratas de America.* The first two English editions were printed in 1684: that of William Crook, based upon the Spanish edition; and that of Thomas Malthus, based on the Dutch edition. *Histoire des Adventuriers,* with some additions, was published in Paris in 1686. In seven years, Exquemelin's book had been printed in all of the main European nations.

Exquemelin seems to have been a descendant of Huguenot apothecaries. Some sources state that he studied surgery in Rouen and Paris for six years, but Louis XIV issued a decree in 1666 forbidding Huguenots from practising medicine. He signed on as an engagé (or indentured servant) to the recently formed La Compagnie des Indes Occidentales (French West India Company), and sailed to Tortuga on the *Saint Jean* in May 1666. Soon after his arrival, the Company was in financial difficulties and he was sold to the Governor's cruel deputy, as he relates in his book. Fortunately he was sold on to a surgeon, and

"$\mathcal{T}$*his work became the inspiration of a vast number of novels, plays, imaginary voyages, and doubtless inspired many an adventurous spirit to turn sea-rover … It has well been called the classic of buccaneering books."*

St. NICHOLAS

★

Above: An illustration by Manning DeVilleneuve Lee on the cover of a popular children's magazine, October 1924.

Opposite: Frontispiece of the 1724 edition of Daniel Defoe's *The History of the Pyrates*—he used the pseudonym Captain Charles Johnson to add gravitas and to keep his earnings.

bought his freedom after a year, thereupon joining the bucaniers (buccaneers). He entered service as a ship's surgeon, although still unqualified, took part in the expeditions to Maracaibo in 1669 and Panama in 1670-71, under the command of Captain Henry Morgan, and also sailed under Roche Brasiliano.

After leaving the buccaneers, Exquemelin left the West Indies on a Dutch ship sailing out of Cuba, and was in Amsterdam in 1672. Between 1672 and 1686 he made at least three other voyages to America. In the spring of 1674 he enlisted at Amsterdam as a chief-surgeon in Admiral de Ruyter's fleet, which set out to attack the French Antilles. France had overrun much of Holland, and it was in revenge for this invasion that de Ruyter arrived off Martinique aboard his flagship *The Seven Provinces* in July 1674, with 18 warships, 9 storeships, and 15 troop transports bearing 3,400 soldiers. Attempting to assault Fort Royal, his fleet was becalmed, and the next day new booms prevented de Ruyter from entering the harbor. Dutch soldiers went ashore without the support of the fleet's guns. Within two hours they were returning to the fleet, with 143 killed and 318 wounded. Exquemelin must have been heavily involved in attending to these casualties.

The fleet then returned to Europe, while disease spread aboard the ships. In 1676 de Ruyter took command of a combined Dutch-Spanish fleet to help the Spanish suppress the Messina Revolt. He fought a French fleet twice in the Mediterranean, at the Battle of Stromboli and at the Battle of Agosta, where he was fatally wounded when a cannonball hit his left leg. It appears that Exquemelin had sailed with de Ruyter again, since his power of attorney was not cancelled until November 30th, 1676 (an uncle had legal power to manage his affairs). In 1677 Exquemelin tried to join the English navy as a surgeon's mate for a second time; but after a parliamentary interdict on foreign surgeons, he returned to Amsterdam.

By this time Exquemelin had completed the manuscript of his experiences, which was published by the Amsterdam printer and bookseller Jan ten Hoorn in 1678—*De Americaensche Zee-Roovers*. However, the printer did not merely translate the manuscript from French into Dutch. He omitted some parts, rewrote others, and added a chapter, to make the book more appealing to its Dutch audience. Amsterdam archives record Exquemelin as a "surgeon and stranger" in September 1679. In October 1679 he passed his surgeon's last examination, which enabled him to practice his profession in Holland as he had done at sea. He is at this time listed on the books of the Dutch Surgeons' Guild and had been granted Dutch citizenship.

The book quickly became successful, with many different editions appearing throughout Europe in the following years, some of them illegally copied, or "pirated." The history of Exquemelin's book is, in fact, better known than that of his life. In 1679, the account was translated into German. In 1681 the first Spanish edition, containing many previously unpublished details, was printed in Cologne. The translator was the Spaniard Alonso de Buena Maison, a doctor of medicine from the University of Leyde. This translator was Exquemelin's housemate and a fellow surgeon—a Christianized Jew who had fled from the Spanish Inquisition. Buena Maison rewrote the book, as he did not want to give too much offence to the Spanish audience. Despite these efforts, a Spanish Marquess later claimed to have had Buena Maison and Exquemelin expelled from Amsterdam for their insults to his country (and perhaps his religion).

Below: There were two English editions in 1684. This second edition portrayed Henry Morgan as a hero instead of a villain.

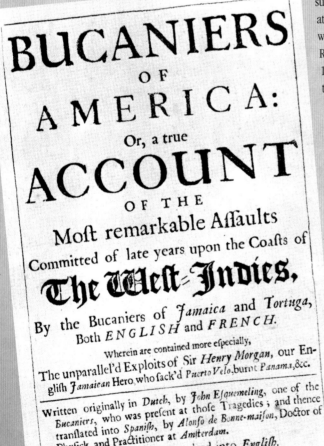

BUCANIERS
OF
AMERICA:
Or, a true
ACCOUNT
OF THE
Moſt remarkable Aſſaults
Committed of late years upon the Coaſts of
The Weſt=Indies,
By the Bucaniers of *Jamaica* and *Tortuga*,
Both *ENGLISH* and *FRENCH*.

Wherein are contained more eſpecially,
The unparallel'd Exploits of Sir *Henry Morgan*, our Engliſh *Jamaican* Hero, who ſack'd *Puerto Velo*, burnt *Panama*, &c.

Written originally in *Dutch*, by *John Eſquemeling*, one of the
Bucaniers, who was preſent at thoſe Tragedies ; and thence
tranſlated into *Spaniſh*, by *Alonſo de Bonne-maiſon*, Doctor of
Phyſick, and Practitioner at *Amſterdam*.

Now faithfully rendred into *Engliſh*.

LONDON:
Printed for *William Crooke*, at the Green Dragon without Temple-bar. 1 6 8 4.

We next find Exquemelin and Buena Maison aboard the *San Jeroboam* in 1681, bound for Jamaica. Exquemelin founded a surgeon's practice in San Domingo, but this proved not to be a success. In 1683 the Spanish tried to capture the Ostend slaver *Martha and Maria*, commanded by privateer Captain Nicholas van Hoorn, and Exquemelin returned to sea as the surgeon of a pirate fleet. Its captains included the Dutch pirate Laurens de Graff and French buccaneer Michel de Grammont.

The London publishers William Crook and Thomas Malthus each printed an English version of the book in 1684, with Exquemelin's name anglicised to "Esquemeling." It was entitled *Bucaniers of America; or a true account of the … assaults committed …upon the coasts of the West Indies, by the Bucaniers of Jamaica … especially the … exploits of Sir Henry Morgan … written originally in Dutch by J. Esquemeling … now rendered into English, London 1684.* A second edition followed within three months.

However, Sir Henry Morgan, the ex-Jamaican privateer and for a time Governor of Jamaica, was offended by some parts of the book. In the first successful libel trial in British history, the two English publishers were prosecuted. There followed a different English version in 1684, vindicating Morgan and absolving him of the cruelties and lusts so obvious in the first two editions. The new book was entitled *The History of the Bucaniers; being an impartial account of all the battels, sieges, and other most eminent assaults committed for several years upon the coasts of the west Indies by the pirates of Jamaica and Tortuga. More especially the unparalleled achievements of Sir Henry Morgan…. Very much corrected from the errors of the original, by the relations of some English gentlemen, that then resided in those parts.*

In 1685, Crook and Malthus were condemned to pay Morgan an indemnity and to rectify the facts in the preface of the book. The publishers made the following public apology: "There have been lately printed and published two works, one by Wil. Crook, the other by Tho. Malthus, both initialled The History of the Bucaniers: both which books contained many false, scandalous and malicious reflections on the life and actions of Sir Henry Morgan, of Jamaica, Kt. The said Sir Henry Morgan hath

Above: This original Dutch edition, from 1678, called the buccaneers *Zee-Roovers* (Sea-Rovers).

There followed a different English version in 1684, vindicating Morgan and absolving him of all the cruelties and lusts so obvious in the first two editions.

Morgan's uncles were the Royalist General Edward Morgan and the Parliamentarian General Thomas Morgan, who took part in the English Civil War. Another of his father's brothers lived in the mansion known as Llanrumney Hall, in Glamorgan, Wales.

by judgment had in the Kingsbench-Court, recovered against the said libel £200 damages. And on the humble solicitation and request of William Crook, hath been pleased to withdraw his action against Crook, and accept of his submission and acknowledgment in print."

Many facts in the book were sensationalized to sell these English editions. For example, it is a matter of Spanish contemporary records that the Spanish governor, not Morgan, fired Panama to stop the privateers from gaining booty and provisions. Also, his description of Morgan as an indentured servant is false. Morgan's uncles were the Royalist General Edward Morgan and the Parliamentarian General Thomas Morgan, who took part in the English Civil War. Another of his father's brothers lived in the mansion known as Llanrumney Hall, in Glamorgan, Wales. There were nine further editions by different London publishers over the next hundred years, testifying to its enduring popularity.

It seems that at last Exquemelin decided to settle down. Not only that, it appears that he renounced his Protestant faith. We can draw these conclusions from his appearance in the 1684 parish records of St. Germain-des-Près (a Catholic church in Paris) as *le Sieur Alexandre Olivier Hessequemelain, chyrurgyen de son estat*. However, the following year Louis XIV revoked the Edict of Nantes, depriving Huguenots of their civil rights and citizenship. It seems that Exquemelin was now forced to rejoin Michel de Grammont's pirates, based in the French West Indies. We find him in Paris again in 1686, where he is working on a commission for the French Royal Navy, an account of the Chagres River. He was presented to the Admiral d'Estrées, whom he possibly first saw 15 years earlier, after the sack of Maracaibo. This same year, the Parisian publisher Jacques Lefebvre printed a new edition of his book under the author's name of Oexmelin. Somehow, through all these vagaries of fortune, it appears that Exquemelin had retained his original manuscript (with maps from the cartographer l'Abbé Baudrand and under the patronage of d'Estrées), as there were ten new chapters in Lefebvre's edition, and extra botanical descriptions. Another possible explanation for the significant changes is that the manuscript may have been rewritten by Exquemelin in the intervening years. *Histoire des Aventuriers qui se sont signalez dans les Indes* was a huge success, leading to a second edition in 1687.

Finally accepted in France, Exquemelin next recorded all his experiences since 1678, which became the third French edition of his book, published in 1699 as *Histoire des Aventuriers Flibustiers*. Exquemelin must have returned to sea yet again, as he is recorded as having taken part in the successful French attack by Baron de Pointis on Cartagena, in Colombia, in 1697. Exquemelin vanishes from history after 1707, but his book remained a bestseller in France, growing to four volumes in new editions over the years. After Henry Morgan's death in 1688 there were many more editions, adding further accounts of buccaneering. By the 1690s, an English edition in four volumes, by the publisher Newborough, was so popular that ten Hoorn, the original publisher, translated it back into Dutch for a 1700 edition.

This version of Exquemelin—and there are hundreds—has been lightly edited, and is in four parts instead of the original three. We can see that each nation had a different version of the book, so the Dutch, French, and Spanish versions have all been used to inform this edition. As the bibliophile Joseph Sabin (1821-1881) rightly said, "Perhaps no book in any language was ever the parent of so many imitations and the source of so many fictions as this."

Opposite: The 1678 Dutch frontispiece openly endorses the English and French sea-rovers, who battled the Spanish in the Americas.

ISLE DE CUBA
aux Espagnols

Caya de Moua · Port de Baracoua · R. de Maran · M. de Baracoua · Pointe de Mayosi · Baye de Tequiry · Porto Descondido

LES FRERES DE LA CÔTE BOUCANIERS DE L'ISLE DE LA TORTUE

1492 1697

1697 1804

I. de Navaza

Cap Dame Marie

Pointe des Irois

Cap Tiberon · B. du C. Tiberon · P.te du vent · P.te des aigrettes · les Basses · Tapion de la Caouane · les Anglois · les Chardonieres · P.ta des Chardonieres · P.ta a Piment · les Damasini · Roche a bateau · l'Ance a Juif · l'Ance à Dric · Port Salut · Pointe a Gravois · Port a Nonet

P.te de la Seringue · Cap Rose · Trou Bonbon · Trou Jeremie · Grande Ance · Petite Caymite · Caymites · B.t de Marsoin · les Baraderes · R. de Nipes · Pointe de Nipes

Pays desert · M. de la Hotte division de la partie du sud · Ligne de division · QUARTIERS du SUD · R. de Cavaillon · R. serpente · Aquin · Cavaillon · les Anses · les 3 Rivieres · les Coteaux · le Fond · LES CAYES · R. de l'Acul · l'Etron de Porc · Isle a Vache · Pointe de l'Abacou · Caycalean · la Folle · Fond des Negres · B. St George · Petite et Grosse Caye · Fort St Louis · Baye du Mesle · B. a Flaman · R. de Cavaillon · Baye d'Aquin · les Grands Cotes de Fer · Benet · Cap de Benet · Jaquemel

Cap St Nicolas · Mole St Nicolas · Cap aux Four · la Plate forme · P.te de Jean Ravel · Port a Piemet · Plaine de Jean Ravel · Ripelou · QUARTIER · Port Paradis · Salines de Corido · Port a Piment · les Gonaives · Baye Tortue · R. de la Pierre · R. de l'Artibonite · Baye St Marc · Pointe de St Marc · P.te a Paturon · R. des Roseaux · Islets Arcadins ou de l'Arcahay · CUL DE SAC DE · ISLE DE GONAVE · R. de Monrou · Ance aux LEOGA · Basses · P.te de Miragoane · la Rouillone · R. de l'Acul · Islet Carenage · Acul · LEOG · P. Goave · PETIT GOAVE · GRAND GOAVE · DEBARQUEMENT DE CHRISTOPHE COLOMB au Mole St Nicola

TOUSSAINT L'OUVERTURE · GOUVERNEUR GENERAL · 1801

PART ONE

How the French first came to Hispaniola, and the origin of the buccaneers, with an account of their life on the island of Tortuga

Left: During the 1700s, Haiti became extremely wealthy, thanks to crops of sugar, rum, coffee, and cotton harvested by 500,000 slaves imported from Africa by French colonists. A violent slave rebellion in 1791 led to a 13-year civil war and recognition in 1804 of Haiti as the second republic (after the U.S.A.) in the western hemisphere.

CHAPTER I

Introduction—The author sails to the West Indies
in 1666, in the employ of the French West India
Company—Our arrival at Tortuga

Introduction

Before I recount my story of the greatest buccaneers of the century, the reader should realize that my first voyage was made not knowing that pirates are abundant in the West Indies. There are three main reasons for this profusion of pirates. Firstly, there are hundreds of uninhabited little sandy islands called cays, or keys, abounding with water turtle, shellfish, and fish. On these keys, the buccaneers can hide from the authorities, provision, and prepare their ships for their new expeditions. Secondly, the ships sailing in these waters, be they French, Spanish, English, or Dutch, are laden with great booty, especially those returning to Europe with the riches of the Spanish Main, and with fortunes made from the slave trade. Thirdly, pirate boats are much more suitable for the many shallow reefs, natural harbors, and inlets than the men-of-war of the navies of Europe.

These pirates usually start off in a small way, infesting the seas all along the coast from the Caribbean to North America, until they gain enough strength and resources to make an expedition via the Azores and the Cape Verde Islands to Guinea in West Africa. They then continue to take advantage of the currents and winds, sailing back to Brazil and the Caribbean.

I sail to the Western Islands

On May 2, 1666, I set sail on the *St. John*, from Le Havre, bound for the Western Isles (the West Indies). We carried 20 mariners, 220 passengers, and 28 guns. The passengers included indentured servants of the French West India Company and free persons with their servants. We anchored off the Cape of

Right: *Marooned* (1909), an oil painting by Howard Pyle, depicts the punishment for not sharing booty, for stealing from a fellow pirate, or for murdering one of "the brethren." The man was left on a deserted island, sometimes with a musket and one ball with which to kill himself. Other punishments for breaking "the code of the coast" were being thrown overboard and "Moses' Law," 39 lashes.

THE FRENCH WEST INDIA COMPANY

In 1664, the *Compagnie des Indes Occidentales* was formed by Frenchman Jean-Baptiste Colbert. A charter from King Louis XIV granted the Company stewardship of: Canada; Acadia (Nova Scotia, New Brunswick, Prince Edward Island, and part of Maine); the Antilles (Guadeloupe and Martinique); Cayenne Island and Guiana; and the mainland of South America, from the Amazon in Brazil to the River Orinoco in Venezuela. It had the trading monopoly in these areas, and also in Senegal and the Guinea coasts of Africa, for 40 years. By 1674, however, the Company was in deep financial trouble caused by the continuing wars with England and the fight to recover its Caribbean possessions from the Dutch. In that year its powers were rescinded by the king and investors reimbursed. The various territories it controlled became part of the French empire.

Jean-Baptiste Colbert (1619–1683) was concurrently Minister of Finance and Secretary of State of the Navy under Louis XIV.

Barfleur near Cherbourg to meet up with seven other ships of the Company, which had sailed from Dieppe. Our convoy was from there protected by a man-of-war of 250 men and 37 guns. Two ships were sailing to Senegal, five to the Caribbean, and our ship was destined for Tortuga. Around 20 more ships joined later, headed for Newfoundland, and some Dutch vessels bound for La Rochelle, Nantes, and St. Martin's Isle in the West Indies. Eventually around 30 French and Dutch ships had assembled. Our Admiral, the Chevalier Sourdis, led us close to the coast of France, as we had word that four English frigates, of 60 guns apiece, were waiting off Alderney in the Channel Islands to attack us. A Flemish ship from Ostend informed our Admiral that she had been raided that morning by a French corsair, so our man-of-war gave chase but could not find her.

We were fortunate to avoid the English warships in the foggy weather, but the peasants all along the coast were greatly alarmed, fearing that we were an English invasion fleet. We ran up French flags, but they showed no faith in them. We took on water and provisions at Le Conquet, near the Isle of Ushant in Brittany, and sailed the more dangerous route, continuing our voyage via the rocky currents of the Raz de Fonteneau to keep away from our enemy.

The wind was fair until Cape Finisterre, where a violent storm dispersed our fleet, and we were separated from the convoy. It lasted a full eight days. Our passengers lay sprawled all over the deck, suffering from sea sickness, and the hands were obliged to step on or over them to carry out their duties to keep the ship from foundering. We later had a favorable wind, which we badly needed as we were running out of water. We were rationed to just one-and-a-half pints of water a day.

Our arrival in Tortuga

Around Barbados, an English frigate chased us, but we saw that she had no real advantage, so we in our turn gave chase, firing with our 8-pound cannons, but she was better rigged and escaped. We came within sight of Martinique and tried to gain St. Peter's roadsteads, but a storm took us away and we resolved to steer to Guadeloupe. Again we were thwarted by the wind, so headed for our original destination of Tortuga, where we anchored on July 7 and landed the West India Company's goods. The ship then went on to Cul-de-Sac in northwest Hispaniola to disembark other passengers. We were fortunate not to have lost one man during the nine-week voyage.

Below: A rusted cannon juts out of the bay near Basse Terre, the lowland in the south of Tortuga, overlooked by Fort de la Roche. Tortuga was, in the 16th and 17th centuries, a main base for pirates and privateers preying on the Spanish plate fleets in the Caribbean.

CHAPTER II

A description of Tortuga and of its fruits, plants, and animals—How the French first settled there and twice were driven out by the Spanish—How I was sold on two occasions and then joined the buccaneers

A description of Tortuga

The Spanish gave this island the name Tortuga-del-Mar, as it resembles a great sea tortoise. It is sixteen leagues in circumference and lies just three leagues off the north coast of Hispaniola. The mountainous, heavily wooded part is uninhabited, and most people live in the southern lowlands, where there is the island's only harbor, Cayona. The richest planters live here. There is also Middle Plantation, only good for growing tobacco, La Ringot in the west, and the Mountain, where the first planters came.

Tortuga's fruits and plants

Trees grow very tall in Tortuga, including fustic, or furstic, which gives a yellow dye, and red, white, and yellow sandalwood. The yellow West Indian sandalwood is called by the inhabitants *bois de chandelle*, or candle-wood, as it burns like a candle and is used for night-fishing. Guaiacum also grows, and is used for the treatment of venereal diseases and for cold and viscous humors, so is known

Above: The green turtle was the favored turtle for eating and was eaten in port and aboard ship. They were kept alive on deck until required for cooking by being placed upside down, unable to move, then shaded from the sun and soaked with water every few hours.

Right: The calabash tree is depicted in a 16th-century Spanish engraving of Tortuga's fruits and plants. It was incredibly important for early settlers, who copied the Indian practice of drying or smoking the tough rind of the large fruits. They were then used as cups, jugs, and bowls, and especially for carrying and storing fresh water.

TORTUGA

Tortuga, discovered by Columbus in 1494, was named after the Spanish for "turtle" because of its humped shape. A few Spanish colonists lived there, but in 1625 French and English settlers arrived on the island after being forced out of Hispaniola. From 1630 onward, Tortuga was divided into French and English colonies, allowing the buccaneers to use the island as their main base of operations, although it was continually contested by the Spanish.

Some of the fortifications that still exist today stand as testament to this wrangling for territory. Basse-Terre, on the south-eastern coast, is home to the remains of Fort de la Roche, once the island's biggest fortress. A lime kiln, three cannons, and the foundations of a wall are all that is left of Fort Ogeron, which was built in the mid-1600s.

Tortuga, 25 miles long, provided fresh water and excellent defensive positions. In the south was a port named Cayona, which allowed several entries to ships and, more than this, easy escape. French governors, like their British counterparts at Port Royal, in Jamaica, relied upon buccaneers for local defense. In their turn, buccaneers needed such safe havens. They too opposed the Spanish.

By the year 1670, as the buccaneer era was in decline, many of the pirates, seeking a new source of trade, turned to log-cutting and trading wood from the island. At this time, Captain Henry Morgan started his expeditions from Jamaica and invited the pirates on the island of Tortuga to sail under him. They were then hired by the French as privateers—a striking force that allowed France to have a much stronger hold on the Caribbean region than they would have had

otherwise. Consequently, the pirates were never really controlled and kept Tortuga as a neutral hideout for pirate booty. In 1680, however, new Acts of Parliament began to limit the freedoms of privateers.

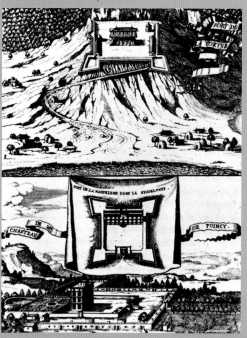

This 17th-century French engraving shows Governor Jean La Vasseur's impregnable fortress (top), Fort de la Roche, on Tortuga, and the fortified estate (bottom) on Guadeloupe belonging to Philippe de Poincy, the Governor General of the French islands in the Caribbean.

The incense-tree and china root also grow in abundance, along with aloes and medicinal herbs. The wild boar subsists on the china root, if it can find nothing else, although it is not as good as the china root of the East Indies. Also common are manioc, sweet potatoes, acajou apples, yams, melons, watermelons, cashew nuts, mammee apples, pineapples, bananas, plantains, guavas, and a lot of other produce. The islanders use palmettos, the small fan palm, to make wine, and the leaves cover their houses instead of tiles.

The animals of Tortuga

There are abundant wild boar, but the governor prohibited the hunting of them with dogs, lest the pigs might be wiped out. He thought this was necessary, as in the case of invasion the inhabitants could retreat to the woods and mountains and still find food. However, because of the rocks and precipices, many a huntsman has fallen to his death there.

Every year, huge flocks of pigeon come to Tortuga. There are far more than the people can consume, and so they do not bother killing other fowl for food. However, once the season is past, these pigeons become lean and exceedingly bitter to the taste, because of a certain type of seed that they consume.

Right: Montbars "the Exterminator" (born c. 1645 in Languedoc, France) was a freebooter based in Tortuga. He hated the Spanish after he saw his uncle killed in battle off San Domingo in 1667. He was famous for never giving quarter and attacked the coasts of Mexico, Honduras, Venezuela, the Spanish Main, Cuba, and Puerto Rico, taking forts and destroying cities.

Along the shore can be found large sea and land crabs, and these are good to feed to servants and slaves, although, when eaten too often, they can cause dizziness and may even produce temporary blindness for about a quarter of an hour.

How the French settled in Tortuga, and were twice driven out

The French had settled on the island of St. Christopher, called by the English St. Kitts. They planted trees, from the timber of which they made longboats and hoys. They then sailed to Hispaniola and found many cows, bulls, horses, and wild boar, but, as the Spanish were settled there, thought it convenient to seize the Isle of Tortuga instead. This was easily effected as no more than 10 or 12 Spaniards guarded it. Alarmed by the number of these new planters arriving, the Spanish set out to dispossess them.

The French, having no women or children to hinder them, vanished into the forests of Tortuga, and many also took canoes to hide on Hispaniola. When the Spanish left a small force to guard the island,

They set upon the Spanish with such ferocity that some leapt down the mountain to their deaths on the rocks below. Only a few escaped Tortuga.

the French again took over and asked the governor of St. Kitts to send provisions and reinforcements. M. Jean le Passeur was sent with a ship full of men, and he built a fortress to hinder any vessels from entering the harbor of Cayona.

This fort was constructed on a rock, with two cannon and a water supply sufficient for 1,000 men. The only ascent was by a ladder, which would be raised in a siege. More colonists now arrived. Some turned to hunting and collecting hides on Hispaniola. Others turned to piracy along the Spanish coasts. The rest, who had wives, grew tobacco, set up taverns, or traded on Tortuga. But by surprise, the Spaniards landed 800 men while many of the French were at sea or hunting. They used Indian slaves, called *matates*, to cut through the forests to haul two cannon onto the rocks above the M. le Passeur's fort. The colonists sent out word to their pirate comrades to return to defend the island. Knowing the forests, a party of Frenchmen climbed the mountain through the rainforest by secret paths and came upon the Spaniards as they were preparing to fire down on the fortress. They set upon the Spanish with such ferocity that some leapt from the mountain down to their death on the rocks below. Others were put to the sword. Only a few escaped Tortuga.

How I joined the buccaneers

In 1664 the French West India Company took possession of Tortuga, appointed M. Bertrand d'Ogeron as its governor, and he arrived in 1665. It had been agreed in France that the hunters, pirates, and planters could buy goods and supplies only from the Company, but it had major difficulty in getting the French in Tortuga to pay for anything, even when they were threatened by armed men.

Thus the Company was forced to sell up all its possessions. Its indentured servants were sold for only 20 or 30 pieces of eight each. As I had left France as a servant of the West India Company, I fell into the hands of the cruel lieutenant-governor of Tortuga. He misused me terribly. As I was starving I had become ill, so he agreed that I could buy my freedom for 300 pieces of eight. However, I became so poorly that he sold me for only 70 pieces. Under my next master I regained my health, and he said that I could buy my liberty for 100 pieces of eight, after I had served him for a year. At liberty, I needed to gain a living, so decided to join the pirates in 1669 and stayed in their company until 1672. I will now give the reader a true account of my time with them, but first a brief description of the Island of Hispaniola.

Left: This 1689 engraving is entitled *Pirates of the South Sea unloading their ill-gotten gains from a boat,* but actually shows them taking on fresh water. Water was mainly used for cooking and was often taken from river mouths by men in the ship's boat, so that the ship was not at risk.

CHAPTER III

A description of the island of Hispaniola and its flora and fauna

ↄ·ↄ

A description of Hispaniola

This abundant and fruitful island was discovered by Christopher Columbus in 1492, being in circumference 300 leagues, in length 120 leagues, and in breadth almost 50. There are many rich plantations and good and strong cities and towns, the capital being San Domingo. This is a walled city with a fort and fine harbor, sheltered from all winds except southerlies. It is on the south coast, 40 leagues from the eastern point of the island, Cape d'Espada. The governor, whom they call the president, lives there, and all the towns and villages receive their supplies from there, and the Spanish will only trade with that port.

Another city is St. Jago de los Caballeros, also called Santiago, or St. James, which has no castle and is surrounded by rich plains, yielding vast numbers of skins and hides for the prosperity of the city. To its south is Nuestra Senora de Alta Gracia, Our Lady of Grace, also called El Cotui, where cocoa is grown for the richest chocolate and also ginger and tobacco. Plenty of tallow is made from its cattle. The nearby island of Savona, or Saona, is the chief fishery for turtles. The Spanish took cattle to breed on Saona, but they were destroyed by buccaneers.

West of San Domingo is the handsome village of Azua, whose people trade with another village named San Juan de Goave in the middle of the island, next to a huge prairie full of wild cattle. This village produces great numbers of hides and quantities of tallow, but the soil is too dry for anything else. Only cow-skinners and hunters live in San Juan, most of mixed blood. Those of Negro and white parentage are called mulattoes, and those of Indian and white descent are mestizos. Those of mixed Negro and Indian blood are named *alcatraces*. The Spanish are fonder of Negro women than their own, so there is a great mingling of races.

Below left: These cannon are on the highly defended walls of the castle of Don Diego Colón, built in 1517, which has 40-inch-thick coral-limestone walls. Santo Domingo de Guzman, now in the Dominican Republic, was an important Spanish colonial city. It was made a UNESCO World Heritage Site in 1990.

Below right: This 1619 watercolor map shows the defenses and surroundings of Santo Domingo de Guzman when it was part of Hispaniola. The Spanish used this settlement as the first point of influence in the Americas, from which they spread and conquered much of the American mainland.

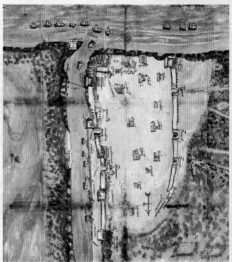

The Spanish possess most of Hispaniola, the rest being occupied by French planters and forest hunters. There are many excellent harbors and the rivers are full of fish. Not many Spaniards live in the north of the island, since it has been pillaged by the Dutch.

The fruits, trees, and animals of Hispaniola

The fields of Hispaniola are commonly five to six leagues in length, full of both sweet and sour oranges and lemons. There are also citrons, tangerines, and limes, which the English call crab-lemons. Date palms grow over 150 feet tall, and the fallen dates are coveted by hedgehogs. There is a sort of white cabbage growing at the top of these trees, which is boiled with all kinds of meat by the Spanish, just like cabbage. From this white bushy part is produced the leaves and seed-vessels. The tree's leaves are around 7 to 8 feet long by 3 to 4 feet wide and are excellent for roofs of houses, proof against the greatest downpours of rain. The Spanish also use these leaves to wrap up smoked meat and to carry water. You can also take the skin off the inner side of the leaf and use it as parchment for writing. If you wound the tree about 3 to 4 feet above the root, the liquid given off becomes liquor in a short time of fermentation, which quickly inebriates men. The French call this tree the frank-palm.

There are four other types of palm. The prickle palm is used by Indians to torture their prisoners. They tie the prisoner to a tree, then take the thorns, wrap them in cotton dipped in oil, and stick them into the sides of the misfortunate, so he looks like a hedgehog. If he sings, they will remember him with valor. If he cries out, they will refuse to remember him, as he has been a coward. The latanier palm is similar, but its leaves are like those of the date palm. The wine palm has an extraordinary shape, being very narrow at its base and much larger above. Its liquor makes good, clear wine, without any trouble, and its fruit are like cherries. They taste good but cause extreme stomach pain and quinsies. The rosary palm is so called because the French and Spanish make rosaries from its seeds.

Above: La Citadelle Haiti, an archaeological site in Haiti. It took Henri Christophe 15 years to build this vast mountaintop fortress, constructed to combat another invasion by the French. It is balanced on top of the 2,952-foot Pic la Ferrière. With 13 foot-thick walls that reach heights of 131 feet, the fortress was impenetrable.

Right: Deforestation in Haiti has meant that by 1990 only two to three percent of the country had tree cover. This caused soil erosion, which lowered the productivity of the land, worsened droughts, and led to desertification. Here we see a few surviving logwood trees.

There is also a type of apricot tree which grows ash-colored fruit, much loved by wild boars. The French hunters eat them instead of bread and call the tree an *abricot*. Trees called *caimitos* are like our European pear trees and produce fruit like Damascene plums or prunes. Genipa trees are like our cherry trees, with big ash-colored fruit, full of prickles under the skin that must be removed before eating. Otherwise one will get griping of the stomach. The juice of the ripe fruit is as black as ink, and can be used to write with, but the message disappears entirely within nine days. Its wood is excellent for shipbuilding and very resilient after years at sea.

The French call the cedar trees *acajou*, and they are used for building canoes, hollowed out and swift. The Indians make them without any iron, just by using fire to shape them. Some stand around to dampen the fire where and when needed, and others scrape out the burnt wood with stone axes, shaping

PLANT DYES

Of huge commercial value in Europe, logwood grew in great quantities in Mexico's Bay of Campeche, the Bay of Honduras (modern Belize), and across the West Indies. This dark-red tree, *Haematoxylum campechianium L.*, produced a black or brown dye, which did not fade in cloth like other existing dyes. The genus *Indigofera* (indigo) was harvested and refined in the West Indies and Spanish America to make a purple-blue powder, of huge value as a commercial dye in Europe. Before its discovery, most people's clothes were black, yellow-brown, or gray.

In the 1600s it was estimated that the average value of merchandise a ship could carry in a year was 1,000 to 1,500 pounds. A single load of 50 tons of logwood was worth more than an entire year's cargo of other merchandise.

the trunk into a canoe, which can put to sea for up to 100 leagues. As to medicinal preparations, there is the tree that gives our apothecaries *gum elemi* or pox-wood, also *lignum sanctum*, aloe-wood, *cassia lignea* (similar to cinnamon), china root, and several more. There are trees for making dyes, three types of sandalwood, and others used for building houses and ships.

The mapou tree is enormous. It is used for medicines but is not as good for making canoes as the cedar, since it becomes too waterlogged. Acoma wood is used to make the hard oars or sails for the sugar mills. Oak is used for houses and shipbuilding as it is not attacked by teredos worms. Brazilete, or brazil-wood, is known as fustic and is used for dyeing. It is common in the south, near the harbors of Jacmel and Jaquina, which can take large ships. The manzanilla, or dwarf-apple tree, grows on the sea shore and has deadly fruits. Its bark and resin are also poisonous. Once I took a branch to fan away insects from my face. The next day my face was swollen and blistered, and I could not see for three days. Icacos or cocoa plums are a fruit like damsons.

A fly that is as big as our European horse-fly sucks the blood until it is full and unable to fly. The Spanish call them mosquitoes. They incessantly torment human bodies, and we needed to constantly use the branch of a tree to fan them away. Most vexing is the unbearable noise they make in one's ears. Another insect is the size of a grain of sand, and it does not buzz and can penetrate linen. Hunters cover themselves with hog's grease and burn tobacco leaves at night to keep these away.

The third nuisance is a red mite—the *bête rouge*—only the size of a mustard grain, but which creates hideous ulcers on the face. The French call them *calarodes* and the Spanish *rojados*. There are also fire-flies, like glow-worms, and once I could read a book by the light of three of these insects in my cottage. There are huge numbers of noisy crickets, and many snakes, some of which are useful for getting rid of rats and mice. Other reptiles are useful for killing flies.

Left: This 16th-century engraving is named *The Spanish Battling Against Haitians*. The Spanish colonization of Haiti quickly wiped out the native Taíno population "in the name of the Holy Trinity." On neighboring Hispaniola, the Taíno population dropped from almost four million in 1496 to just 125 slaves in 1570.

CHAPTER IV

The animals of Hispaniola and the men who hunted them—The French tobacco planters on the island and their indentured servants

The caiman

The species of crocodile known as the caiman, or cayman, can grow to 70 feet long and 12 feet in breadth. They lie like an old tree fallen in the side of a river, waiting for a wild boar or cow to drink there. Then they seize the victim and drag it under. Before this they eat nothing for three to four days, but fill themselves with one or two hundredweight of stones to make sure they can drag down their prey underwater. After waiting for the corpse to putrefy, they devour it in a frenzy.

A reliable person told me that he was near a river and a caiman started dragging his tent into the water. The man put a knife in his mouth and started tugging back at the tent, but he was pulled into the water and the caiman attacked him. The man stuck his knife in the animal's belly, and it died of the wound. After dragging the caiman out of the water, the man found that there was a hundredweight of stones in its belly, all about the size of a fist. Caiman cannot hide, as they give off a strong smell of musk, produced by two glands in the throat, two below the forelegs, and two between the hind legs. Hunters send these glands to Europe for sale.

Every May, the caiman lay eggs on the sandy shore, cover them with sand, and leave them to hatch. The eggs are white, the size of goose eggs, and taste good. When hatched, the young go straight to the water, where they float on the surface for a few days. Their mother protects them from birds by taking them into her mouth. If the weather is fine, she will lie in the sun, and the young ones will come out to play on the sand, but if anyone approaches they scuttle back inside their mother's mouth. I have seen this myself when throwing a stone at a caiman on the far side of a river.

Wild dogs and horses

Apart from horses, cows, bulls, wild boar, and others, there are huge packs of wild dogs which every year destroy newly born calves and foals. They will even attack an entire herd of wild boar, until they have torn apart two or three of them for food. One day, when hunting with a French buccaneer, we saw that a pack of wild dogs had surrounded a wild boar, which was fighting them off next to a tree. We ourselves had climbed trees for safety, as well as being desirous to see the sport. With his tusks the boar had killed and wounded several dogs, but after an hour or so, still could not escape. Then, when he again attempted to flee, one of the dogs landed on his back and fastened upon the testicles, which at one pull it tore into pieces. The other dogs then fell upon the boar and killed him. They then lay on the ground around the beast, while that first bravest of the dogs ate his fill. Only then did the others begin to feed.

In 1668 Governor d'Ogeron of Tortuga brought large quantities of poison from France and laid poisoned corpses of horses all around the island for six months. Many dogs died. However, numbers soon grew back to normal. Their pups prove to be better than domestic dogs if trained to hunt by a buccaneer. These dogs were used to hunt native Indians when they hid in the forests. When found, the Indians were hacked to pieces by the buccaneers, then fed to the dogs. When the Indians had been exterminated, the Spanish had no use for the dogs, so the dogs took to the woods and fields and became

CAIMAN OF THE ISLANDS

The Spanish word for alligator is *caiman*, but the accounts of buccaneers and pirates from these times use the terms crocodile, caiman, cayman, and alligator interchangeably, and we are never sure of the species. There are 23 species of these reptiles in total, all of them endangered, found in tropical parts of Africa, Asia, Australia, and Central America.

The largest is the saltwater Indo-Pacific crocodile *Crocodylus porosus*, which can grow to 23 feet, and is found in eastern India, Australia, and the western Pacific, in both freshwater and saltwater habitats. The widespread American crocodile *Crocodylus acutus*, which can grow to 16 feet in length, still had some habitats in Jamaica, Cuba, and the Dominican Republic in the 17th century, but across the Caribbean Islands this species is now extinct. It is now found from the southern Florida coast to Ecuador.

The Cuban crocodile *Crocodylus rhombifer* has a short snout, grows up to 11½ feet long, and lives in freshwater swamps in Cuba. Morelet's crocodile, *Crocodylus morelett*, which also grows up to 11½ feet, is found in Central America, where it is over-hunted. The *Caiman Crocodylus* has two subspecies, the Brown and Yacara Caiman, and there are also a Black and a Rio Apaporis Caiman in South America. Caiman are usually smaller than crocodiles or alligators. When Exquemelin speaks of a caiman being 70 feet long in Hispaniola, he was probably referring to the saltwater crocodile.

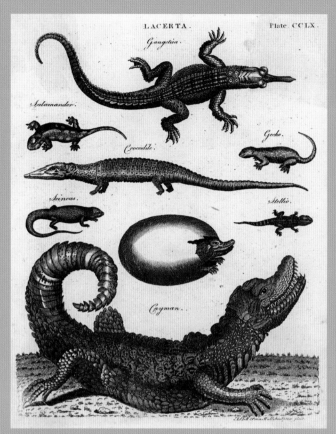

In the Florida Everglades and across the Caribbean, alligators were a useful food source for both Indians and European settlers.

unacquainted with their former masters. There are also herds of up to 300, short and sturdy wild horses. Sometimes the hunters catch them for their leather or to smoke-harden their meat as food for going to sea. They are easy to tame and are used for carrying meat or hides to the coast. To catch the horses, the hunters stretch a rope across a narrow forest track, tied to a bent sapling, and when a horse treads against it, the rope springs up and checks the animal. The horses are then tied up and beaten, and made to drag something heavy around in order to break them in. After eight days they are tame enough to carry loads, and the hunters can untie them.

Wild cattle and boar

There used to be large herds of wild cattle and huge wild bulls on Hispaniola, but they are becoming scarce. The Spanish are trying to wipe them out, in order to starve the French of this lucrative source of hides—a bull's hide can measure up to 13 feet long—but the French still manage to slaughter huge quantities of them. It is a wonder that there are any bulls or wild swine left on Hispaniola.

For the past 81 years, more than 1,500 wild pigs have been killed every day by the French and Spanish hunters. Indeed, I would say that the French alone slaughter more than this, but there are still incredible numbers of them on the island. The pigs are medium-sized and generally black, running in herds of 50 or 60. The males take the lead, with the females and young ones in the rear.

Above: Early Spanish engraving of a busy Indian market at Cartagena in Colombia. There are tobacco leaves alongside vegetables and skins for sale.

When attacked by dogs they scatter in all directions as fast as they can. They can be tamed, from my own experience. We have caught piglets in the forest, and brought them up on meat, and when grown they followed us like dogs. They would run ahead of us into the trees, and would start grunting and squealing on finding any wild swine. Our dogs would then rush in and kill the wild pigs, and our tame pigs would eat the flesh just like the dogs.

The birds of Hispaniola

There are too many birds to describe, most of them edible, so I shall only mention the main species. There are wood-fowl or wild pullet, parrots, wild pigeons, crab-eaters, herons, ravens, West Indian turkeys, flamingos, fishers, frigate-birds, snipe, duck, geese, teal, humming-birds, *cabreros* (small birds known as goat-keepers), and many others unknown to me.

The wild pullet is called the *pintada* by the Spanish because of its black and white plumage, painted like the skin of a tiger. It does not have a comb on its head like other fowl, but a sort of horny crest. It is as big as our largest home-bred chickens and tastes as good. In the woods it runs in flocks of 50 to

They would run ahead of us into the trees and start grunting and squealing on finding any wild swine. Our dogs would then rush in and kill the wild pigs, and our tame pigs would eat the flesh just like the dogs.

60 and flies up squawking into the trees when disturbed. Its eggs are laid on the ground and are easy to find. They can be hatched under an ordinary hen, but when the chicks hear their breed in the woods, they run off to them and become wild once more.

Our parrots in Europe are transported from this part of the world. The parrots nest in holes in palmetto trees, although their curved beaks cannot peck out a hole; they rely on others for this, such as the carpintero, or carpenter birds, woodpeckers the size of sparrows, which excavate the holes for them. There are vast flocks of pigeons, like those described on Tortuga, but these are only good to eat at a certain time of year. They are bigger than Tortuga pigeons, and when the trees are fruiting they grow so fat that when you shoot them, their crops burst open when they fall.

Herons are the same as our European variety, and there are also crab-eaters, which are the same size as the herons and good to eat. Multitudes of ravens gather when shooting is going on, screeching so loudly that the hunters cannot hear themselves speak. They look the same as our European ravens and can be eaten if there is nothing other available.

The West Indian turkeys have a big body and look similar to turkeys at home, except for their head, feet, and plumage. Their beaks and feet are like those of storks, and they are totally white except for two black patches on the wings. Flamingos live in the south of Hispaniola and their body is similar to that of a stork, the neck almost six feet long and the legs in proportion. Their beak is like a goose's, but more thick and curved, and they have an inch-thick tongue. They fly in flocks of 50 to 60 and are extremely delicious to eat. When they are on the shore seeking food, one always keeps watch. If he sees danger, he gives a warning cry and flies off, the whole flock following him. Fisher birds live on the banks of rivers and eat only fish. They are white, about the size of a duck, with red feet and a curved red beak, and are about nine inches long.

Frigate birds are the size of a turkey, very nourishing to eat, and taste of beef. They fly very quickly and so delicately that it is impossible to discern any movement in their wings. Found far out at sea, they eat only fish. No one has ever seen frigate birds on land, although they make their nests in those trees which grow in the water, mangroves, with as many branches in the water as above it. If these birds have not caught enough fish to feed their young, they fly around the crags and strike at the birds nesting there with their wings until they are forced to flee. To make themselves lighter for their sudden flight, the attacked birds tend to disgorge their food, and the opportunistic frigate birds dart beneath them and catch the food before it drops into the sea.

The birds they attack are a type of tern called the noddy, perhaps because of their nodding behavior during courtship. These noddies are the size of ducks, with a beak like that of a heron, with a saw on either side. Although their beaks are stronger than those of the frigate birds, the noddies yield to birds less powerful than themselves. They live on fish and inhabit the trees which grow in the water. They let themselves be taken by men without any other resistance than screeching. When ships sail by the islands, noddies come and perch on the yards. Sailors often catch them but they are not good to eat, having an oily smell and taste. A bird with a similar taste is the great-throat, which can swallow a fish as big as a man's head, although its throat is like that of a goose. Its beak is eight inches long and four wide, and it frequents river banks, the seashore, and rocky inlets.

Snipe are bigger and fatter than ours at home. There are immense numbers of ducks, which come into season at a certain time of year, just as at home. However, they are so fat that you have to burn the grease off them before you can eat them, and the same is true of teal. Geese come once a year and stay three to four months. They stuff themselves with certain seeds until they become too fat to fly and can easily be caught as they waddle along, a thing I have often done. We used to come across a flock on the open plains and follow them until they were too tired to fly or walk, when we could kill them easily with a stick. After gorging thus, for a month after they apparently eat nothing, living only on their fat, until they become light enough to fly.

The tiniest of all the birds on the face of the Earth is the humming-bird. It lives only on flowers and has plumage of extreme beauty. Only the Indians are swift enough to shoot them with their arrows, then they dry them and sell them to the Christians. When shooting the tiny birds, they put a drop of wax on the end of their arrows and aim with great skill, so that the bird is undamaged.

The French on the island—the origin of the Tortuga buccaneers

The French who inhabit the island follow one of three professions—hunting, planting, or roving the seas in the manner of pirates. I have already told how the French came to the island, bringing with them their bondservants and keeping them in service for three years. When he finishes this service, it is the custom for each man to seek out a comrade or partner to share their fortunes, with whom they draw up an agreement for mutual gain. These articles are agreed and signed, leaving the surviving companion as absolute heir of all the joint possessions. Others, if married, leave all their estates to their wives and children. Others leave everything to relatives.

Left: This 1686 engraving shows a typical *boucanier* of the Spanish Main, a superb marksman who practiced every day after he had completed his work, invariably accompanied by his hunting dogs.

The hunters are divided into *boucaniers*, or buccaneers, who hunt only wild bulls and cows, and others who hunt wild boar. Numbers of buccaneers have dropped from 600 to 300 because there are fewer wild cattle, and the buccaneers have to be quicker and more skilful. They go into the woods in Hispaniola for a year or two and divide the spoil before sailing home to Tortuga. Here they buy shot, powder, and guns and spend their days in drunken debauchery before returning to the hunt. They will drink brandy like water and buy a whole cask of wine, broach it, and drink until it is empty. The tavern-keepers and strumpets make great gain from the buccaneers, who stay until they have spent all their money and can get no more credit. Then they return to the woods for another year to eighteen months.

The hunters rendezvous and separate into groups of five or six, with their indentured servants. They seek a place in the open fields, where they set up tents and make a hut in which to store the dried hides. At dawn, they go with their hounds into the forest, along the trails where they are most likely to shoot bulls. After shooting one, they immediately take what they call their "brandy"–sucking the marrow from the bones while it is warm. After this they flay the animal and take the hide back to camp. They carry on like this until every man has a hide, perhaps until around noon. At their camp, if they have bondsmen, these servants stretch the hides out to dry and prepare food. They all eat only meat.

After eating, each buccaneer takes his musket and goes off to shoot horses or birds for sport. Sometimes they shoot at targets for a prize, typically at an orange tree, to see who can shoot down the most oranges without damaging them. I have often seen them do this, by nicking the stem with a single bullet. On Sundays they carry the hides to the beach and put them in their boats. Once a bondsman complained to his master that the seventh day should be for rest, and the buccaneer thrashed him mercilessly, saying, "Get on, you scoundrel! My commands are that six days thou shalt collect hides, and the seventh thou shalt bring them to the beach."

A servant turns hunter

These men are extremely cruel to their servants—there is more comfort in three years in a galley than one year in the service of a buccaneer. One hunter hit his servant so badly that he thought he had killed him and went away. The bondsman staggered after him but could find neither his master nor his camp. He was forced to stay in the forest, with no weapons and only a hound that had luckily stayed by his side.

BARBECU

*B*arbacoa and *barbecu* were the Taíno Indian words for a fire-pit used for cooking. A framework of green wood was used as a grill, called by the Caribs a *bukan*, and then by the French a *boucan*, so men who cooked meat in this manner became known as *boucaniers*. Meat was slow-cooked over a fire of green twigs and animal dung. Wild hogs were salted before being placed on the bukan, but other meat was dried in the smoke to a reddish-colour. *Barbacoa* and *arjoupa* became the Indian names used for the rough house of leaves and skins used by boucaniers.

Jacques Le Moyne de Morgues painted How to Grill Animals *following a French attempt to settle in Florida. Engraved after his death, it was published in 1591.*

As the pups grew into hounds, he let them kill and open up any animal, then he tore off lumps of raw flesh with his hands, relishing it as much as the best food he had eaten in all his life.

After two or three days he came across some wild pigs, and caught a young one, but had nothing to cut it with. Eventually he managed to cut strips of flesh off with a flint and ate them raw. He gave a lump to the hound and carried the rest with him as he wandered through the forest. One day he saw a wild bitch carrying a piece of meat in her mouth. He followed her until he came to her den and pups and stoned her until she was dead. He took the meat she was carrying and ate it. He also took two of her pups, for his hound had recently whelped and was still in milk. He found a place in the forest where there were enough young pigs to feed him and his dogs. As the pups grew into hounds, he let them kill and open up any animal, then he tore off lumps of raw flesh with his hands, relishing it as much as the best food he had eaten in all his life.

After about 14 months of living like this, he came across a band of hunters. At first they were afraid of him, for he looked utterly wild, being fully bearded and naked apart from a strip of tree-bark covering his loins. He had a piece of raw flesh dangling at his side. He told them how he had been left by his master, and the hunters wanted to take him along with them, but he insisted that they must release him from his bondage. Otherwise he refused to return to his master, saying he would rather live as he was. This they promised to do, and they brought him back with them, advancing him enough money to buy his freedom. I was there when they brought him back, and I was amazed. He was fat and sleek and healthy, far more so than when he was with his master. But he was so used to raw meat that he would not eat it cooked, nor could his digestion tolerate it. If he tried cooked meat, he groaned with stomach ache for an hour or so and then vomited up all he had eaten, as whole as when he had eaten it. We tried to keep raw meat from him, but he managed to get it when we were not looking.

The same thing happens with wild dogs. When a month or two old, they do not want cooked meat. I have recounted this story to show the cruelty of the hunters to their bondsmen, and also to show that a man can become accustomed to all kinds of food. In fact, I believe that a man can live on grass just as well as animals, and I shall give further examples elsewhere in this account.

The Spaniards and the hunters

The Spaniards on Hispaniola keep constant observation of the buccaneers and murder them if they get a chance. Five companies have been sent from San Domingo to find them, but are praying that they do not. They have no courage to take them on in the open field, as the hunters are excellent marksmen. Thus the Spaniards try to spy their whereabouts, in order to kill them in their sleep. I will recount incidents on this subject.

One morning, a hunter was out with his bondsman, and 12 Spaniards were hidden along the forest trail. He noticed their horses' hoof prints, so took a different path, but still could not escape their attention. They heard his dogs barking and rode him down in an open field. The hunter stood back to back with his servant, putting powder and bullets in their hats by their feet. The Spanish horsemen encircled them, lances pointed, and called on them to surrender, offering mercy. The hunter had played many tricks on the Spanish before and did not trust them. He knew that they would burn him alive. He said he wanted no quarter, but that the first one who attacked him would be killed. On this he dropped to one knee and aimed his musket, primed to fire. Seeing him so determined, the Spaniards rode off.

On the return of the hunting party, each man flays the animals he has caught, taking the flesh from the bones. The meat is cut into strips about six feet long, strewn with salt, and left for three to four hours.

On another occasion, a solitary hunter was surprised by a troop of Spaniards. He ran toward them, calling on his non-existent colleagues to back him up, and aiming his musket. The Spaniards fled.

The wild boar hunters are just as debauched as the other hunters and go to designated places to hunt with five or six friends, for a period of four to five months or even a year. They live in the same manner as the cow-killers, but they catch wild boar very differently to the methods used in Europe. The site where they live is called a boucan. The indentured servants are often provided to the hunters by planters, and they assist in carrying supplies to and from the hunters. The planter is obliged to keep the bondsman in powder, shot, and hounds. All other needs the hunter must supply himself. The buccaneers agree to provide the planters with a certain amount of meat for a year at a fixed price, usually paid for by 20 or 30 hundredweight of tobacco leaf.

When the hunters have finished their morning's work, they shoot horses in the afternoon, and melt the fat to make lamp-oil. A pot of this tallow is sold to planters for a hundredweight of tobacco. They also earn more by rearing hounds, and a good hunting dog will fetch a set price of six pieces of eight.

Other hunters, who are not part of such an agreement with planters, set off in groups of seven or eight. One man leads the hounds and another carries the guns. One stays at the boucan to guard the goods, smoke flesh, grind salt, and cook for when the others return. They kill large numbers of animals, sometimes 100 swine in a morning, only to take seven or eight of them. They generally prefer to take sows as they are fatter than the boars. Wild pigs are very dangerous and can do great damage to dogs and men. A man must always carry a staff to fend off a wounded animal. Once it has passed by, there is safety because the hogs never turn in their tracks, always charging straight ahead.

On the return of the hunting party, each man flays the animals he has caught, taking the flesh from the bones. The meat is cut into strips about six feet long, strewn with salt, and left for three to four hours. It is then hung on beams and sticks in a nearby hut. A fire is lit under it and the meat smoked until it is sufficiently dry and hard, then it is packed away. When they have accumulated 20 or 30 hundredweight, it is sold for two pounds of tobacco for every pound of meat.

The arrival of the planters

Having described the hunters, we will now consider the planters. The planters began to cultivate Tortuga in 1598, being very successful with tobacco, but the island is small and some parts were not suitable for that crop. Sugar was also attempted, but with little success. There was no money for a sugar refinery. When hunting grew slack on the island, some turned to agriculture once again, choosing the best place on Hispaniola for planting tobacco. They chose Cul-de-Sac in the north-west of the island, where the Spaniards could not get at them. There grew to be 2,000 planters of tobacco on Hispaniola, and they at first suffered much back-breaking work in clearing the trees and roots of the rocky terrain.

There was only forest when the planters arrived, full of wild boar, and so two or three men would join together to buy tools such as axes, mattocks, and knives, along with five to six hundredweight of provisions. They would then build a small hut of branches and clear the undergrowth, which they gathered in small piles and burnt. Then they proceeded to cut down the tall forest trees and burnt the branches with brushwood, keeping the trunks.

Opposite page: In 1492, Columbus was offered "fragrant leaves" by native Indians, but threw them overboard—they were tobacco leaves, as portrayed in this 1613 engraving. In the same year, Rodrigo de Jerez and Luis de Torres were in Cuba and first observed smoking. The natives wrapped dried tobacco leaves in palm or maize leaves "in the manner of a musket formed of paper." They lit one end and "drank" smoke through the other. Jerez brought the habit back to Spain, but the smoke billowing from his mouth and nose so frightened people that he was imprisoned by the Inquisition for seven years. By the time he was released, however, smoking had become popular.

I.
Tabacum latifolium.

From bananas they make wine, which easily causes drunkenness, but which also produces dangerous diseases of the throat.

The first crop planted was beans, which ripen and can be dried in the space of six weeks. The planters also needed to plant sweet potatoes, which take four to five months to ripen, and which they eat boiled for breakfast. The third crop planted was manioc, and from its roots flour is made. It takes between eight months and a whole year before it can be eaten. The planters make bread-cakes, by scraping the roots with tin or copper graters; the shavings are put in sacks of coarse cloth and all the moisture pressed out. It is then passed through a large parchment sieve until it looks like sawdust, then baked on an iron griddle into cakes and placed on the rooftops to dry. This may be where an old story originates, about a land where the houses are covered with pancakes. The planters use the coarse meal left over, which would not pass through the sieve, to make cakes five or six inches thick. These are piled on top of each other and left to ferment, and a beer called veycou is made from the liquor, similar to English beer. From bananas they make wine, which easily causes drunkenness, but which also produces dangerous diseases of the throat.

The beans are cooked with meat, and a potage is made together with eggs. The sweet potatoes are cooked in a pan with a little water and covered with a cloth. In about half an hour they are ready, dry like chestnuts, and served with a sauce made from lard, lemon juice, and red peppers. The planters also make alcoholic liquor called *maiz* from sweet potatoes, which they learned about from the Indians, who call it *maby*. Slices of sweet potato are covered with hot water, and the liquor is strained into a cauldron. In a few days it ferments, and although sour, it is not unpleasant.

The tobacco plantations

When the planters had cultivated their basic needs for living, they began to plant tobacco for trading. First they prepare a bed of earth 12-foot square, sow the seeds, then cover the area with palmetto leaves so that the sun cannot ripen any weeds in the ground. They constantly water the ground, and when the young tobacco plants are about the size of a lettuce, they transplant them into long rows, three feet apart, in big fields. When the tobacco is about 18 inches high and grown into a thick bush, the tips are snipped off to prevent it growing taller. This way the leaves get more nourishment from the soil and grow more vigorously. The planters keep them well-weeded until they have grown and ripened. The plants sprout more leaves once they have been cut, and this is done about four times a year.

Near their houses the planters prepare drying-sheds, apartments 50 to 60 feet in length and 40 feet in breadth. The green leaves are laid on the branches of trees and rafters to dry. When thoroughly dried, the leaf is stripped from the stalks and rolled up. The people who undertake this work tend to do nothing else and are paid with one tenth of what they roll. Most of the tobacco goes to France for dye or chewing-tobacco.

In 1664 the French West India Company proclaimed the citizens of Tortuga French citizens, but the planters refused to work for them, thus causing the company's dissolution. The governor thus decided to work with the planters in Hispaniola and Tortuga rather than against them, allying with merchants from France to supply them with what they wanted, on condition they did not inform on this deal.

Opposite page: These hog-hunters of Hispaniola and Tortuga wore leather caps with brims to protect their eyes from the sun. They were clad from head to toe in leather skins. Because of the blood and grease on their clothes, and the smoke from their *barbecoas*, their clothes became so black that they looked as if they had been tarred.

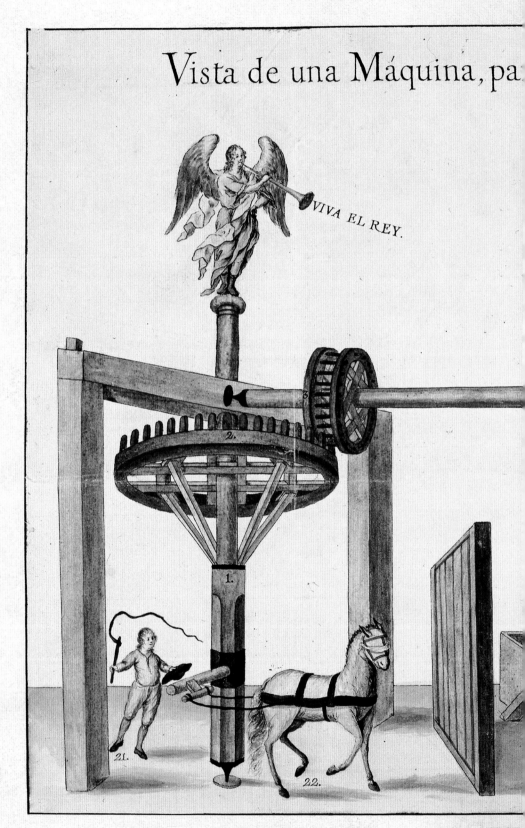

Vista de una Máquina, pa

VIVA EL REY.

Right: This 18th-century drawing of a tobacco mill of the "Royal Factory of Mexico" shows how the use of technology and slaves had enabled the rapidly expanding tobacco industry to move out of Cuba into the rest of the Americas.

nír Tabáco enla R.¹ Fabrica de Sigarr.ˢ 18.

He would arrange for ships to buy their merchandise and carry it back to France four times a year, which would be better than doing business irregularly with foreign traders. He brought together the most important planters to agree to this, and the rest were excluded from the deal. These were not allowed to buy so much as a yard of linen without begging him and they could not export their produce. The ships used were under his orders, and he was one of the shipowners. His own goods were always loaded first, and then those of his friends, and if there was any room left onboard, other goods could be loaded only with his written permission.

Two Dutch ships traded with Hispaniola planters in 1669, and many planters defied the governor, deciding to deal in future direct with the Dutch rather than the governor of Tortuga. The governor arrived in a ship to call a halt to the trading, but the planters fired on him, and he could not land. He was forced to send his ships to France only half-laden. Trade with the Dutch carried on, and friends of the governor were forced to keep quiet and not interfere, on threat of death. The Dutch had full cargoes of hides and tobacco and promised to return for more. Negotiations had broken down with the governor, and the French planters on Hispaniola set forth in canoes determined to kill him. They wished to set up a new Commonwealth, independent of France. However, news came that war had been declared between France and Holland, which forced them to rethink.

The governor now sent to France for two men-of-war, which landed parties at Hispaniola to ruin the homes of the French planters, until the governor offered them a pardon, hanging only two of the ringleaders. His new policy was to allow the planters to deal with any nation whatsoever, and tobacco production increased to 20,000 or 30,000 rolls a year.

TOBACCO

Tobacco was "the cocaine of the 17th century." In 1493 Colombus noted the habit of the (now extinct) Taíno Indians of lighting rolls of dried leaves and inhaling the smoke through their nostrils. In the early 17th century, smoking had become so popular it was said that "many a young nobleman's estate is altogether spent and scattered to nothing in smoke [and] a man's estate runs out through his nose, and he wastes whole days, even years, in drinking of tobacco; men smoke even in bed."

The leaf's value equalled that of silver. At first growing wild in Virginia, the tobacco plant was subsequently cultivated by the Virginia Company for profit. However, after three to four tobacco crops the land would be exhausted and more ground would have to be cleared and replanted. The Virginia Company struggled for enough workers and life expectancy among their laborers was short.

In the 17th century, smoking was the height of fashion, and it retained that status until the 1970s. The practice of "drinking smoke" was prohibitively expensive until the Virginia tobacco plantations began large-scale exports in the 18th century.

Left: This painting by Abraham Storck (1635–1710) depicts the Four Days Battle of June 1–4, 1666, in which the English lost 8,000 men and 17 ships fighting the Dutch in the English Channel. In the reign of Charles II, Henry Morgan's successes were the only English victories against foreign powers, which made it difficult for the Crown to punish him for piracy.

The indentured servants and their cruel masters

The planters have few slaves, but they do have servants who are bound to them for three years. However, their masters sometimes traffic them as if they were horses at a fair, or sell them like slaves from Guinea. To advance the trafficking trade, persons go to England and France and make great promises to young men or boys, who they then transport to the West Indies. They are then forced to work like horses, being worked much harder than the Negro slaves.

This is because it is in the owners' interests that the Negroes stay alive as their perpetual bond-slaves, while they do not care if the white men live or die, as they are their servants for only three years. Whether sick or well, they are forced to work in the heat of the sun, and their backs are often full of sunburn sores, like horses chafed with heavy loads. Sometimes their hard usage induces a coma in the white youngsters, called after the French *mal d'estomac* (bad stomach). They become sleepy, full of dropsy, and short of breath, and this is caused by harsh treatment, poor diet, and the intolerable sunshine. Some of these sufferers are beaten so cruelly that they fall down dead. The planters complain that the rascals would rather die than work. This I have often seen.

One planter was so cruel to a servant that the servant ran away. When he was caught he was strapped to a tree and had so many lashes on his naked back that the ground around the tree was covered in blood. To make the wounds smart worse, the planter anointed them with lemon juice mingled with salt and pepper and left him tied there for 24 hours. Then the treatment started again, and the dying wraith gave up the ghost, saying "I beseech the Almighty God, Creator of Heaven and Earth, that he permit the wicked Spirit to make thee feel as many torments before thy death as thou hast caused me to feel before mine." Just four days passed when the Lord enforced His punishment, and the tyrant planter began to whip himself into a bloody pulp until he himself died.

They become sleepy, full of dropsy, and short of breath, and this is caused by harsh treatment, poor diet, and the intolerable sunshine. Some of these sufferers are beaten so cruelly that they fall down dead.

INDENTURED SERVANTS

There were only two ways to get much-needed labor from Britain before the slave trade: By the transportation of criminals and by indentures, such as the one Henry Morgan was supposed to have signed. A new life in the New World, where one could easily obtain ownership of one's own land, was an attractive and well-marketed proposition, but people could not afford the crossing. Consequently, a modified version of apprenticeship called the indenture was devised.

Named from the Latin *indentare* or *indentura* (to give a jagged edge, to cut with teeth), it was a contract drawn on parchment, signed by two or more parties, and then cut into two pieces. The fit between the two parts proved that the agreement between the master and the servant was authentic. In theory, an indenture bound a British person as a servant for a period of four to seven years, or, for a minor, until he or she reached 21. However, life in the plantations was a nasty, brutish, and short affair.

When, in 1618, Governor Thomas Dale of Delaware took offence to his servant Richard Barnes uttering "base and detracting words" against him, he ordered that Barnes be "disarmed and have his arms broken and his tongue bored through with an awl, and he shall pass through a guard of 40 men and shall be butted by every one of them, and at the head of the troop be kicked down and footed out of the fort; and he shall be banished out of James City and the Island, and he shall not be capable of any privilege of freedom in the country." Banishment outside the colony was, in effect, a death sentence. Seamstresses who sewed their ladies' skirts too high were whipped. Men who tried to escape were tortured to death. Piracy must have seemed a welcome release from the life of an indentured servant if the opportunity presented itself. For this reason bondsmen were a source of manpower for the pirate captains.

This agreement concerns the relocation of a servant from County Kent, England, to the colony of Virginia. By the terms of this contract, the master was obliged to supply "Meat, Drink, Apparel, Lodging and Washing," but in reality many servants were denied even basic needs.

Caribbean planters are cruel to their servants. In St. Kitts a man named Bettesa has killed over 100 of his servants with blows and whippings, a fact well known to Dutch merchants. The English do the same. The mildest cruelty is that after six years of service—the English have to complete seven years before they are free men—they treat them so badly that the servants plead for another master. They are then bound for another three, four, or seven years, and it can happen again and again. I have known men bound for 15 and 20 years before they gained their freedom.

The English celebrate Christmas and let their slaves have whatever they ask for—drink, food, or whatever—but the bondsmen pay for it dearly. The English have a strict law that when anyone owes 25 shillings and cannot pay, he can be sold as a slave for six months to a year. I will now relate the famous actions of pirates, not taken from any source but from enterprises upon which I was an eye-witness.

Palatium Reguli in S. Dominici Insula ab Hispanis inventi.

LAMINA XII

Left: Columbus landed on Hispaniola in 1492, and it became the first Spanish colony in the West Indies, until it was claimed by the French in the 17th century. The Spanish governor's palace in Santo Domingo, shown here, demonstrates an Islamic influence on the garden design.

PLACES AROUND THE CARIBBEAN

After first settling Hispaniola, the Spanish took Cuba and the larger islands in the Caribbean before colonizing Mexico, Florida, Louisiana, Texas, and Central and South America. Between Columbus' first landing in 1492 and 1650, the native population of the Americas fell from around 50 million to 8 million. This decimation, assisted by European diseases such as smallpox and measles, was worst in the West Indies, resulting in the extinction of the Indians on many islands. The expansion of agriculture was hindered by the subsequent shortage of labor, so African slaves were then imported to work the sugar and tobacco plantations in the Americas.

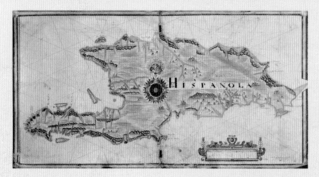

HISPANIOLA

Today shared by Haiti and the Dominican Republic, in 1492 Columbus called this island—the second largest in the Antilles—*Isla Espanola* (Island of Little Spain). Hispaniola was the Anglicized version of that name. The original Arawak name was *Ayiti*. Santo Domingo, today capital of the Dominican Republic, is the oldest European settlement in the Americas.

Left: *Map of Hispaniola by Nicholas Comberford, 1633.*

CUBA

In 1493, Pope Alexander VI commanded Spain to conquer, colonize, and convert the pagans of the New

World to Catholicism. The Spanish of Hispaniola began to settle Cuba in 1511. The indigenous Taíno Indians were effectively exterminated in Cuba, as in Hispaniola. Desperate for labor to work in the new plantations, the conquistadors sought slaves from surrounding islands and the continental mainland. The Spanish established sugar and tobacco as Cuba's primary products and the island soon supplanted Hispaniola as the primary Spanish base in the Caribbean.

Above: *A 1683 engraving of Havana, founded in 1515.*

JAMAICA

Cromwell's 1654-55 expedition to take Hispaniola was poorly executed, and the leaders of the campaign decided to take Jamaica instead. The island was taken despite the inadequacies of the offensive, simply because there were very few Spanish settlers or defenses. French, Dutch, and English buccaneers flocked to Jamaica's capital, Port Royal. The French had forced them out of their Tortuga stronghold, but the English authorities saw the pirates both as a source of considerable trading wealth and as their main defense against the Spanish. By 1662, there was so much looted silver and gold in Port Royal that the government considered establishing a mint there.

Below: Lignum vitae *flowering in Jamaica's Blue Mountains.*

OLD PROVIDENCE ISLAND AND SANTA CATALINA

A pirate haven 250 miles off Puerto Bello, this pair of islands, so close together they are almost adjoining, lay on the Cuba to Venezuela trading route. The larger island is now called Old Providence Island (or Providencia), but in Exquemelin's time (and in his account), the term Santa Catalina referred to both the larger island and the pair. The pirates there successfully beat off a Spanish attack in 1635, but it was taken in 1640. Henry Morgan used the islands for his attack on Panama in 1670–71.

CARTAGENA

Cartagena, or Carthagena, was the treasure port between Panama and Venezuela, now part of Colombia. It was one of only three treasure ports visited by the annual Spanish *flota*, or Plate Fleet, which carried pearls, precious woods, gold, silver, and emeralds. The others were Santo Domingo and Nombre de Dios. Founded in 1533, Cartagena was heavily defended and was the only major Spanish port never taken by the buccaneers.

Above: Plan of Panama City, 1673. After Morgan's attack in 1671, the city was rebuilt several miles away from the original site.

PANAMA

Because Francis Drake had sacked Cartagena, Santo Domingo, and Nombre de Dios, the Spanish developed Puerto Bello as their main Caribbean treasure port from 1595. Every year, silver was carried on mule trains from Panama City across the Panama Isthmus to Nombre de Dios, and then to Puerto Bello on the Caribbean coast. If the Chagres River was full, the silver would be carried by water instead. Henry Morgan sacked Panama City in 1671, just three years after he had taken Puerto Bello.

Left: The Palace of the Inquisition, in Cartagena, was finished in 1770.

45

PART TWO

How the buccaneers arm their ships, their way of life and some notable pirates—Pierre le Grand, Pierre François, Bartholomew the Portuguese, Rock the Brazilian, Lewis Scot, Edward Mansveldt, and John Davis

Opposite page: This painting by Howard Pyle (1853-1911) is titled *Which Shall Be Captain?*. It shows pirates fighting over buried treasure. Even today, men are still searching for the buried treasure of buccaneers and pirates such as Henry Morgan, Captain Kidd, Black Bart Roberts, and Olivier "the Buzzard."

CHAPTER I

How the buccaneers man and victual their ships, and how they regulate their voyages

Before pirates go to sea, they tell everyone when and where to embark and what each man must bring in terms of powder and bullets necessary for the expedition. Then a council is held as to where meat and other provisions should be obtained. They scarcely eat anything other than meat, mainly pork. Sometimes they raid Spanish hog-yards, which contain up to 1,000 swine, and threaten their keeper with death until they have killed enough for their voyage. They also take lightly salted turtles with them. The allowance onboard is meat twice a day—as much as one can eat. All, including the captain, eat exactly the same food, with no limit on quantity.

The next council decides where the expedition shall head, and articles are agreed in writing by all the voyagers. They specify what each participant should receive as a share from the booty taken. So it is the same law for these people as with pirates—"No Prey, No Pay."

BRETHREN OF THE COAST: THE ORIGIN OF BUCCANEERS

Since the 1530s, Europeans had formed settlements on the coasts of Jamaica, Cuba, and Hispaniola. They caught wild cattle and pigs, and exchanged hides, meat, and tallow for guns, clothes, provisions, and alcohol. In retaliation against Spanish attacks on their settlements, they attacked Spanish shipping in pirogues or piraguas—canoes made from hollowed-out tree trunks. The Spanish tried to massacre their herds, which turned the "Brethren of the Coast" even more toward piracy and buccaneering. From 1630, the island of Tortuga became their unofficial headquarters.

The buccaneers evolved a strict code, the "Custom of the Coast," whereby they shared booty evenly and did not know each other's pasts or surnames. Crossing the Tropic of Cancer "drowned" their former lives, according to superstition. A council of equals decided where they would get provisions and where they would attack under an elected captain. Exquemelin recorded these negotiations from his own experiences. Buccaneers attacked ships, but not usually those of their own homeland. Their favored form of attack was in long canoes or small, single-masted barques. They would pack their boats with sharpshooters so they could attack anyone trying to fire cannon at them and would approach from astern of the prize ships, giving their opposition a minimal target. Although they called themselves "privateers," they rarely had letters of commission or marque, although they sometimes carried expired commissions or forgeries.

This contemporary engraving shows the unglamorous life of an early buccaneer, one of the hunters on Hispaniola or Tortuga. Hunting with their "mates," they lived in an early form of social democracy.

Firstly, they state what the captain should have for his ship, then secondly an amount for the shipwright or carpenter who has careened, repaired, and rigged the vessel, which is usually around 100 to 150 pieces of eight. For provisions and victuals, around 200 pieces of eight are taken from the proceeds. Then the surgeon is given about 200 to 250 pieces of eight for his salary and medicine chest. Lastly, they stipulate recompense for injuries. For a right arm, 600 pieces of eight or six slaves, and for the left arm, 500 pieces or five slaves. For the right leg, 500 pieces of eight or five slaves, and for the left leg, 400 pieces or four slaves. For an eye or a finger, 100 pieces of eight or one slave. These sums are taken out of the money they make from piracy. Of the remainder, it is shared so that the captain gets five or six times as many shares as the ordinary seaman, the mate two shares, and the other officers also have proportions. All seamen then get equal parts, but the boys get half shares.

They observe good order. When a prize is taken, it is severely prohibited that any man takes anything for himself. Hence everything is equally divided, according to their articles agreed before. They make a solemn oath not to abscond, nor to conceal anything they find. If pirates contravene this oath, they are turned out of the society, so they stay very charitable and committed to each other. Indeed, if one wants something another has, it is given with great liberality.

Above: This painting, *Peasants in an Inn* (1635) by Molenaer, shows a typical 17th-century tavern. Pitchers and drinks containers were often made of leather, so they did not break during the celebrations.

They make a solemn oath not to abscond, nor to conceal anything they find. If pirates contravene this oath, they are turned out of the society, so they stay very charitable and committed to each other.

The LIBERTY of the SUBJECT.

Publish'd Oct.r 15.th 1779. by W.Humphrey N.o 227 Strand

Above: This James Gillray engraving from *1779* is entitled *The Liberty of the Subject* and shows the press gang taking impressed men to serve on British ships. Some were made so drunk that they had no idea they were on a ship until they were at sea. Men were captured not just for the Royal Navy but also for the Merchant Navy, especially in times of war when labor was scarce.

If a man has nothing, the other pirates will generously allow him credit until he can pay it back. Disputes are settled with duels, but if someone kills someone treacherously in a quarrel, he is tied to a tree and shot dead himself. However, if he has killed his opponent in a duel, after giving him time to load his musket, then the man is allowed to go free.

The types of turtles

As soon as pirates take a ship, they set ashore the prisoners, detaining a few where necessary to assist them, but release these after two or three years. They often put in for refreshment in the isles to the south of Cuba, when they careen their vessels and hunt. Some go to sea in canoes, seeking their fortune. Many times they take poor turtle fishermen and force them to work for them for a time.

There are four distinct types of turtle. One grows to between 2 and 3,000 pounds, but its scales are so soft they can be cut with a knife. These Leatherback turtles are not good to eat. Another smaller one is green, and its flesh is pleasant to taste. The third turtle is the same size, called the loggerhead, with a large head and not good for food. The fourth is named a caret, being similar to our European tortoise, keeping amongst the rocks and mainly living on sea apples. The others feed on sea grasses. Their eggs are like those of a crocodile, but without any shell. They are found in prodigious quantities but are frequently destroyed by birds; otherwise the sea would abound with tortoises. They return every year to the same place to mate and to lay their eggs, mainly to the three Cayman Islands, south of Cuba.

Most of the turtles come from the Gulf of Honduras, about 150 leagues away. Sometimes ships, having lost their latitude in bad weather, follow swimming turtles to the Cayman Islands. The green turtles are easy to catch on the beach. Two men turn one over with a hand-spike, so they cannot move, and in the length of 500 paces one may see as many as 100 upturned turtles. At the Caymans the turtles eat nothing, then they head toward Cuba and fatten up. The Spanish then go out and fish for them, fixing a long nail or dart on a pole with a long rope attached, to wound the tortoises when they appear above the water to breathe fresh air. They then harpoon them again when they resurface, and can haul them aboard.

The main pastime of the buccaneers is target shooting with pistols and muskets, and they keep their guns very clean. Their muskets are four-and-a-half feet long, and 16 bullets are made from a pound of lead. They always carry a cartouche of 30 cartridges, being ever prepared for action.

Below left: This engraving depicts green turtle hunting. On a calm night pirates could see the turtles' heads breaking the surface for air. The "striker" fired a dart or harpoon into the turtle's back. When it came up again for air, another harpoon was fixed. Muffled oars were used, as turtles have poor sight but excellent hearing.

Below: Flintlock pistols, such as these from c.1660, used a flint inside a device called a lock to strike sparks into the priming pan when the trigger was pulled. The sparks ignited gunpowder in the priming pan, which ignited gunpowder in the barrel, firing the lead ball.

PERSONNEL

Discipline onboard was usually very good, as both pirates and privateers signed up to articles of agreement. Interestingly, the names for the lower ranks onboard ship, such as boatswain, coxswain, and seaman, all derived from the people's language, Anglo-Saxon. The titles of the officers—admiral, captain, and lieutenant—are all derived from the language of the court in medieval times, which was French. Incidentally, so many men from the west of England went to sea that their distinctive dialect influenced the pronunciation of words such as boatswain, which became "bo'sun." Similarly, coxswain is pronounced "cox'n," bowline is pronounced "bo'lin," gunwale is pronounced "gunnel," foresail is "fors'l," and main sail is "mains'l."

CAPTAIN

A pirate captain had remarkably few rights or benefits and was in charge only when the crew was fighting, chasing, or being pursued. During such action, he was allowed to strike, stab, or shoot any man who disobeyed his orders. He was usually chosen for being "pistol-proof": Having a dominating and daring character. Any man could enter his cabin, drink from his punch bowl, swear at him, and take his food with little come-back. Pirate captains were usually deposed by popular vote, just as they were elected.

Below: *A Howard Pyle illustration of a pirate captain.*

GUNNER

The gunner led the group who were manning the cannon. His greatest skill was in aiming from one rolling ship at another rolling ship. The gunner would train and oversee each group of four to six men who were responsible for loading, aiming, firing, resetting, and swabbing (cleaning out the burning powder residue) for the next load and fire. He would also check that guns were not dangerously over-heating (when they could burst their barrels) or recoiling excessively and would coordinate timing, especially for broadsides.

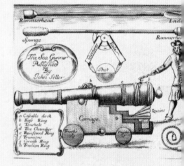

Above: *An illustration from the manual* The Sea Gunner *by John Seller, published 169*

QUARTERMASTER

On pirate ships the quartermaster was democratically elected. It was his job to represent the interests of the crew to the captain and to be in charge of the operations of the ship when it was not in action. As the virtual equal of the captain, when a prize was captured, the quartermaster usually took it over. He kept order, judged disputes, and dispersed food and cash. Because he was second-in-command, he usually received a larger share of plunder than other crew members. When a prize vessel was taken, it was often given to the quartermaster, who then became a captain himself. Usually, only the quartermaster could flog a seaman, and then only after a vote by the crew.

Above: To run the ship efficiently, the boatswain gave orders by pipe calls.

BOATSWAIN

The boatswain, often shortened to bo'sun, was in charge of the rigging, sails, cables, and anchors, making sure they all worked efficiently. He was also usually in charge of stores and provisions. On deck, he translated the captain's operational orders into tasks for the crew.

SAWBONES

The sawbones was the ship's surgeon, who was usually not much more knowledgable than a barber. In fact, one role developed from the other—barbers became surgeons because they had the sharpest implements for cutting. Surgeons were in huge demand on pirate ships. They could extract bullets, treat venereal disease, set bones, staunch wounds, and amputate to prevent gangrene. For major procedures, such as amputation, the ship's carpenter was often employed for his knowledge and his equipment. Exquemelin himself was a ship's surgeon.

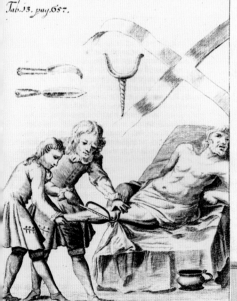

Left: A 17th-century engraving of an amputation. Onboard pirate ships, rum would have been the only anesthetic available.

ARTIST

The term "artist" was used to describe skilled men, such as surgeons, carpenters, or navigators, who were sometimes "forced" to join the pirates, to cover gaps in the crew. Pirate captains then issued them with a notification that they had been forced, for use at any possible trial by the Crown. While most pirates at trial would say that they had been forced, usually only skilled men would be acquitted.

Above: Ship carpentry was an ancient art even in the 1600s. This French engraving dates from the 15th century.

CARPENTER

Carpenters were vital not only for ship repairs and careening, but also for stripping prizes to be used as pirate ships. Often the carpenter would have separate quarters combined with a workshop. He repaired battle damage to masts, yards, hatches, and the hull and also kept leaks out with wooden plugs and oakum fibers. The sawdust he created was kept onboard and liberally sprinkled around the gun deck, so that men would not slip on blood in battle.

CHAPTER II

*The origin of the most famous pirates of the coasts of
America—A notable exploit of Pierre le Grand*

I have told you why I was forced to adventure among the pirates of America. The Kings of Spain have
often sent their ambassadors to the Kings of France and England, complaining of pirate molestations
and troubles in America. Those ambassadors have always been answered that those pirates were not
subjects of France or England, so Spain could treat them as they wished. The King of France said that
he had no fortress or subjects on Hispaniola, and the King of England stated that the people of Jamaica
had never had any commissions to be hostile to Spain. The King of England did, however, recall his
Governor of Jamaica and replace him. None of this affected the pirates of the Americas.

The first known pirate on Tortuga was Pierre le Grand, or Peter the Great, from Dieppe in Normandy.
In 1602, with a single barque and a crew of only 28, he captured the Vice-Admiral of the Spanish fleet
off Cape Tiburon, west of Hispaniola. This was when the Spanish had not yet discovered the Bahamas
Channel and sailed off the Caicos Islands. According to a trustworthy journal, the pirates had been at
sea for some time, running low on food, and their ship was becoming unseaworthy. Pierre sighted a
flagship which had become detached from its fleet, and closed on her, deciding to attack. When it was
dusk, the buccaneers approached the flagship. Pierre's surgeon bored a hole in his own ship to scuttle

BURIED TREASURE

Very few buccaneers or pirates ever buried plunder. They
shared it out and usually spent it within days on women,
gambling, and alcohol. The Dutchman Roche Brasiliano
(known to the English as "Rock the Brasilian"), when tortured
by the Spanish Inquisition at Campeche, told them about
treasure he had buried on the Isla de Pinos, off Cuba.
Spanish soldiers retrieved over a hundred thousand pieces of
eight, upon which the Spanish
put "Rock" out of his misery.

Legend persists that Black
Bart hid treasure inside a cave
on Little Cayman Island after his
pillaging of the Portuguese fleet
at Bahia. The first recorded story
of buried treasure was by William
Williams in his novel *The
Journal of Penrose, Seaman*,
written in the late 18th century

but not published until 1815. The concept was later copied
by Edgar Alan Poe for *The Gold Bug*, his most financially
successful short story.

In New Providence in the Bahamas, in 1733, Edward
Seward found several bags of gold doubloons in a cave.
The value of his haul was estimated at 700,000 dollars. In
the early 20th century an archaeologist, Mitchell Hedges,

was one of the first people to
explore the underwater ruins of
Morgan's Port Royal. He discovered
four chests filled to the brim with
gold doubloons, which he sold for
six million dollars.

*Silver, gold, jewels, and pearls kept their
value buried in any type of container, as
they are resistant to salt and corrosion.*

As the pirates' barque had sunk, some Spaniards cried that the pirate demons must have fallen from the sky.

her, and without a sound they clambered aboard the Spanish ship. There was no resistance, and they found the captain playing cards in his cabin. Some buccaneers had secured the gun room to stop the Spanish getting arms, and some Spanish were killed as they tried to prevent them. The captain had seen the strange barque in the day, but dismissed her as being too small to attack his flagship.

As the pirates' barque had sunk, some Spaniards cried that the pirate demons must have fallen from the sky. Pierre le Grand put some prisoners ashore but kept others to help man the ship, crossing to France where he remained, never going to sea again. Because of this success, the buccaneers and planters of Tortuga sought ships to plunder the Spanish. They used canoes to intercept the barques used for trading along the coast, and which also carried hides and tobacco to Cuba. Back at Tortuga the pirates sold these goods to merchant ships and bought more arms, before setting off toward the Gulfs of Campeche and of New Spain. Here they acquired more booty, including two ships sailing for Caracas with silver. Using these two ships, they acquired at least 20 ships in the next two years, to enable them to gather more plunder. The Spaniards now had to use naval frigates to protect their shipping and to cruise against this new threat to their power in the area.

Above: This painting by Howard Pyle shows Pierre le Grand catching a Spanish captain off guard in his cabin. According to Exquemelin, the pirates had taken the galleon by surprise at night after it had lagged behind the rest of the treasure fleet.

CHAPTER III

The pearl fleet and Pierre François

Below: The *volcanitos* (air volcanoes) of Turbaco, near Cartagena in Colombia, are today known as mud volcanoes. They are mentioned in several pirate accounts because of the heat of the ground in the area. The volcanitos are now a tourist attraction.

When they have been in any place for some time, the buccaneers agree where to make their next expedition. If one of them is familiar with the coasts where the merchantmen trade, he will offer his services as a guide. For instance, the Spanish of New Spain and Campeche load up huge ships and in winter these ships head for Caracas, Trinidad, and the Isle of Margarita. In summer the winds are contrary, bearing north to Campeche on the Yucatan in Mexico. Thus the pirates usually can guess when and where Spanish ships are sailing. Pierre François had been a long time at sea with his crew of 26 men, waiting for ships returning from Maracaibo in Venezuela to Campeche.

Frustrated, he then sailed to the Rancheria River (in modern Colombia), where there is a rich pearl bank offshore. Every year a dozen fishery vessels go there from Cartagena, protected by a man-of-war. Each vessel has a couple of Negro divers who can reach depths of six fathoms to get the pearls. Pierre François rode at anchor off Riohacha, the town at the mouth of the Rancherias, just half a league from the Pearl Fleet. The wind was calm, so he furled the sails of his ship and began to row his vessel, pretending to be a Spaniard from Maracaibo, merely passing the fleet.

So doing, he ordered the eight-gun flagship to surrender, but she fired on his ship. The pirates opened up accurate fire, killing some of the gunners and boarding the 60-crew Spaniard before she could reload. The vice-admiral surrendered his ship, probably believing that the man-of-war would soon come to his rescue. However, François then sank his own ship and flew the Spanish flag on the Spanish flagship. He tied up his prisoners and prepared the battered ship for sailing. Meanwhile, the man-of-war fired a victory salute to celebrate what looked like a "victory" over the pirates.

A disaster befalls the pirates

François now weighed anchor and set off under full sail for the open seas. Quickly, the captain of the Spanish man-of-war realized his error. He immediately cut the anchor cable and began chasing the French. Dusk fell, and the man-of-war was gaining all the time. The pirates crowded on more and more canvas, until the mainmast crashed to the deck under the weight and force of the sail that was upon it. The 22 remaining pirates manhandled the broken mainmast overboard and rigged more sails on the foremast and bowsprit, but the man-of-war still closed with François. He was thus forced to surrender.

François asked for terms that the crew would not have to slave in the stone or lime quarries and that they should be sent to Spain when possible. In Spain captives were kept in hard labor for three to four years before being allowed freedom. Terms were agreed, so Pierre François gave up pearls valued at 100,000 pieces of eight—all owing to the loss of his mainmast.

Left: This engraving dates from either the late 16th or early 17th century. It depicts slaves digging for gold and silver on the Guinea Coast of Africa, to enrich the Spanish Empire.

CHAPTER IV

The pirating career of Bartolomeo el Portugesa, or
Bartholomew the Portuguese

Above: This engraving of Bartholomew the Portuguese appeared in the original 17th-century editions of Exquemelin's book. Bartholomew escaped capture on numerous occasions and was responsible for many robberies on the Caribbean coast. The last information about him was that his ship was sunk off the coast of Jamaica.

Another famous buccanner is Bartolomeo el Portugesa, or Bartholomew, who hailed from Portugal, and who left Jamaica in a four-gun barque with just 30 men. He was rounding Cape Corrientes on western Cuba when a Spanish ship was sighted. She was en route from Maracaibo and Cartagena to Havana, and then heading for Hispaniola. The Spaniard carried 20 guns, other armaments, and 70 passengers and crew. Bartholomew's first attack was beaten off, but he tried again and quickly took the ship, losing ten men and four wounded. The Spanish had only 40 men left alive, including their wounded. The plunder totalled 20,000 pounds of cacao, used for making chocolate, and also 70,000 pieces of eight.

Prevailing winds prevented his return to Jamaica, so Bartholomew sailed a few leagues west to Cape San Antonio to get water. However, three Havana-bound warships from New Spain came alongside Bartholomew's heavily laden ship. The pirates had to surrender. Two days later, the four ships were separated in a storm, and the one carrying Bartholomew and the other prisoners put in at Campeche. The port's traders knew Bartholomew, who had previously murdered people and burned houses along the Mexican coast. The town's justice officers came aboard and agreed that the pirate captain should be handed over for hanging the next morning, and a gallows was erected.

Bartholomew escapes his captors

However, Bartholomew could speak Spanish and overheard his captors discussing his execution. In his cell he had found two empty wine jars and fashioned stoppers for them out of cork. That night everyone slept except his guard, and Bartholomew managed to slit his throat with a hidden knife. He could not swim, but lowered himself over the side with his jars and, using their buoyancy, paddled to the shore. He hid in the forest for three days, watching search parties from the shelter of the woods.

When his pursuers eventually returned to the city, he made his way along the coast toward El Golfo Triste on the eastern tip of the Yucatan Peninsula, over 30 leagues from Campeche. It took him 14 days, clambering over trees and through mangrove swamps, as he did not dare to take any roads. He had

That night everyone slept except his guard, and Bartholomew managed to slit his throat with a hidden knife. He could not swim, but lowered himself over the side with his two jars and, using their buoyancy, paddled to the shore.

hardly any water and lived off raw periwinkles on the rocks. He had rivers to cross, so used an old nail-studded plank, washed up on a beach. He hammered the nails flat with stones and ground their edges so they could cut creepers. He tied the creepers around driftwood, fashioning a raft to cross the rivers. Starving, at last he came to El Golfo Triste, where he found a pirate ship from Jamaica.

Bartholomew recounted his adventures, and the buccaneers agreed to give him a canoe and 20 men to take his prison ship, which was at anchor in Campeche. In the dead of the night, they silently boarded the ship. Its crew had thought the canoe was a trader from the city, carrying smuggled goods to them. The pirates took the ship, cut the anchor cable, and sailed away. However, the gold had been removed from the ship.

Setting course to Jamaica, Bartholomew was near the Isle of Pines, south of Cuba, when a southerly gale forced the ship onto the reefs of Los Jardines de la Reina. Bartholomew and his crew were thus forced to take to a canoe and eventually came to Jamaica. He was soon off after booty again and made many attacks on the Spanish, but made no great profit. I saw him dying in wretched circumstances.

Below: Sunset at the Fort of San Miguel in Campeche, Mexico. As well as city walls, Campeche had an outer defense system of forts, including San Miguel, which still has its moat, drawbridge, towers, and cannon.

Above: The original 17th-century editions of Exquemelin's book featured this engraving of Rock the Brazilian. Born in the Netherlands, he emigrated to the Dutch colony of Bahia in Brazil. When the Dutch were driven out of Bahia by the Portuguese in 1654, he moved to Port Royal and joined ranks with the English buccaneers.

CHAPTER V

The exploits of Roche Brasiliano, or Rock the Brazilian

Another pirate presently lives in Jamaica. He was born in Groningen in the United Provinces, but his name is unknown. The French pirates call him Roche Brasiliano, and the English know him as Rock the Brazilian, as he lived for a long time in that country. He was forced to flee when the Portuguese took that country in 1654, from the West India Company of Amsterdam. Other nationalities then inhabiting Brazil, such as French and English as well as Dutch, were also forced to seek new fortunes.

Rock the Brazilian went to Jamaica, and to gain a living was forced to join the society of pirates. As an ordinary mariner he was loved and respected by all. One day certain pirates disagreed with their captain and deserted the ship. Rock followed them, and they elected him captain and fitted out a small vessel. A few days later he captured a great ship out of New Spain, full of silver plate, which he then sailed back to Jamaica.

He was famous in Jamaica, but his behavior changed wildly, so that he no longer had any self-control. When drunk he was even worse, hitting out at anyone in the street. His greatest atrocities were reserved for the Spanish. Some he tied on wooden stakes and roasted alive between two fires, as you would roast a hog. This was because they would not show him the way to the hog-yards to steal swine.

Right: This 1659 painting by Jacob van der Ulft (1627-1689) shows Dam Square, in Amsterdam, as it appeared in Rock the Brazilian's time. The Republic of the United Provinces was officially recognized in the Peace of Westphalia in1648 and was a major maritime trading nation.

Left: This depiction of the 1629 reconquest of St. Kitts was painted by Felix Castello (1602–1656). The Spanish drove out the English and French settlers, but Spanish resources were too thinly spread to prevent their return to the island.

After many more cruelties, Captain Rock was cruising along the coast of Campeche when a storm forced his ship aground. The crew managed to get ashore only some muskets, powder, and shot. They struggled overland toward El Golfo Triste, where pirates often put in to effect repairs or to careen their ships. After three or four days, starving and thirsty, Captain Rock's little party was eventually spotted by a troop of 100 Spanish cavalry.

Captain Rock urged his 30 men to fight to the death, as he had no intention of being taken prisoner by his most hated enemies. The men agreed, and in the cavalry charge, every pirate bullet found its mark. The battle lasted an hour, and the surviving Spaniards took flight. The sea-rovers killed the wounded and took their horses and food. They had lost only two men killed and two injured. The pirates rode along the coast road, where they noticed a Spanish barque, which had come to cut logwood.

The buccaneers hid in the forests, sending six men to spy on the Spanish. Next morning, as most of the Spanish were ashore cutting logwood, the six men took one of their canoes, rowed to the barque, and captured it. Rock the Brazilian now had a reasonable ship to sail home to Jamaica. There were few provisions aboard, so the pirates slaughtered some of their horses, salting them with some salt they found on the ship. Soon after, they encountered a ship sailing from New Spain, laden with meal and pieces of eight. It was bound for Maracaibo to buy cacao. Captain Rock took it and now sailed home to Jamaica, where he debauched with his crew until the money was spent. They spend their days whoring, drinking, and dicing until they had nothing left. Some might spend up to 3,000 pieces of eight in a day. I once saw one of Morgan's men in Jamaica give 500 pieces of eight to a whore, just to see her naked.

The man who paid to see the harlot naked had at that time 3,000 pieces of eight, but only three months later was himself sold for his debts, by the keeper of the tavern where he spent most of his money.

Rock was my own captain, and he used to buy a butt of wine, stand it in the street, and stand barring the way. Every passerby had to have a drink with him, or he promised to shoot them. Once he bought a cask of butter and threw the stuff at anyone who came near, covering their clothes or head.

The unscrupulous tavern-keepers

The pirates are generous to each other. As I have said, if a man has nothing, others will help him. But Jamaican tavern-keepers extend a great deal of credit, and you cannot trust them. I have often seen them sell a man for a debt. The man who paid to see the harlot naked had at that time 3,000 pieces of eight, but only three months later was himself sold for his debts, by the keeper of the tavern where he spent most of his money.

Returning to our story, Captain Rock had soon squandered all his money and took his crew to sea again, heading for the Campeche coast. After 14 days without a prize, he took a canoe into the Campeche roadstead to reconnoitre the shipping there. However, he and his ten seadogs were captured by the Spanish instead. The governor shut the captain in a dark hole with hardly anything to eat. The governor wanted to hang him, but Rock had cleverly written a letter, which appeared to have been delivered from his comrade buccaneers to the governor, and promised that if Rock was killed, no quarter would be given to any captured Spaniards in future. The governor feared that he might suffer the same fate, as Campeche had previously almost fallen into the hands of buccaneers led by Captain Mansveldt.

Captain Rock was therefore sent to Spain with the galleons of the treasure fleet, the flota. The governor made the pirate give his oath that he would never return to piracy, threatening Rock that he would hang him if he caught him transgressing again. On the voyage from the West Indies, Rock earned 500 pieces of eight by fishing, with which he bought clothes and necessities and was able to return to Jamaica, where he carried on harassing the Spanish at every opportunity.

Above: This 19th-century depiction of Rock the Brazilian shows him in a more heroic pose. The previous engraving (see page 60) depicted him as a cruel monster, for the benefit of its Spanish readers.

PORT ROYAL—PIRATE HEAVEN

When Cromwell's force took Jamaica in 1655, they amended the Carib-Spanish name of the town Cayagua to Cagway. It lay on the tip of the Palisadoes sand spit, which forms Kingston Harbor. The place was renamed Port Royal in 1660 on the restoration of Charles II, but was still called Cagway by Morgan and his men for some time after. Because of the fear of a Spanish invasion, buccaneers were asked to come from Tortuga to bolster its defenses.

After the 1660 peace with Spain, many buccaneers were granted letters of marque to attack shipping. By the early 1670s, Port Royal—a city of 7,000 people—rivaled even Boston in wealth and population. It was "pirate heaven," with a huge harbor that could accommodate up to 500 ships. At the heart of all the West Indies shipping routes, this was an easy market for pirate plunder. The waters were 30 feet deep just a few yards offshore, allowing for easy anchorage. Port Royal was also known for its "grog shops," gaming houses, and brothels, earning it the moniker "Sodom of the

New World." In 1661, in one month alone, the council issued licenses for 40 new grog shops, taverns, and punch houses. Among them were the "Black Dog," "Cheshire Cheese," "Sign of Bacchus," and "Sin of the Mermaid."

Around this time Jamaica's Governor Modyford was making a fortune in bribes from Henry Morgan and other buccaneers. On June 7, 1692, a combined earthquake and tidal wave destroyed this buccaneer capital, probably killing two-thirds of its population and sweeping Captain Morgan's grave into the sea.

This is a contemporary article about the earthquake and subsequent tsunami in 1692 that destroyed most of Port Royal and swept Henry Morgan's grave into the sea.

CHAPTER VI

The daring exploits of the pirates Lewis Scot, Edward Mansveldt, and John Davis

Seeing the difficulties of getting rid of the pirates, the Spanish reduced their number of voyages, but the buccaneers simply started attacking them on land, plundering villages and towns. The first sea-rover to start these new attacks was Lewis Scot, who plundered Campeche and forced its citizens to pay ransoms before he gave it back. He retired to Tortuga. After Scot came the Admiral Mansveldt (Edward Mansfield), who attacked Granada in Nicaragua in 1666 and attempted to ravage as far as the South Sea. He was forced to turn back for lack of food. First he had captured the island of St. Catalina, where he took prisoners who then led him to Cartagena, but he was unsuccessful.

The sea-rovers take to land

There was John Davis, who was waiting in the Gulf of Boca del Toro, hoping to capture a ship en route from Cartagena to Nicaragua. Being unlucky in this endeavor, he left his ship in the mouth of the Nicaragua River and took his crew upstream in canoes. The ship was concealed among trees, so as not to alert the Indians who fished in the area. He left ten men to guard the ship and took ninety others in three canoes. They traveled upriver by night, hiding in the forests in the daytime, and aimed to plunder Granada at night. On the third night, at midnight, they reached their goal and were mistaken for returning fishermen from the lagoon, as some of the buccaneers spoke good Spanish. They had an Indian with them who had escaped the Spanish, who wanted to enslave him. He approached a sentry and killed him, enabling the crew to land without any other force. They went to the mansions of three or four principal citizens and also plundered the churches. Some Spanish citizens managed to raise the alarm. The pirates fled with their booty as the garrison was being roused, taking some prisoners to use to obtain quarter, if the Spanish should catch up.

Just 90 men had struggled 40 leagues inland, taken a city garrisoned by 800 men, and seized 40,000 pieces of eight, silver, and jewels. At the river mouth, the buccaneers ransomed their prisoners for fresh meat to sail to Jamaica. While waiting for the meat to arrive, 500 armed Spanish rose up but were repelled by the ship's cannon fire. In Jamaica, they spent their loot, and John Davis was elected captain of a fleet of pirate ships. They agreed to cruise along the north coast of Cuba to wait for the fleet from New Spain, but missed it. Thus they set sail for the town of San Augustin in Florida. It had a fort, garrisoned by two companies of soldiers, but was plundered without any harm to the pirates.

They had an Indian with them who had escaped the Spanish, who wanted to enslave him. He approached a sentry and killed him, enabling the crew to land without any other force.

Above: Howard Pyle produced this idealized painting, *Buccaneer of Hispaniola in the Caribbean*, in the late 19th century. In truth the buccaneers were never this clean, nor as glamorous.

THE PIRATES' WOMEN AND THE GERMAN PRINCESS

Jamaica and Barbados were both home to huge numbers of transported criminals, including many prostitutes, who found no problem in carrying on their business in the infant colonies, where women were scarce. The most famous was "The German Princess," Mary Carleton, who was convicted of theft and bigamy and transported to Jamaica in 1671, where she gained some renown. Mary would pretend that she was born in Cologne, but was in fact English—born in Kent. She eventually returned to London and was hanged at Tyburn around 1673.

The sex trade gave rise to some colorful language in the West Indian colonies. A "punch house" was a common term for a brothel where alcohol was sold. In ports, "the stews" was a raucous area of narrow alleyways, gambling dens, taverns, and brothels frequented by sailors spending their money. "Catting" was chasing harlots. "Fishmonger" was another term for prostitute, probably derived from "fleshmonger." A "pitcher-bawd" was a former prostitute who took pitchers of beer to a tavern's customers. "Lap-clap" was the 17th-century term for copulation.

This 17th-century engraving depicts the embarkation of Parisian prostitutes bound for the colony of New Orleans.

Left: This photograph shows an aerial view of Castillo de San Marcos, in St. Augustine, Florida. This massive stone fortification was built by the Spanish between 1672 and 1695. John Davis attacked the previous settlement in retaliation for the Spanish attack on New Providence Island.

PIRATE WEAPONRY

The objective of privateers was to take ships without inflicting too much damage, either upon the ships themselves or their cargo. Both were too valuable to ruin. Rich passengers could be ransomed and the crew were expected to surrender immediately. If not, they were expendable and pirate weapons were developed to do the maximum damage. After firing their single shot muskets and pistols, pirates would use cutlasses and daggers to board an enemy ship. Caribbean cutlasses could be up to three feet in length. As the curve was slight and the tip was sharpened, a pirate with strong arms could also use it as a rapier when needed. Ammunition was carried in a cartouche—a leather or canvas bandolier worn over the shoulder which carried up to 30 cartridges.

BOARDING HOOK AND AXE

Boarding hooks with lines attached were used to haul two ships together. After that, the ship's rails were lashed together for easy boarding. Axes had a sharp blade on one end of the head and a blunt hammer on the other. The blade was used defensively, to cut the ropes of boarding hooks and the other ship's rigging and spars; the hammer was used offensively, to break down doors and bulkheads in the melee of boarding.

Left: The two sides of this axe head were designed to perform different functions.

Right: Muskets like the one in this illustration were single-shot weapons.

MUSKET

A musket was a single-shot rifle used to "pick off" the helmsman and officers of opposing ships prior to boarding. For short-range work the barrels were sawn off. An effective load of one musket ball and three heavy buckshot pellets was then inserted. The stock was sawn off so pirates could attach them to sashes across their chests.

GRENADE

A pirate's grenade, also called a *grenado* or *granado*, was a square bottle of glass, wood, or clay filled with pistol shot, glass, bits of iron, and gunpowder. Grenades were lit and thrown at the men on the opposite deck before boarding.

Left: An early metal grenade—illustrated in La Pyrotechnie, *published in France, 1630.*

DAGGER

A pirate's dagger was used for both eating and killing. Its straight blade was designed to thrust and puncture, not to slash like a cutlass. A cross-bar or hilt prevented the hand from slipping onto the blade and also deflected the strike of an enemy's cutlass, allowing the pirate to use his own cutlass against his undefended opponent in a split second. The dirk was a small, sharp knife used for throwing.

Left: An ornate dagger like this would not be used for fighting, but would fetch a high price as booty.

GRAPNEL

A grapnel, or grapple, was a light anchor with very sharp flukes, which could be thrown at a ship with the intention of boarding. The barbed flukes, once hooked into the ship, were difficult to extract and pirates could then climb the attached ropes.

Left: This small anchor made a perfect grappling hook.

POWDER HORN

Powder boxes and powder horns were small containers used for carrying gunpowder and keeping it dry. They were made of wood, leather, or ivory. In battle, the less able men, such as the cook, would use powder boxes to reload weapons for the men who were fighting. All fighting guns were single shot in those times—a pirate would drop his musket and use his cutlass until his gun was reloaded. He could not keep a powder box on his person, as any spark or shot would send him to kingdom come.

Right: Powderhorns were originally made from the horns of cattle.

CUTLASS

A cutlass was a short, curved sword ideal for close-range fighting on deck. Rapiers and "small swords" had long, thin blades that could slide between an opponent's ribs and puncture the heart or lungs. The cutlass was shorter, thicker, and wider and was used like a machete for hacking at limbs. A "basket-guard" covered the handle to protect the hand.

Right: A cutlass or "cut-lash" was used in a lashing out, slashing motion, not to thrust and pierce.

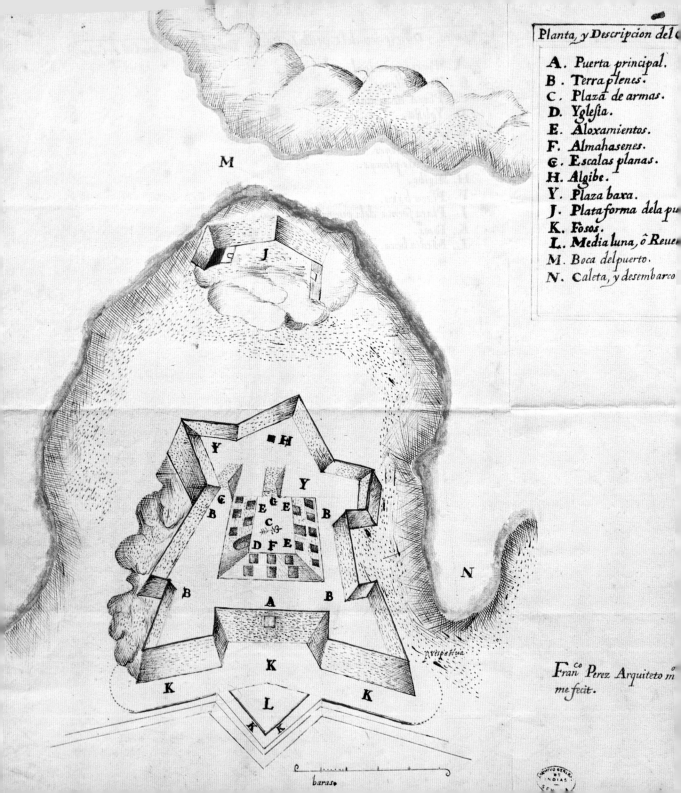

M

J

Y   H

Y

G   E G   B
B   E
C
D F E

B   B

A

N

perspectiva.

K

Franco Perez Arquiteto iñ
me fecit.

K   L   K

K   K

baras.

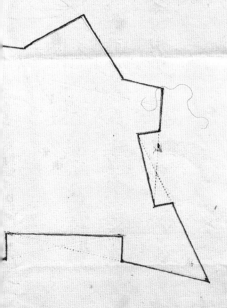

Sⁿ Pedro del puerto dela Ciú de Cuba.

dela Isla de Cuba y Ciu de Sⁿ X^ptoual dela Haū porsu Mag^d

PART THREE

The story of François L'Olonnais—From his origins and the beginning of his robberies to his famed cruelty and gruesome demise

Left: San Pedro de la Roca castle in Santiago, Cuba, shown here in a plan, was built between 1638 and 1643 and is now a World Heritage Site.

CHAPTER I

The origin of François L'Olonnais, and the
beginning of his robberies

Above: "The man from Olonne,"
François L'Olonnais, gained a
reputation for brutal atrocities in his
treatment of prisoners.

FRANCIS LOLONOIS.
Part. 2. Page. 1.

Jean-David Nau was born in the port of Les Sables d'Olonne in Bas-Poitou. In common with many buccaneers he hid his original name and became known as L'Olonnais, the man from Olonne. He was shipped out from La Rochelle to the Caribbean as a boy, serving as an indentured servant, or slave. After serving his time, he joined the hunters on Hispaniola, but he later committed unspeakable atrocities on the Spaniards. I will describe his main exploits, up to his death.

After L'Olonnais had sailed two or three times with the buccaneers, M. Frederick Deschamps de la Place, the governor of Tortuga, noticed his great courage. As France was at war with Spain, he gave his fellow Frenchman a ship with which to plunder the enemy. L'Olonnais made enormous gains and became known through the whole Spanish Main. Whenever the Spanish encountered him, they

PRIVATEERS AND LETTERS OF MARQUE

Privateers were semi-official pirates, who supplemented a country's navy with their own private warships. They were allowed to attack the enemy in times of war and keep a large percentage of any plunder. Privateers cost nothing to the governments that hired them. Their only reward was what they could take or "purchase," as in the term "no purchase, no pay." Francis Drake and Henry Morgan were noted privateers. Privateer was also the name given to a privately owned, armed vessel with a letter of marque.

Letters of marque were documents, commissions, or licenses given to privateers by governments, giving permission for privately owned ships to attack enemy merchant vessels. From 1589, 10 percent of the value of prizes went to the Crown, and 90 percent to the owner. Sometimes a commission given to a commander could extend to the hire of ships from other nationalities. For instance, Henry Morgan used to take French pirate ships from Tortuga under his own commission when attacking the Spanish. Privateers didn't always attack only the nations stipulated

in their letters of marque: Mansveldt and Morgan attacked the Spanish although their letter of marque was directed toward the Dutch. There were no naval frigates posted to protect Jamaica—a British outpost surrounded by Spanish colonies—so Jamaica needed extra defense from privateers, as well as the cheap goods they brought with them.

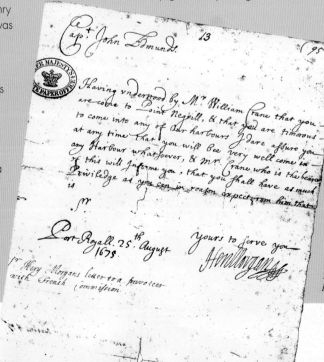

The Spanish lacked resources to protect their vast empire, so employed costagardas, who owned their own ships. English governors had minimal protection from the Royal Navy, so privateers were given written permission to attack the King's enemies.

fought until they could fight no more, as they knew he gave them no quarter. Fortune had favored him greatly, but he then lost his ship in a northerly gale on the coast of Campeche on the Yucatan in Mexico. They were forced ashore and all survived, but most of his men were then killed by the pursuing Spanish. L'Olonnais was wounded and had no chance of escaping the bloodshed, so he smeared himself with sand and blood from his wounds and hid under the corpses of his men on the beach. He waited motionless for the enemy to leave and then hid in the forest to recover and gain strength.

He bound up his wounds and in Spanish clothes ventured to the outskirts of the city of Campeche. He found some slaves, to whom he promised freedom if they followed him. The slaves stole one of their master's canoes and made for Tortuga with L'Olonnais. Meanwhile, the Spanish had interrogated some of the captain's shipmates in prison. They told the Spanish that L'Olonnais was dead, as they thought. The Spaniards thanked God and lit bonfires to celebrate.

L'Olonnais "returns from the dead"

In Tortuga, L'Olonnais entertained no thoughts of entering a more peaceful career. He obtained a small ship by trickery and sailed off with 20 well-armed men toward Cuba. On its coast there is a village called De los Cayos, which exports hides, tobacco, and sugar to Havana. Barques are used for trading there, as it is shallow along this coast. L'Olonnais' intention was to take some of these ships, but he was seen by fishermen. They traveled overland to Havana and told the governor that the French corsair was on the coast with two canoes and that they dared not go to sea until he had gone.

The governor had received news from Campeche that the French corsair was dead, but nonetheless he sent a ship with 90 well-armed men and ten cannons. Its captain was told not to return until he had destroyed the pirates, and a Negro was sent along as an executioner to hang the villains. However, he stipulated that L'Olonnais was to be brought back to Havana for a public hanging. The warship sailed to De los Cayos. L'Olonnais captured some fishermen and they told him about the ship and where it was located, hoping that he would free them and flee the area. However, the Frenchman had other ideas.

All the Spaniards were beaten back by the buccaneers, forced below deck, and the hatches secured tightly. L'Olonnais then allowed them to be brought onto the deck one by one, and he ordered their heads be lopped off.

The devious buccaneer wanted a new ship, in order to make a bigger fortune, and he forced the captured fishermen to show him the way into the port of De Los Cayos.

The taking of the man-of-war

The warship was anchored in the estuary, and one of the fishermen was forced to lead the pirates toward her. The sea-rovers approached along the shoreline, under the cover of trees. At two o'clock in the morning they approached the Spanish ship and were heard. They were hailed and asked if they had seen the pirates. The corsairs called back in Spanish saying that the pirates had fled, as they had been warned of the coming of the man-of-war. In the pitch-black, the Spaniards relaxed their guard, until at the break of dawn they heard the warlike cries of the pirates.

The Spanish took up battle stations, firing broadsides at the canoes on either side of them, near the river banks. After two or three rounds of cannon fire, the pirates judged their moment when the cannon were being reloaded and swarmed onboard, brandishing their cutlasses. All the Spaniards were beaten back by the buccaneers, forced below deck, and the hatches secured tightly. L'Olonnais then allowed them to be brought onto the deck one by one, and he ordered their heads be lopped off. After some time, the Negro, who was to have been the sea-rovers' executioner, came up, pleading "Senor Capitan, no me mateis! Os dire la verdad!" ("Don't kill me! I'll tell you the truth!"). L'Olonnais heard his confession, had him executed, and carried on killing all the men onboard except for one.

Right: Matanzas Bay, on the Straits of Florida, was once a pirate haven, but in 1693 the Spanish established a settlement there. By 1820 it had become Cuba's second city, mainly because of the growth of the sugar industry.

He gave this man a letter for the governor of Havana and also a verbal oath that he would never give quarter to any Spaniards he captured, no matter how many. He also told him that he would kill himself rather than fall into Spanish hands. The letter expressed the same sentiments and added that L'Olonnais hoped to hang the governor just as the governor had hoped to hang him.

Receiving this news, the enraged governor swore to kill every pirate that came into his hands, but the citizens pleaded with him not to do so. They argued that they had to go to sea every day to earn their living, and the corsairs could kill a hundred of them for every buccaneer the Spanish could take. They implored the governor not to start such a vengeful policy.

L'Olonnais now had the powerful ship he wanted, but there was little booty onboard as it was equipped for war, not trade. He therefore decided to get more men and go cruising for prey. Next he took a ship in the Gulf of Venezuela, which was bound for Maracaibo to buy cacao, so had both money and merchandise aboard. The corsairs returned to great rejoicing on Tortuga, and L'Olonnais soon decided to take a fleet to raid the Spanish coast. Some prisoners had promised to act as guides, providing he could gather 500 men, as he wished to take Maracaibo and plunder all the nearby coastal towns and villages. The prisoners knew the region well, especially a Frenchman whose wife lived there.

Below: This 18th-century depiction of the French pirate Robert Surcouf taking the English man-of-war *Kent* shows the disparity between small, maneuverable pirate craft and naval warships. In order to defeat a larger ship, the pirates usually had to forcibly board it and use their superior manpower and musketry.

CHAPTER II

L'Olonnais equips a fleet to land upon the Spanish islands of America, with intent to rob, sack, and burn whatever he meets

To carry out his grand design, L'Olonnais let his intentions be known to all pirates, either at home or abroad, and eventually over 400 men had joined him. There was also another famous pirate on Tortuga called Michel de Basco, who had gained so much booty that he could live at ease and never go to sea again. He was a Basque and had the office of Major of Tortuga. Seeing the preparations, Michel entered into friendship with L'Olonnais. The freebooter offered to take part if he was offered the captaincy of any land operations, as he knew the area very well. They agreed upon this, to the great joy of L'Olonnais, who knew that the Basque had performed great actions in Europe and had a reputation as an excellent soldier. He thus gave Michel land command, and they embarked in eight ships, that of L'Olonnais being the greatest, having ten cannons of varying size.

They set sail about the end of April 1667, having a considerable number of men for those parts— more than 630. A course was steered toward Bayaha on the north coast of Hispaniola (now Fort Liberté, in Haiti). Here they took on some French hunters, who volunteered their service. Also victuals, water, and other necessities were taken onboard for the voyage. On the last day of July, they sailed for Punta d'Espada, the eastern cape of the island, where they caught sight of a ship from Puerto Rico, bound for New Spain, carrying cacao. Admiral L'Olonnais gave orders for the rest of the fleet to rendezvous at the Isle of Saona, on the south side of the Cape, while he pursued the ship.

After being chased for two hours, the Spanish turned broadside on, and a battle ensued for three hours. The Spanish ship carried 16 guns and 50 fighting men, but at last was forced to surrender. Onboard, the corsairs found 120,000 pounds of cacao, but also 40,000 pieces of eight, and jewels worth

FORCED TRANSPORTATION

There was a continual need for labor in the colonies, and Britain's jails were full to overflowing, so a Royal Proclamation of 1617 allowed any felon, except those convicted of murder, witchcraft, burglary, or rape, to be transported to Virginia's tobacco plantations, or to the West Indian sugar plantations. Women were particularly required as "breeders." Thousands of children were also rounded up off London's streets and sent on the terrible journey. A 1627 letter noted that 1,500 children had been sent to Virginia in the previous year. A 17th-century word for seizing was "napping," thus the seizing of children to go to America as servants gave rise to the term "kidnapping."

Huge European demand for tobacco in the 17th century meant that large Caribbean tobacco plantations were set up to compete with those of Virginia. Plantations were labor-intensive, so workers had to be imported.

at least 10,000 pieces of eight. The Admiral sent the prize ship to be unloaded in Tortuga, and told his men to then return with her to Saona.

In the meantime, at Saona, the fleet had chanced across another Spanish vessel, en route from Cumana in Venezuela, laden with military provisions for Hispaniola, and also carrying money to pay the island's garrison. Although she carried eight guns, she was taken without resistance. On her were 7,000 pounds of gunpowder, great numbers of muskets and fuses, and 12,000 pieces of eight. The pirates were greatly encouraged to be so reinforced with provisions, arms, and money so early in their voyage.

When the ship laden with cacao had arrived at Tortuga, the governor had speedily unloaded and reprovisioned her with fresh provisions and sent her back to the rendezvous at Saona. He also sent more men, and all this was effected within a fortnight of the ship being taken. L'Olonnais now commandeered this ship as his own and gave his former flagship to his comrade Antony du Puis. The Admiral now had two extra ships, more provisions, and new recruits to replace those he had lost or who were wounded in taking the two prizes. His men were now ready and motivated for the expedition to begin, and he led the fleet to Maracaibo Bay, on the coast of New Venezuela. The bay is 20 leagues deep and 12 across. To seaward lie the islands of Onega and Los Monges; the bay's eastern headland is Cape San Roman, and its western is the Cape of Caquibacoa. Some call this bay the Gulf of Venezuela, but the pirates know it as the Bay of Maracaibo.

A description of the bay of Maracaibo

In the strait through which you enter the bay are two islands, lying east to west. The eastern one is Isla de las Vigilias, or Look-Out Island, because in its center is a high hill where a watchman is perpetually stationed. The other is Isla de las Palomas, Pigeon Island. Behind these islets, inland, is a great freshwater lake, a little sea being 60 leagues long and 30 wide, which disgorges into the ocean around the two islands. The best passage for ships is between the two islands, but the channel is no wider than the range of an eight-pounder cannon. There is a fort on Pigeon Island to impede entry to the lake and Maracaibo, and any ship wishing to enter must pass close to it, as there are two sandbanks in only 14 feet of water which must be avoided. Inwards there is another sandbank known as *El Tablazo*, The Great Table, which is no deeper than 10 foot, but this is one league further on in the lake. Others are no more than six, seven or eight fathoms deep, as far as Rio de las Espinas, about 40 leagues along the lake. All are dangerous, especially to those unacquainted with the lake.

A description of Maracaibo and Gibraltar

Six leagues along the western shore of the lake lies the pleasant city of Maracaibo, with fine houses ranged along the waterfront. The city may contain three to four thousand persons, including slaves. Of this population, about 800 are able to bear arms, all of them Spanish. There is a finely adorned parish church, four monasteries, and one hospital. Commerce consists mainly of hides and tallow, and the city has a deputy-governor, who is subordinate to the governor of Caracas. There are great numbers of cattle on the plantations of Maracaibo, which extend to the space of some 30 leagues into the country.

Below: The Gulf of Venezuela was known to the buccaneers as the Bay of Maracaibo. There were difficult sandbanks to negotiate to enter the Lake of Maracaibo. The largest lake in South America, it extends 110 miles inland, and the strait connecting it with the Gulf of Venezuela is 34 miles long.

After being chased for two hours, the Spanish turned broadside on, and a battle ensued for three hours.

Below: This engraving by Theodor de Bry (1528–1598) shows English traders in the West Indies around a century before Morgan's exploits. The Indians are using hollowed logs as *canoas*, or canoes, to take goods to the ships.

There are also plantations on the other side of the lake, around the great and populous town of Gibraltar. Here there are immense quantities of cacao-nuts and all sorts of garden fruits, which are sent to sustain the inhabitants of Maracaibo, where the lands are much drier. Maracaibo sends great quantities of meat to Gibraltar, and these boats return every day carrying oranges, lemons, and several other fruits. The fields of Gibraltar are not suitable for rearing sheep or cattle.

Maracaibo has a fine harbor, where all sorts of vessels can be built, as timber can be brought down from the forests at little cost. Near the town goats are reared on the small islet of Borica for their skins and tallow, not their flesh or meat, except the kids may be eaten. Many sheep are in the fields around Maracaibo but the ground is dry and the sheep are small.

In some of the islands of the lake live unconquered Indian tribes, whom the Spanish call Indios Bravos. They will not agree to any accord with the Spaniards, by reason of their brutish and untamable behavior. They live mainly on the west side of the lake, in small huts high in the trees which grow in the

water, to try to escape the innumerable mosquitoes which plague them night and day. On the eastern side are Spanish fishing villages, also built in the mangrove trees. Another reason for dwelling thus is the frequent floods, for after great rains the land is often flooded to the distance of two or three leagues, and no less than 25 great rivers and 50 streams flow into the lake.

Gibraltar is about 40 leagues along the coast of the lake and has 1,500 inhabitants, of which about 400 can bear arms. Most of the inhabitants keep shops, where they exercise one trade or another. The adjacent fields are cultivated with plantations of cacao and sugar, in which there are tall, beautiful trees useful for building houses and ships. Among the trees are huge cedars, from which they make piraguas, which can carry a topsail. Gibraltar is frequently drowned in the inundations, so the inhabitants have to leave and retire to their plantations.

There are plentiful rivers and streams, and in times of drought the inhabitants channel the water via sluices along ditches to water the crops. Much tobacco is exported, highly regarded in Europe, and known there as *Tabaco de Sacerdotes*, or Priests' Tobacco. The fertile land stretches 20 leagues, being bounded on one side by swamps and on the other by high mountains, which are always covered with snow. On the other side of the mountains is the great city of Merida, to which the town of Gibraltar is subject. All sorts of merchandise is carried by mule-train from Gibraltar to Merida, but only in one season of the year, on account of the unbearable cold and ice at other times. On the return from Merida the mules bring meal-flour, sent from Peru by way of Santa Fe.

A Spaniard once told me of a strange tribe who are said to live on these mountains, of the same stature as the Indians but with short curly hair, and with long claws on their feet, like apes. Their skin is reputed to resist arrows and sharp instruments, and they are agile climbers, with tremendous strength.

In some of the islands of the lake live unconquered Indian tribes, whom the Spanish call Indios Bravos. They will not agree to any accord with the Spaniards, by reason of their brutish and untamable behavior.

The Spanish tried to kill some of them with lances, but their iron could not pierce the skin. No one has ever heard them speak. Sometimes they come down to the plantations and carry off women slaves. I have read various descriptions of America, so I believe that they must be some type of Barbary ape, for I have seen such apes in the forest, but several Spaniards have assured me that these creatures are human, and that they have seen them frequently, so I recount it here, for what it is worth. Truly, God's works are great, and these things may well be.

The attack on El Fuerte de la Barra

I thought it convenient to describe the Lake of Maracaibo, so my reader is better able to comprehend the event which took place. When he arrived at the Gulf of Venezuela, L'Olonnais made his fleet cast anchor out of sight of Look-Out Island. The next day, very early, they sailed to the mouth of Lake Maracaibo, setting anchor in front of the sand-bar. It was impossible to enter the lake without passing under the fort known as El Fuerte de la Barra, which commanded the passage, so men were landed to attack it. The fort consisted of 16 great mounds of earth, placed on rising ground, each with a great gun, and gabions—earth-filled wicker containers—protected its soldiers. The pirates landed a league away, but seeing them approaching the governor of the fort had placed some men to ambush them from behind, while he attacked them with a frontal assault.

However, an advance guard of 50 corsairs discovered the ambush party and attacked the Spaniards, cutting off their retreat to their fort. Now L'Olonnais and his comrades could advance on the fort. After a battle lasting three hours, armed only with pistols and swords, the buccaneers took the fortress. During the fighting, survivors from the ambush party fled to Maracaibo, telling its citizens that 2,000 pirates would be there soon. The citizens panicked, remembering its sacking of 10 to 12 years previously, and began packing to move out. Those with boats headed for Gibraltar, spreading the news, and others took their goods inland on horses and pack-mules.

A pistol and coins salvaged from the 1724 wreck of the Conde de Tolosa, *in the Casas Reales Museum, Santo Domingo, Dominican Republic. The* Conde de Tolosa *was struck by a hurricane in Samana Bay along with the* Nuestra Senora de Guadalupe. *Both ships were wrecked on a reef.*

SPANISH WRECKS

Of the hundreds of Spanish colonial shipwrecks that occured from the 16th to the 18th century, only a few were treasure ships. The oldest recovered galleon is the *Nuestra Señora de Atocha* (or *Atocha*), which left Cuba in 1622 in a fleet of 28 ships that was making the return journey to Spain carrying gold, silver, coins, jewels, and logwood for dyes. The whole fleet sank. The loss of this fleet had a huge impact on Spain, forcing it to borrow more money in order to finance its role in the Thirty Years War. The *Atocha* was discovered off Florida in 1985, with a treasure of gold and silver bars and coins intact.

In 1715 a fleet of eleven galleons carrying gold and silver, valued at almost fifty six million reales, was struck by a hurricane off the east coast of Florida, near Cape Canaveral. The ships broke apart and sank—their cargo scattered over the ocean floor. Five of these wrecks have been located and a great deal of treasure recovered.

THE "JOLLY ROGER"

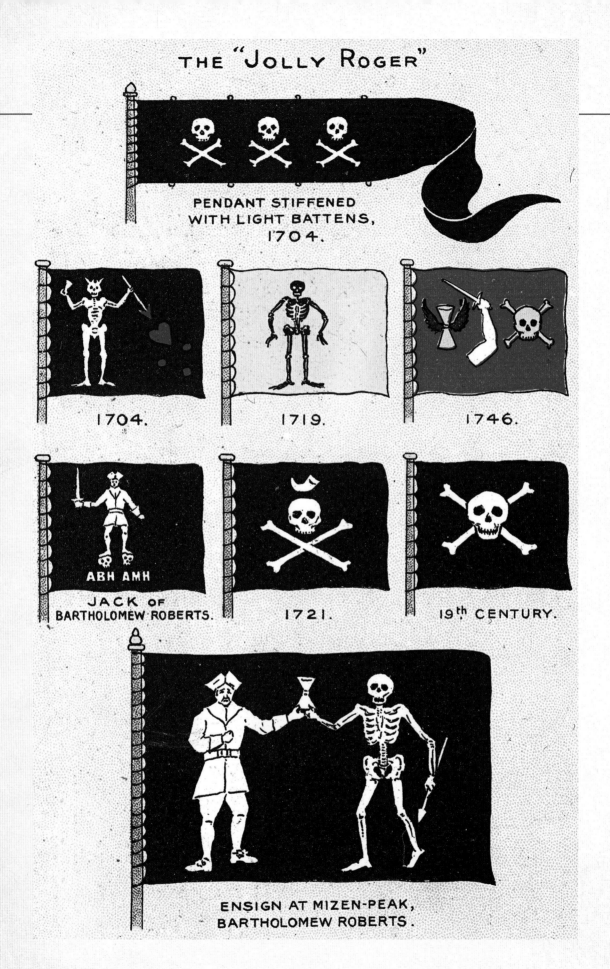

PENDANT STIFFENED WITH LIGHT BATTENS, 1704.

1704.

1719.

1746.

JACK OF BARTHOLOMEW ROBERTS.

1721.

19th CENTURY.

ENSIGN AT MIZEN-PEAK, BARTHOLOMEW ROBERTS.

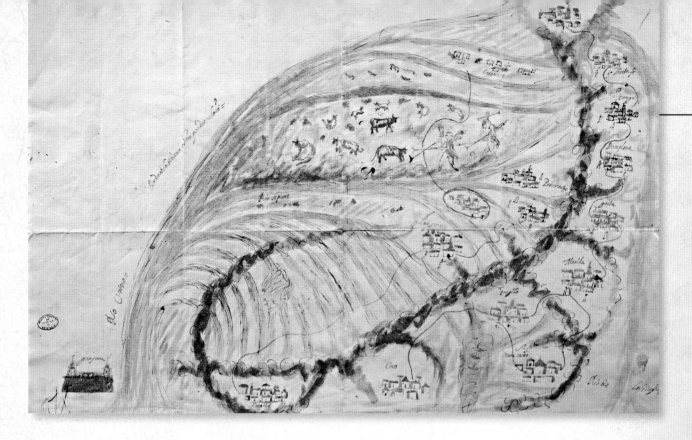

Above: This 1675 map shows the Orinoco River, Venezuela, in 1675. The exact length of the river is even now unknown, with estimates ranging between 1,500 and 1,700 miles, making it one of the world's largest river systems.

The buccaneers hoisted a flag when they had taken the fort, as a signal that their ships could pass through safely into Lake Maracaibo. The rest of the day was spent demolishing the fort, spiking its guns, burning the gun-carriages, burying their dead, and taking the wounded to the ships. However, very early next morning the fleet was ready to weigh anchor and sailed the six leagues to Maracaibo. Progress was slow because of the lack of winds, but eventually the ships ranged in formation outside Maracaibo, in order to give the landing parties maximum support with their cannon. The landing was made in canoes, and it was agreed that half the men in each canoe should stay in it, while the other half landed under covering fire from the ships into the woods. However, there was no response whatsoever, and the corsairs gathered all their forces and marched in good order into Maracaibo.

The sack of Maracaibo, 1667

The city was deserted, but there were plenty of provisions—wine, brandy, chickens, pigs, bread, and meal. The best houses were used as the buccaneers celebrated their victory, after four weeks of abstinence and short rations. Sentries were posted and the church was used as their guardhouse. Next morning a party of 150 men was sent into the woods to find prisoners, and to discover where the wealth of the city had been hidden. They returned later that day with 20,000 pieces of eight, 20 prisoners—men, women, and children—and several mules laden with household goods and merchandise.

Some prisoners were put to the rack, but no useful information was obtained from them. Then L'Olonnais drew his cutlass and hacked a prisoner to death in front of the others, saying "If you do not confess and declare where you have hidden the rest of your goods, I will do the like to all your companions." One prisoner was so terrified that he promised to take the pirates to where the fugitives were hiding. However, the Spaniards in the forest, realizing that a prisoner would inform on them, constantly changed their hiding places, and the sea-rovers had no chance of finding them. The citizens were so fearful that a father would not trust his son with any information.

The attack on Gibraltar

Finally, after 14 to 15 fruitless days in Maracaibo, the pirates decided to attack Gibraltar. Spanish spies warned its citizens that the buccaneers intended to cross over the mountains to Merida. The governor of Merida had seen active service as a colonel in Flanders, and when informed of the buccaneers' plans,

*S*ome 200 Spanish charged after them, but at a command the
buccaneers turned, fired their muskets unerringly, and then charged
with their cutlasses, killing most of the Spanish.

he headed for Gibraltar with 400 men and mustered another 400 in Gibraltar. He quickly mounted
a battery of twenty cannon facing the sea, all protected by baskets of earth. A further battery of eight
guns acted as a redoubt, and the narrow highway into the town was also blockaded. He then opened up
another pathway into the town, through the wood, which was unknown to the pirates.

L'Olonnais had embarked all his prisoners and booty and now saw that the royal standard of Spain
was flying over Gibraltar and the town had been heavily defended. He called a council of war with his
captains and then with his men. He told his men that the task would now be difficult, but roused his
men to follow him. They agreed, and he told them, "Tis well, and I will lead you, but know ye that the
first man who shows any fear or lack of courage in battle, I shall shoot down."

The fleet then anchored a quarter of a league from the town, and next morning 380 men landed,
each armed with a cutlass, a musket, and one or two pistols, and sufficient powder and a cartouche
or cartridge belt of 30 bullets. The men shook hands, swore oaths of comradeship, and were led by
L'Olonnais, who cried, "Allons, mes frères, suivez-moi, et ne faites point les lâches!" ("Come on,
brothers, follow me, and let's have no cowardice!")

They followed their guide, but the way he knew had been barricaded by the governor. They thus had
to take the muddy path through the wood and marshes, where the Spaniards could shoot them at will.
Nonetheless, the pirates slashed branches from trees so that they could step on them and not sink in the
mud. The guns from the fort kept up continuous fire, so the sea-rovers could hardly see for the smoke,
or hear each other because of the noise. Coming at last out of the wood, they met with firm ground, but
a battery of eight guns fired small bullets and grape-shot at them. Taking advantage, the Spanish sallied
forth and forced the pirates to retreat. The great guns kept firing continuously, and many buccaneers lay
dead or wounded. The living tried to find another way through the forest, but the Spanish had cut down
many trees to block any paths, and they were eventually forced to retreat.

L'Olonnais saw that his men could not get near enough to scale the gabions and used a stratagem
to outwit the Spaniards, pretending to retreat. Some 200 Spanish charged after them, but at a command
the buccaneers turned, fired their muskets unerringly and then charged with their cutlasses, killing
most of the Spanish. They carried on, forcing the Spanish behind the earthworks to flee into the forests
and killing every man they found. The pirates next advanced upon the redoubt, and its defenders
surrendered on the promise of quarter.

The pirates tore down the Spanish flag, setting up their own, and herded prisoners into the church.
They dragged up most of the cannon and placed them behind a breastwork, expecting another attack
when the Spaniards rallied. However, on the next day they realized that they were relatively safe. They
gathered the dead for burial, to prevent a stench, and found the corpses of more than 500 Spanish, not
counting those wounded, who had fled into the woods and died there. As well as this, there were 150
Spanish male prisoners, plus 500 women, children, and slaves. Their own losses totaled just 40 dead and
30 wounded. Most of these wounded died on account of fever brought on by the unhealthy atmosphere
and of their wounds soon turning gangrenous. The prisoners were forced to bury the pirate corpses. The
Spanish dead were thrown into two old boats, which were lying on the beach, taken out about a quarter
of a league toward the lake, and sunk.

Right: Most Spanish losses of treasure were caused by storms in the Caribbean. This treasure was salvaged from the *Conde de Tolosa*, which sank in a hurricane in 1724 off Samana Bay, in the Dominican Republic.

The sack of Gibraltar

The pirates then gathered all the silver plate, household stuff, and merchandise that they could carry away, although the Spanish had hidden most of their valuable possessions carefully. The pirates began to seek more booty, not sparing even those who lived in the fields, such as the hunters and planters, and brought in more goods and slaves. After only 18 days, most of their prisoners had died of hunger. In the town very few provisions could be found, especially meat. There was some flour, but the pirates took this for themselves to make bread. Likewise, they killed and ate any cows, swine, sheep, and poultry they could find. The poor prisoners had to make do with the flesh of mules and donkeys, or die of hunger, for they were given nothing else. The only people to get better food were the women, whom the pirates used for their own pleasure, some by force and others of their own free will, because they were driven to it by hunger. Prisoners suspected of concealing money or jewels were stretched on the rack. If they would not, or could not, confess, they were then killed.

After four weeks, four of the surviving prisoners were sent to the Spaniards who had fled into the woods, demanding a ransom of 10,000 pieces of eight for not burning the town to ashes. They were given just two days, and after this parts of the town were set alight. The inhabitants begged them to stop, telling them that if they did so, the ransom would somehow be paid. However, several houses had been damaged and the monastery church burnt to the ground by this time.

The return to Maracaibo

After receiving the ransom, L'Olonnais embarked all the booty and many slaves who had not been ransomed. The other prisoners had been all been ransomed. The pirates sailed back to Maracaibo, which was still in a distressed state. There they sent three or four of the prisoners, who had been taken from Maracaibo, to the governor, demanding 30,000 pieces of eight be brought to the ships as ransom for their houses; otherwise the city would be burnt to the ground. Meanwhile, raiding parties went ashore, stripping statues, bells, and paintings out of churches and marine stores from the warehouses. The Spanish prisoners returned with orders to negotiate a deal, and a sum of 20,000 pieces of eight and 500 cattle was agreed upon.

The pirates left, to the great joy of Maracaibo's inhabitants, which was only to turn to despair just three days later, when the pirate fleet returned. However, a pirate came ashore stating that L'Olonnais demanded a skilful pilot to help him negotiate his large and heavily laden flagship around the dangerous sandbanks at the entry of the lake. This request was willingly granted, to rid themselves of the buccaneers after two months on the lake. The fleet sailed out of the gulf, and eight days later anchored at Isla de la Vaca, Cow Island, to the south of Hispaniola.

The sharing of the booty

A few French hunters live here and sell meat to the buccaneers who use the island. All the loot was brought on shore and shared out according to pirate custom. There were 260,000 pieces of eight, 10,000 crowns worth of tobacco, and the silverware was weighed and assessed at ten pieces of eight to a pound of silver. The value of the jewels was roughly estimated, as they had no exact knowledge of their value. Apart from this, there were at least 100 pieces of eight for each man in the value of linen, silk goods, and other trifles. Those who had been wounded were compensated first, before all the rest. Then, after every man had sworn an oath that he had hidden nothing, each was given his allotted share. For those who had died in battle, their shares were given to their partners or friends or lawful heirs.

The buccaneers now sailed for

Tortuga and arrived a month later, to scenes of great joy. However, some had their money for only three days before it was gambled away at cards or dice. A short time before, three French ships had arrived with wine and brandy, so alcohol had been cheap. However, prices rose to meet the new demand from the newly rich buccaneers, and soon the corsairs were paying four pieces of eight for a flagon of brandy. The governor bought the ship full of cacao for a twentieth of its value. The tavern-keepers made a fortune, and the harlots took the rest. Thus, soon the buccaneers, including their captain, L'Olonnais, had to seek more money by the same unlawful means as before.

Above: The old Spanish monastery at Antigua, Guatemala is now a hotel. Monasteries like this were attacked and looted during pirate attacks.

NEW-WORLD SHIPS

Privateers and pirates preferred fast, small ships of 30–50 tons and often redesigned the sails and rigging for better airflow and speed. All deckhouses would be cut down to streamline the ship, leaving the deck clearer to allow cannon and resources to be shifted from one side to the other during a fight. The gunwales would be raised to give the crew extra protection. If a large boat was taken, it was usually used to store plunder, before being destroyed, sold, or set adrift. In the shallow waters of the Caribbean, captured galleons were useless for pirates. Neither were naval men-of-war any use. Three-masted frigates of around 360 tons were preferred, carrying 195 men and 26 guns. Fast warships like these were not big enough to be "ships of the line" but were often used against pirates. The Royal Navy had a limited presence in the New World, so most of the defense of Jamaica had to be carried out by privateers.

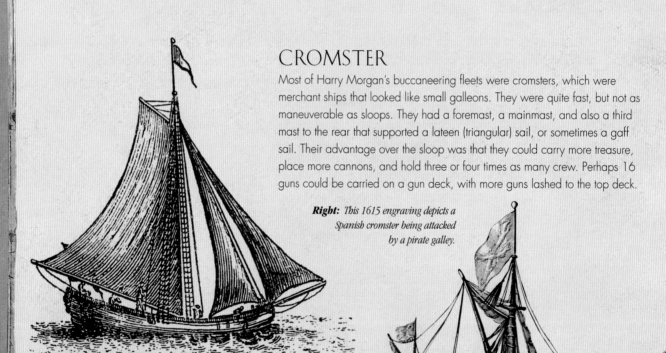

CROMSTER

Most of Harry Morgan's buccaneering fleets were cromsters, which were merchant ships that looked like small galleons. They were quite fast, but not as maneuverable as sloops. They had a foremast, a mainmast, and also a third mast to the rear that supported a lateen (triangular) sail, or sometimes a gaff sail. Their advantage over the sloop was that they could carry more treasure, place more cannons, and hold three or four times as many crew. Perhaps 16 guns could be carried on a gun deck, with more guns lashed to the top deck.

Right: This 1615 engraving depicts a Spanish cromster being attacked by a pirate galley.

Above: The barque—small and fast—was a popular pirate ship.

BARQUE

A Barque (or Bark) was a smallish ship with three masts. The foremast and following mast were rigged square and the aftermast (mizzen mast) rigged fore and aft. This type of ship, fast and with a shallow draft, could hold 90 men. Before the 1700s, the term barque was applied to any small vessel.

MERCHANT SHIP

In the 17th and 18th centuries, all commercial ships were referred to as merchant ships, but seamen usually reserved this term for a specific three-masted, square-rigged vessel, which could carry passengers or cargo. A typical ship weighed about 280 tons, measured 80 feet in length, and took 20 crew. Merchant ships might carry 16 cannon, but it is unlikely that the "short-handed" crew could handle more than four at a time. With excellent sail power, these ships could cross the Atlantic from Britain to America in about four weeks.

Right: A replica of Francis Drake's Golden Hinde, *built during a transitional phase, when galleons were replacing their predecessors, carracks.*

Above: Galleons like this were favored by the Spanish for both trade and war.

GALLEON

Used for either trade or war, these huge ships had three or four masts, square rigged on the foremast and mainmast, and latine-rigged on the after-mast(s). Whereas an average sailing ship weighed around 400 tons, the weight of a galleon on the transatlantic route might vary between 400 and 1,000 tons. Sailing qualities varied, with speeds of four to eight knots. They could carry 20–76 guns, of varying caliber. If used as a man-of-war, there would be 36 guns mounted on each side, with two remaining guns mounted aft, making 74 cannon, plus numerous swing guns mounted along the rail used to repel boarders. Galleons were usually terribly over-crowded, often carrying an infantry company of at least 100 troops under an army captain. Because of their high sides and even higher poop deck, galleons were easily rocked by the sea and pitched and rolled more than other ships.

DUTCH FLUYT

The fluyt was an early-17th-century ship: Cheap to build, with a large hold, and easy prey for pirates. She was about 300 tons and 80 feet long, and needed only a dozen seamen to man her. With a flat bottom, broad beams, and a round stern, this type of ship became a favorite cargo carrier, having about 150 percent of the capacity of similar ships. However, it was slower and less wieldy than the normal merchant ship, so was more easily taken.

Right: Fluyts such as the one pictured here were important in West Indian trade.

CHAPTER III

*L'Olonnais makes new preparations to take the city of
St. James de Leon; and also that of Nicaragua, where he
miserably perishes*

Discussing his new expedition with his lieutenants, L'Olonnais decided to sail for Lake Nicaragua and plunder the area. Because of his great renown, and the profits made from his last voyage, L'Olonnais had no problem in attracting around 700 men to serve under him. He put 300 on the large ship he had taken before Maracaibo, off Punta d'Espada, and the other 400 men were shared around five smaller ships. They rendezvoused at Bayaha, in Hispaniola, to take on salted meat and provisions for the fleet. An agreement was drawn up and they set sail for the Gulf of Matamano, on the south of Cuba. This was a center for turtle fishing, from where salted turtles were sent to Havana. They took the fishermen's canoes, which they would need to head upriver in Nicaragua, the river being too shallow for their ships.

Having stolen these canoes, they sailed for Cape Gracias a Dios, 100 leagues from the Isla de los Pinos, the Island of Pines. However, a flat calm meant that the fleet drifted into the Gulf of Honduras instead. The prevailing wind and currents were then against them regaining their course, and L'Olonnais' flagship became separated from the others. Worse still, he was running out of provisions, so was forced by hunger and thirst into the first river mouth available. A few canoes were sent up the Rio Xagua (Aguan) in Honduras, six leagues east of Trujillo, where they robbed and destroyed Indian villages. They returned to the ship with some Spanish wheat, or maize, and pigs, hens, turkeys, and whatever they could find.

The taking of Puerto de Caballos

There were still not enough provisions for their expedition, so they held another council and decided to wait in the area until the bad weather had passed. They cruised along the coast, carrying on plundering food supplies, and even shot forest apes for food. At last they came to Puerto de Caballos in Honduras, west of St. James de Leon (now Puerto Cortes), where the Spanish had two storehouses of goods awaiting embarkation. Here they seized a Spanish ship of 24 guns and 16 *pateraras,* or swivel-pieces. The warehouses and the hides inside them were all burnt, and the unfortunate Spanish prisoners were tortured abominably. If a victim was on the rack and would not confess, L'Olonnais would cut him to pieces with his sword, and lick his blood off his cutlass, wishing that the poor wretch had been the last Spaniard in the world that he had killed. Sometimes, driven by the cruel torture, a Spaniard would offer to show where others were hiding or goods were hid, but then could not show, the way. He would then be inflicted with a thousand torments before being killed.

Ambushed!

Every one of the prisoners was tortured and killed, except for two who promised to lead the corsairs to San Pedro, ten or twelve leagues inland from Puerto de Caballos. L'Olonnais led 300 men, leaving the remainder under the command of Moise van Wijn. After three leagues, they were ambushed by a troop of

Opposite page: This engraving from an early edition of Exequemelin shows L'Olonnais tearing the heart out of one of his Spanish captives and forcing another to eat it. Such depravity ensured that the other prisoners would confess where they had hidden their riches.

Spaniards. After a hard fight, when many on both sides were killed and wounded, the pirates put them to flight. L'Olonnais questioned the Spanish wounded about the strength of their forces and killed them if they would not talk. He then turned his attention to the unwounded prisoners. He asked each in turn if there were more ambushes in front of him. They all told him there were. He asked each if there was another way to the town, avoiding the ambushes. They all told him that there was no other way. Enraged, L'Olonnais drew his cutlass and cut open the breast of one of the prisoners. He pulled out his heart and began to bite and gnaw it, like a ravenous wolf. He then threw it into the face of a Spaniard, shouting "I will serve you all alike, if you show me not another way."

Thus the miserable wretches told him that there was another way, but it was very difficult and laborious. They began to lead the pirates, but it proved inaccessible, so L'Olonnais was forced to go back to the original route, swearing that the Spaniards would pay for it. He shouted "Mort Dieu. Les Espagnols me le payeront!" ("By God's death, the Spanish shall pay for this!") The next day there was another ambush. L'Olonnais was so furious that within an hour his men had killed the majority of the Spaniards. No quarter was given. The Spanish tactics were to wear down the buccaneers by degrees, posting men in several places, so that eventually the attackers would become too weak and too disheartened to succeed.

A third ambush was laid, with yet more Spanish troops, but the pirates threw fireballs or hand grenades to force their foes to take flight. There was such a loss of life that the majority of the Spanish were killed or wounded before they could retreat to their town. There were barricades on the approach road to the town, and all around it certain shrubs called raquettes, or prickly pear, were planted, full of sharp-pointed thorns. It was almost impossible for the pirates to traverse these spiny shrubs. They were even worse than the spiked caltrops used in European warfare to obstruct roads.

The taking of San Pedro

As the attackers approached, the Spanish fired their great guns, but the pirates dropped down flat onto their stomachs and attacked after the volley had been discharged. With muskets and hand grenades they killed many Spaniards but could not break through and retreated. Another attack was made with fewer men, who held their fire until sure of hitting a target. Eventually, toward evening, the Spanish waved a white flag, asking for a truce to parley. They asked for quarter, surrendering the town on condition that they had two hours grace to move some possessions out of the town. L'Olonnais kept his promise, but as soon as the two hours had expired the pirates chased them and made most of them prisoners, taking all their goods. However, the greatest part of the town's possessions had been removed and hidden previously, and the buccaneers found nothing there except a few leather bags containing anil, the dye called indigo.

The buccaneers stayed a few days, committing the usual atrocities, before they burnt the town to ashes and returned to their ships. Here they found that their comrades who had been guarding the ships had captured some Indian fishermen. The prisoners told them that a ship from Spain was expected at the Guatemala river-mouth. Two canoes were left there to keep a look-out for the ship,

Above: Prickly pear cactus is also known by its Aztec name, *Nopal.* It was cooked and eaten by Native Americans and also used in medicine.

Enraged, L'Olonnais drew his cutlass and cut open the breast of one of the prisoners. He pulled out his heart and began to bite and gnaw it, like a ravenous wolf.

CAREENING

To careen a ship is to haul it over on its side, or "heave to," to allow for cleaning or repair to the wooden hull. Pirates were most vulnerable when they careened their ships (Bannister's 36-gun *Golden Fleece* was destroyed by the Royal Navy while he was careening in Hispaniola in 1686), so they would take them to a quiet, isolated place.

Guns would be set up to guard the bay and provisions taken off the boat. The masts would then be pulled to the ground to present the ship's bottom for inspection. The hull was scraped of barnacles, patched, and coated with tallow and pitch for protection from marine borers and weeds, which made vessels slow and awkward to steer. The worst borer was a mollusc known as the teredos, or shipworm. In warm waters like the Caribbean careening had to take place at least once every two or three months.

The West Indies was full of coves and cays where pirates could careen their ships in relative safety. Speed was of the essence, as they were defenseless when their ship was beached.

while the buccaneers took their fleet to some islands on the other side of the gulf to careen them ready for action and to catch turtles for provisions.

They made nets from the fibrous bark of macao trees, which they also used for making ropes for the ships. The buccaneers are alert to any opportunity to use materials for their own purpose, wherever they are. On some islands, for instance, they find pitch, with which they make their boats water-tight. To make tar, they dilute pitch with sharks' oil. This pitch is washed up by the sea in such quantities that whole islands have been formed from it. It is not like the ship's pitch used in Europe, but is a scum from the sea, which naturalists call bitumen. In my opinion, it is bee wax thrown into the sea by storms and great rivers and washed up on shore and mixed with sand, smelling like the black ambergris which comes from the east. There are great multitudes of bees in this region, and their honeycombs are blown down from the trees and carried seaward. Some naturalists consider that water causes a separation in this honey, which results in the formation of ambergris. This is easily credible, for when found ambergris is still soft and smells like wax.

The Indians of Yucatan

The careening was effected quickly, to be ready for the arrival of the Spanish ship. In the meantime the pirates cruised in canoes along this coast, where many Indians live, looking for ambergris. For over a hundred years the Indians of this coast of Yucatan have been under the dominion of the Spanish, and whenever the Spanish need their labor, they carry them off and treat them very cruelly. Every six months a priest is sent there, and they claim to convert the Indians, but the visit furnishes more ungodliness than honor and service to God, for they come only to rob these simple folk of what they possess.

When the priest arrives, the *cacique*, or chief, has to give him his daughter or another woman of his family, for his use as long as he stays. Also, every day the Indians must give as many hens, eggs, or turkeys as the priest demands. Should he see them practicing their own religion, the priest and his colleagues seize and punish them, casting their chiefs into prison. When the priest sees that they have nothing left to give him, he leaves. As soon as he has gone, they return to their own religion.

When a child is born, he is taken to a temple where the Indians sacrifice to their gods. A hole or circle is made and filled with clean ashes. The naked baby is placed in the middle of the circle and left for the night.

The animal guardians

Every Indian has a god whom he serves or worships. When a child is born, he is taken to a temple where the Indians sacrifice to their gods. A hole or circle is made and filled with clean ashes. The naked baby is placed in the middle of the circle and left for the night. Their temple is open on all sides, so animals can wander in at will, and next morning the baby's father and relations come to see if any animals have entered in the night. If not, the child is left there until tracks are left showing that an animal has entered the temple. They know what animal it is—a dog, cat, lion or whatever—by its prints, and that animal becomes the child's patron and protector, to help him in any adversity. To honor the guardian they burn a sweet resin known as copal.

When the child is old enough, his parents tell him the name of the beast that he must worship in the temple, and he makes offerings there. After, if anyone injures him or harm happens to him, he complains to his guardian and makes offerings to it in the temple. Many times the wrong-doer is found killed, maimed by the relevant animals. A Spaniard told me the following tale. He had come to trade with the Indians and was obliged to live with them for some time. As Spaniards cannot live for long without a woman, he took an Indian wife to look after him and use for his pleasure. She went one day to the plantations to pick some fruit, and being gone a long time he searched after her. He saw her in the plantation, with a lion doing his will with her. He ran back to his house, and when she came home he asked what she had been doing with the lion. At first she seemed ashamed, then confessed that the lion was her patron. The Spaniard sent her from his house and would have no more to do with her.

The Indians of all the islands of the Gulf of Honduras and those that dwell on the mainland of Yucatan follow these customs. They have strange marriage ceremonies. A suitor approaches the girl's father. The father will ask if he has any other wife, whether he has a large plantation, if he is a good fisherman, and other useful questions. Being satisfied, he gives the young man a bow and arrow, and the suitor takes the maid a garland of green leaves, interwoven with sweet-smelling flowers. This she places on her head and rids herself of the braided flowers virgins wear in their hair. The couple then go to the temple and make offerings to their patrons, asking that the wedding shall come to pass. They then meet at the father's house and drink liquor made from maize. There, before the assembled company, the father gives away his daughter. The next day the bride goes to her mother, takes her head-piece off, and tears it to pieces, wailing, as is the custom when a maid loses her virginity. The new husband appears with his bow and arrow and weapons and shows great friendship to his new parents-in-law. Many things I could relate about the Indians, but I shall return to my story of piracy.

The pirates break up

Our pirates had captured many canoes from the Indians of the isle of Sambale (now Ambergris Cay, off Belize), five leagues from the coasts of Yucatan. On that island can be found large quantities of ambergris, especially when a storm blows from the west, and many other things can be found on its beaches, such as parts of canoes from the Caribbean, over 500 leagues away. In the lands surrounding this sea are huge quantities of Campeche wood, or logwood, and other trees and shrubs used for dyeing.

Opposite page: "Carib" was the European term given to the Kalinago Indians in the Antilles. This engraving of the Carib King Quoniambet is from *La Cosmographie Universelle* (Paris, 1575) by André Thevet (1502–1590).

The smoke of gunpowder still lay thick about the Spanish ship, as four canoes full of buccaneers approached it. They swarmed up her sides and forced the surrender.

I believe that these trees would be much more esteemed back at home in Europe and much use would be made of them, if we only had the knowledge and skills of the Indians, who are able to make beautiful dyes or tinctures that never fade, unlike ours.

The buccaneers had been waiting for three months when they received advice that the Spanish ship had arrived. They hastened to the port, where the ship was unloading, with the intention of taking it at the right time. Before attacking, they sent some of their smaller boats to wait in the estuary for another barque that was expected, laden with silver plate, indigo, and cochineal. The great Spanish ship had been warned that the corsairs were raiding along the coast, and they had taken every care while unloading, to ensure they would not be taken by surprise. Thus they had ready 130 armed men, as well as 42 cannons and other armaments onboard.

L'Olonnais cared not for their defenses, but assaulted the ship directly with his own 22-gun ship, assisted only by a small saetia, or flyboat. There was such resistance that he was forced to retire from the engagement. The smoke of gunpowder still lay thick about the Spanish ship, as four canoes full of buccaneers approached it. They swarmed up her sides and forced the surrender. Unfortunately, there was not the booty that they had expected, as the ship had been unloading rapidly and the goods had been taken away. The Spanish had intended to strip the ship of all nonessential goods, sail into the middle of the estuary, and await the pirate attack. Nonetheless, onboard the corsairs found 50 bars of iron, 50 bales of paper, many earthen jars of wine, and some other goods.

A pirate council is convened

Next, L'Olonnais called a council with his whole fleet and proposed that they head for Guatemala. For many, this had been their first voyage of piracy, and they had thought that pieces of eight were to be shaken off the trees. Now they just wished to go home. Others, more used to the life of buccaneers, said they would rather starve than return home with no booty. The majority felt L'Olonnais' proposed voyage would be of little purpose, and they left him. Moise van Wijn, who was captain of the ship taken at Puerto de Caballos, took course toward Tortuga, to cruise in those seas.

He was joined in leaving by Pierre le Picard, who had decided to do the same when he saw van Wijn leave. Le Picard sailed along the mainland coast to Panama, making a landing on the River Veragua. He took his men to the town of that name and pillaged it, defeating fierce resistance from a force of Spaniards. Several prisoners were carried for ransom to his ship, but there was little plunder. Its inhabitants were poor people, who worked in the mines. There are several gold mines in the area, and slaves are forced to dig in them.

After it is dug out, the earth is washed in the river, commonly yielding tiny pieces of gold the size of peas, sometimes bigger and sometimes smaller. All the corsairs found were about seven or eight pounds of gold. Thus they returned to the ship, deciding in council to go across to the South Sea coast to the town of Nata. There resided most of the rich merchants whose slaves worked in the mines. However, the Spanish forces had been alerted and were waiting in great numbers, so Le Picard was forced to abandon the attempt.

This drawing by Jacques le Moyne de Morgues was engraved by Theodor de Bry and appeared in Johannes Lerii's Account of the Caraibe Indians *in 1593.*

CARIBS AND ARAWAKS

In the 17th century the Carib Indians lived all over the Lesser Antilles, a chain of islands formerly known as "The Caribbees." They were a warlike tribe. In attempting to expand their territory they were known to torture and kill all non-Carib males, taking the females as slave-wives. Arawaks were native to the West Indies. These were the people Christopher Columbus encountered when he first landed in the Americas.

Their numbers included the Taíno, who occupied the Greater Antilles and the Bahamas, and the Ciboney. The Taíno used the Ciboney for slave labor. Both Arawak and Carib societies suffered drastic decline following European settlement as the result of diseases, such as smallpox, attacks between tribes, and harsh treatment by the Spanish. Only very few descendants of these native tribes survive today.

Opposite page: The sweet potato is commonly called a yam in parts of the United States, but it is not the true yam. It is a crop plant whose starchy, sweet-tasting tuberous roots are an important vegetable in the Americas. The young leaves and shoots are sometimes eaten as greens. It is only a distant relative of the potato.

L'Olonnais, abandoned by his comrades, remained in the Gulf of Honduras, with 300 men in his great ship. She was too heavy and laden to beat against the wind and tide and heavy seas as the other, smaller ships had done. Being unable to leave the Gulf, provisions were running very low, and his men had to come ashore to shoot monkeys and anything else that they could eat. At last he found a group of islands called the Islas de las Perlas, south of Cape Gracias a Dios, which is the border of Honduras and Nicaragua. Among them are two larger islands, and near these the ship ran aground on a sandbank, where she stuck so fast that they could not float her. In desperation they threw overboard great guns, the iron bars, and all the weighty goods that they could spare, but to little effect. Therefore they were forced to start breaking up the ship, to use her timber, plants and nails to build a longboat.

The Indians of the Islas de las Perlas

While the pirates are engaged in this work, I will briefly describe these two islands and their inhabitants. The islands called De Las Perlas are inhabited by Indians, who are proper savages, never having at any time known or conversed with any civil people. There are plenty who have lived six or seven months on these islands and have never found their dwellings. They are tall, very nimble, and can run almost as fast as horses. They are also dextrous and hardy divers. I saw them take from the bottom of the sea an anchor weighing 600 pounds by tying a cable to it with great dexterity and pulling it from a rock. They use no other arms than those made from wood, without any iron, unless sometimes they fix a crocodile or shark's tooth to serve as a point. They do not use bows and arrows, like other Indians, but instead a kind of lance, about a fathom-and-a-half in length.

Their plantations are in various parts of the forest, where they grow sweet potatoes, bananas, plantains, pineapples, and many other fruit and vegetables, but there are no houses near their plantations, as in other places in the Indies. Some are of the opinion that they eat human flesh, which seems to be confirmed by what happened when L'Olonnais was there. Two of his sea-rovers, one French and one Spanish, went into the woods for about a league and were surprised and pursued by a troop of Indians. They had only one musket, and the Frenchman fired it and ran off, but the Spaniard was not such a good runner. The first man made it to the beach, but the Spaniard was never seen again.

Some days after, a party of 12 well-armed pirates set off into the woods to see what had become of their comrade. The Frenchman led them to where he had seen the Indians. Near there, they found that the Indians had kindled a fire, and a small distance away they found the bones of the Spaniard, which had been well-roasted. They found some more of him, with the flesh scraped off the bones, and one of his hands, with two fingers remaining.

They marched on, seeking the Indians, and captured five men and four women to take to the ship. The pirates had some Indians with them already, but these did not know the language of the island Indians. They offered the Indian prisoners corals, knives, beads, and axes, which they accepted. The pirates also offered them food and drink, which they would not touch. All the time they were prisoners, no one saw them speak a word to each other. Seeing how afraid they were, the pirates gave them some knick-knacks and let them go, and the Indians indicated that they would return, but they vanished from that island. No boats were seen, so it was supposed that they swam to some of the smaller islands.

Near there, they found that the Indians had kindled a fire, and a small distance away they found the bones of the Spaniard, which had been well-roasted.

PL. II.

PATATES

de diverses Sortes

G.S.D. pinx. ex nat.

They decided to head into the forest to find food, but they were unsuccessful and forced to chew the leather of their shoes and the sheaths of their knives.

The gruesome end of L'Olonnais

Breaking up the ship was time-consuming, so the buccaneers cultivated some ground and planted French beans, which ripened in six weeks, and other vegetables and fruit. They also had maize, wild bananas, and plantains for sustenance, so were in no danger of starvation. They used their portable ovens off the ship to make bread. After five to six months they completed the longboat and sent an expedition along the River Nicaragua to try and steal canoes to fetch the rest of the men off the islands. They also had the ship's skiff with them. To prevent disputes, lots were cast to see who went in the longboat and skiff and who stayed on the islands, and half went and half stayed.

After a few days sailing, L'Olonnais arrived at the mouth of the river, and his ill-luck continued. His party was attacked by a force of Indians and Spaniards, and most of the pirates were killed. L'Olonnais and the survivors fled, and he determined not to return to the islands to rescue his comrades. A council was held, and the pirates voted to take their longboat along the coast of Cartagena instead to try and capture a ship. On arriving in the Gulf of Darien (between Colombia and Panama), they were attacked and taken by the savage and untamable Indians known as Indios Bravos. One of his comrades managed to escape and described L'Olonnais as being torn to pieces while alive and his limbs roasted. Thus ended a man who had spilled so much innocent blood and caused so many grisly atrocities.

The men left on the islands were fortunate in that a pirate ship from Jamaica found them. The pirates were intending to land at Cape Gracias a Dios, heading upriver in canoes and taking Cartagena. The pirates on the islands were pleased to have been rescued after ten months, and the Jamaican pirates were happy to have reinforcements, making their force 500 strong. They took canoes and began heading upriver. However, they had no provisions with them, believing that they could provision the ship from coastal plantations. This plan went awry as the coastal Indians had fled, taking everything with them. The pirates grew faint, after 14 days of travel with only fruit from the river bank to eat. They decided to head into the forest to find food, but they were unsuccessful and forced to chew the leather of their shoes and the sheaths of their knives. If they had met Indians, they would have eaten them, such was their hunger. At last they returned to the sea, but the majority had died. Thus ended the deeds and cruelties of Francois L'Olonnais and his crew. Now we shall describe the actions and exploits of Henry Morgan, a man as merciless as L'Olonnais, but more successful in his achievements.

Left: A 1592 engraving by Theodor de Bry showing cannibalism amongst the Caribs in the West Indies. There is, however, no evidence that they were cannibals. This may be early European propaganda designed to make a better case for their enslavement.

S.ʳ HEN: MORGAN

PART FOUR

The remarkable pirating career of Captain Henry Morgan—His famous raids and prizes

CHAPTER I

Of the origins and the descent of Captain Henry Morgan—His exploits and a continuation of the most remarkable actions of his life

❧

Henry Morgan was born in the Principality of Wales, the son of a well-to-do farmer. As a young man, he signed on a ship for Barbados, where he became an indentured servant. When at liberty, he went to Jamaica, where he found two pirate vessels readying themselves for an expedition. He made three or four voyages with the pirates, which made enough money for a group of them to purchase their own ship. Morgan was made captain and they sailed along the coast of Campeche, capturing several ships.

The taking of Santa Catalina

On his return to Jamaica, Morgan was invited by the Admiral of the Brethren of the Coast, Captain Edward Mansveldt, to be his vice-admiral in a fleet to raid the mainland. It was a fleet of 15 vessels, manned by Frenchmen, Walloons, and English. Soon they arrived at the islands of Santa Catalina, around 35 leagues from the Chagres River. Santa Catalina is much the larger island, and almost

Right: This commission was issued in 1670 by the Jamaica Council under Governor Charles Modyford. It allowed Henry Morgan to attack the Spanish in his raid on Panama. King Charles II had agreed peace with Spain, but news had not yet reached the West Indies.

SLAVERY IN THE WEST INDIES

To extract precious ore and jewels from deposits in Mexico, Peru, and Colombia, the Spanish used slaves to work the mines. However, war, disease, overwork, and suicide caused the native Indian population to plummet, in one of the worst population decimations in history. In the Antilles alone, the native population dropped from 300,000 in 1492 to 14,000 in 1514. Millions more died on the South American mainland.

To help save the Indians from extinction, a former explorer, Bartolomé de Las Casa, proposed that the King of Spain introduce African slaves, believing that "the labor of one Negro is more valuable than that of four Indians." In 1517, the first *asiento* (assent) to this end was agreed, enabling 4,000 slaves to be imported into the West Indies over the following eight years. By 1540, an estimated 30,000 men, women, and children had been transplanted from Africa to Hispaniola alone. From the 1560s, Richard Hawkins, Francis Drake, and others also began trafficking slaves to Spanish America.

From the 16th to the 18th century, slave ships from England sailed to Africa's west coast with rum, firearms, and brass goods, which were bartered for slaves, who were then shipped to the Spanish West Indies and later the southern

After the deposits in the Hispaniola gold mines were exhausted, the Spaniards forced the Taíno Indian slaves to cultivate sugar.

states of the U.S.A. From there, slaves were exchanged for rum and sugar in the Caribbean and tobacco and cotton in America. Each of the three passages was extremely profitable, bringing great wealth to Liverpool and Bristol, the major English slaving ports.

adjoins a smaller island. In a short time they had seized the Spanish garrison. Mansveldt ordered some fortifications to be demolished and others reinforced and left a garrison of 100 pirates there, together with the slaves who had been used by the Spaniards. They built a bridge from Santa Catalina to the smaller island and most of the artillery was transferred there. The houses on Santa Catalina were burned, and the sea rovers put to sea again with their Spanish prisoners.

The prisoners were put ashore near Puerto Bello on the mainland, and the buccaneers cruised along the Costa Rica coast. Landing by the River Colla, Mansveldt planned to plunder villages and head for Nata, which was on the other side of the isthmus in the Bay of Panama, on the Pacific. However, the governor of Panama had been warned and arrived with a strong enough force for the buccaneers to retreat to their ships. As the whole coast was in arms, Mansveldt returned to Santa Catalina. He had left Le Sieur Simon in command and had made the island almost impregnable. He had also planted the small island so that provisions could be supplied to the pirate fleet, not only for the present but also for a new voyage. Mansveldt wished to keep these two islands, as they were strategically near the Spanish and had a good harbor but could be easily defended. He decided to return to Jamaica and send back forces to ensure that the islands could be kept as a buccaneer base. However, the governor of Jamaica was unwilling to displease the English king by taking Spanish property and was afraid that the defenses of Jamaica would be weakened if Jamaican resources were used elsewhere.

"The pirates fired three volleys of bullets, which were met in like by our forces. The major sent one of his officers to summon the pirates to surrender."

Above: In this engraving from the late 16th century, *Indians Battling on San Maro* by Theodor de Bry, the Spanish are armed with muskets, while the native Indians wield bows and arrows.

The Spaniards retake Santa Catalina

Mansveldt now headed to Tortuga to ask for help but died before he could effect this mission. Le Sieur Simon was left alone with his men, while the new governor of Costa Rica, Don Juan Pérez de Guzmán, prepared to take Santa Catalina back. He sent a strong force and also a letter to Simon, offering a reward if he willingly surrendered the islands and severe punishment if he refused to do so. Le Sieur Simon saw no real prospect of keeping the islands and of making profitable use of them without any reinforcements. After some resistance, he agreed to the Spanish terms and surrendered.

A few days later, a ship arrived from Jamaica—secretly sent by the governor—containing fourteen men and two women. The Spanish flew the English flag over the fort, and Simon was made to go down to the shore to guide the Jamaican ship into the harbor. All were captured. A certain Spanish engineer has laid down an exact account, which has fallen into my hands and which I reproduce here:

A true Relation and particular Account of the Victory obtained by the Arms of his Catholic Majesty against the English Pirates, by the direction and valor of Don Juan Pérez de Guzmán, Knight of the Order of Saint James, Governor and Captain-General of Terra Firma and the Province of Veraguas [in present-day Panama].

The Kingdom of Terra Firma, which of itself is sufficiently strong to repulse and extirpate great fleets, but more especially of the Pirates of Jamaica, had notice from several hands imparted to the Governor thereof, that fourteen English vessels did cruise along the coasts belonging to his Catholic Majesty. The 14th day of June, 1665, news came to Panama that the English Pirates of the said fleet had come to Puerto de Naos, and had forced the Spanish garrison of the Isle of Santa Catalina, whose Governor was Don Esteban del Campo; and that they had possessed themselves of the said island, taking the 200 inhabitants as prisoners, and destroying all that they met. Moreover, about the same time, Don Juan Pérez de Guzmán received particular information of these robberies from the former prisoners, whom he ordered to be brought to Puerto Bello, where they gave a detailed account to His Excellency.

They told him that the pirates had come to the island on the 27th day of May, by night, without being seen, and at six o'clock next morning had possessed the fortifications without any struggle, and had taken the people prisoner. Don Juan declared a council of war on 27th June, wherein he declared the great progress the pirates had made in the dominions of his Catholic Majesty. He propounded that the island must be retaken or the Pirates might in the course of time possess themselves of all the countries thereabouts. Some council members said that it was not worth the effort of fighting them, as they would leave of their own accord, being unable to subsist on the island. However, Don Juan, who was an expert and valiant soldier, ordered military provisions to be supplied to Puerto Bello. He went there, with no small danger to his life, and arrived on the 7th day of July, with most things necessary to the expedition in hand.

In the harbor was a good ship, the St. Vincente, belonging to The Company of Negroes, well provided with the munitions of war, and he chartered this for the expedition. He manned and victualed it and gave command to a fine soldier, the Major of Puerto Bello, Captain José Sánchez Ximénez, and

gave him the following men. There were 270 soldiers; 47 of those previously taken prisoner on Santa Catalina, going back like lions to regain their honor; 34 Spaniards belonging to the garrison of Puerto Bello; 29 mulattoes of Panama; 12 Indians very dextrous at shooting with bows and arrows; seven expert gunners, two adjutants or lieutenants; two pilots; one surgeon; and a monk of the order of St. Francis to confess them.

Don Juan then gave his orders to each officer, telling them that the Governor of Cartagena would supply them with men, boats, and all things necessary for success, if they should need them. A letter of requisition had been signed to that effect. A letter of credit was give to the commandant, to show to the richest merchants of Cartagena to equip the ships with extra munitions of war. On 14th July the Governor commanded the ship to weigh anchor and sail to Cartagena, but first he went onboard, encouraging the men to fight against the enemies of their king and their religion, saying that they would be well rewarded. On 22nd July, the ship arrived at Cartagena, and Captain Ximénez presented his instructions to the Governor. The Governor, seeing these bold plans, gave a frigate, a galliot, one boat, and 126 men, half from his own garrison and half of them mulattoes.

They sailed from Cartagena on August 2nd, Santa Catalina was sighted on 10th August, and despite a headwind the fleet managed to land in the port, having lost one boat in a storm, on the Quita Sueños reefs. The pirates fired three volleys of bullets, which were met in like by our forces. The Major sent one of his officers to summon the pirates to surrender, as they occupied it contrary to the laws of peace between England and Spain, and that should they prove intransigent, they would all be put to the sword. The buccaneers replied that it had belonged to the English crown until 1641, when it was taken by the Spanish, and that they would rather die than surrender.

On Friday, 13th August, three Negroes deserted the enemy and came aboard the Admiral's ship, telling him that there were only 72 defenders, who were full of fear on seeing such a powerful invading force. With this intelligence, the Spanish prepared to land and advance towards the fortresses, which kept up heavy cannon fire until dark. On Sunday, 15th August, the feast of the Assumption of Our Lady, the weather was calm and clear, and the Spanish began their attack. The St. Vincente exchanged two whole broadsides upon the island battery known as La Concepción. The vice-admiral on the St. Pedrito, together with the galliot, exchanged cannon-fire with the St. Jago battery.

Above: Rusting cannon remain in the ruins of the castle at Puerto Bello, now in the Colon province of Panama. Members of its garrison were involved in the retaking of Old Providence and Santa Catalina from Le Sieur Simon. At that time, the term Santa Catalina referred to both the larger island and the pair of islands together.

Meanwhile, our people were landing in small boats, and headed for the St. James battery, towards the fort called Cortadura. The adjutant, Francisco Cazeres, was desirous to view the strength of the enemy, and approached the position. However, he was compelled to retreat in great haste, as the enemy fired batteries of 60 muskets fastened like organ pipes, which fired simultaneously, as well as cannon firing iron pieces and heavy musket fire. Notwithstanding the heat of the enemy fire, Captain Don Joseph Ramírez de Leyva, with 60 men, made a strong attack, and after a desperate struggle forced the fort to surrender.

Captain Juan Galeno, with 90 men including half-breeds and Indians, passed over the hills to advance towards the castle of St. Teresa. In the meantime, Major Don José Sánchez Ximénez, as commander-in-chief, took the rest of his men towards the battery of St. James, passing in front of the fort with four boats, and landing despite enemy fire. About this time Captain Galeno began his assault on the castle of St. Teresa, so the enemy were being attacked at three places at the same time. The pirates, seeing six of their number dead, others wounded, and the great forces against them, retreated towards Cortadura, where they surrendered themselves and the whole island into our hands. Our people set up the Spanish flag, and gave thanks to God Almighty for the victory on such a holy day. Six pirates were killed, with many wounded, and there were 70 prisoners. On our side we lost one man, and four were wounded.

There was found on the island 800 pounds of powder, 250 pounds of musket bullets, 800 pounds of fuse, and many military provisions. Among the prisoners were two Spaniards, who had borne arms for the English against his Catholic Majesty. The Major, as was his bounden duty, commanded them to be shot next day. On 10th September an English vessel arrived at the isle, having been seen a great distance away by the Major. He ordered the Frenchman Le Sieur Simon to tell them the island still belonged to the English. It contained 14 men and a woman and her daughter and they were instantly made prisoners.

The English pirates were all taken to Puerto Bello, except for three who were sent to Panama to work on the castle of St. Jerome. This fortification is an excellent piece of workmanship, and very strong. It is raised in the middle of the port, of quadrangular form, and made of very hard stone. It is 88 feet high, the walls being 14 feet thick and the curtain walls or ramparts extend 75 feet in diameter, making a total diameter of 300 feet with storehouses and all the works included. It was built at the expense of private persons, the Governor providing the most money—it did not cost their King any sum at all.

I have given a word-for-word translation of this account, so that the reader can see what an outcry the Spanish make of a business of little importance and what a performance they made of ousting 70 men from an island they were quite willing to leave. Notwithstanding the might of the Spanish, if the buccaneers had wished to hold on to the island they could have easily driven them off.

Below: A 1927 find of jewels in the tunnels of San José church, in Panama, has been linked to the attack by Captain Morgan. The discovery featured as the lead story in this Swedish journal at the time.

NAVIGATION

A derroterro was a set of sailing directions used by the Spanish. The equivalent Portuguese word, *roteiro*, became the French *routier* and the English "rutter." These were of incomparable value in the New World and East Indies. A captain could see on his rutter views of the coast drawn from seaward, with instructions added. In 1680 Captain Bartholomew Sharp captured one in the South Pacific from the Spanish ship *Rosario*. This was unusual, because rutters were usually weighted and thrown overboard in the face of attack. When Sharp was tried for piracy, he gave Charles II the translation of this priceless *derroterro*. Because of this he was acquitted and made a captain in the Royal Navy. English rutters held details of anchorages, harbors, courses, and so on, and were continually updated,

Erasmus Habermel (1550–1606), a German based in Prague, made this specially commissioned compass in 1600. Until the invention of a mariners' compass around 1300, mariners had to rely upon celestial bodies to help them fix positions and directions.

often being passed down from father to son. Because of the lack of knowledge about longitude before the invention of Harrison's Chronometer in the 18th century, merchant ships clustered upon well-known routes, where they were more at threat from pirate attack. Suitable chronometers were not widely used until the late 18th century, making the navigational feats of pirates and circumnavigators like Black Bart Roberts and Woodes Rogers truly remarkable.

CHAPTER II

Some account of the island of Cuba. Captain Morgan attempts to preserve the island of Santa Catalina as a refuge for the English——He arrives at and takes El Puerto del Principe

ে৯

Admiral of the Brethren of the Coast

Captain Morgan succeeded the dead Mansveldt as Admiral of the Brethren, knowing that his predecessor had wished for the island of Santa Catalina to be under buccaneer control and agreeing fully with this strategy. It would have been used as a refuge and sanctuary for pirates and could be used as a storehouse for their robberies. Morgan wrote to several merchants in Virginia and New England asking for supplies to be sent to the island, to help make it secure from any Spanish invasion. His plans came to nothing, however, when the island was retaken by the Spanish.

However, Morgan refused to be discouraged. He prepared a ship for an expedition and gathered a great fleet in a plan to attack some part of the Spanish dominions. He called a rendezvous in the southern cays of Cuba, and then held a council of captains to decide where to attack. So that my readers can better understand this account, I will give a small account of the island.

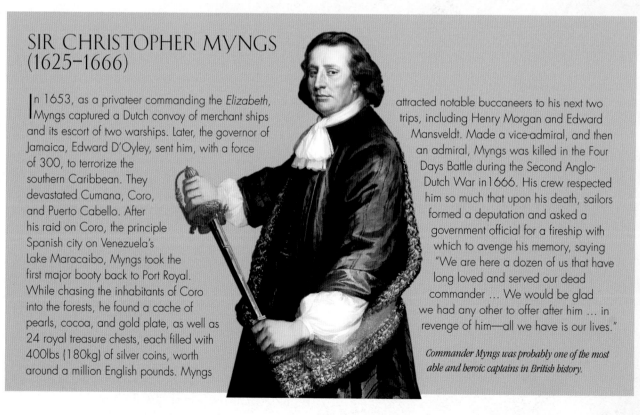

SIR CHRISTOPHER MYNGS (1625–1666)

In 1653, as a privateer commanding the *Elizabeth*, Myngs captured a Dutch convoy of merchant ships and its escort of two warships. Later, the governor of Jamaica, Edward D'Oyley, sent him, with a force of 300, to terrorize the southern Caribbean. They devastated Cumana, Coro, and Puerto Cabello. After his raid on Coro, the principle Spanish city on Venezuela's Lake Maracaibo, Myngs took the first major booty back to Port Royal. While chasing the inhabitants of Coro into the forests, he found a cache of pearls, cocoa, and gold plate, as well as 24 royal treasure chests, each filled with 400lbs (180kg) of silver coins, worth around a million English pounds. Myngs

attracted notable buccaneers to his next two trips, including Henry Morgan and Edward Mansveldt. Made a vice-admiral, and then an admiral, Myngs was killed in the Four Days Battle during the Second Anglo-Dutch War in 1666. His crew respected him so much that upon his death, sailors formed a deputation and asked a government official for a fireship with which to avenge his memory, saying "We are here a dozen of us that have long loved and served our dead commander … We would be glad we had any other to offer after him … in revenge of him—all we have is our lives."

Commander Myngs was probably one of the most able and heroic captains in British history.

Left: Havana, *Ciudad de las Habana*, was founded in 1515 and is one of the oldest cities founded by Europeans in the western hemisphere.

An account of the island of Cuba

Cuba extends 160 leagues from east to west and 40 leagues in width, and its fertility rivals that of Hispaniola. It exports tremendous quantities of hides, known as Havana Hides, to Europe. On all sides it is surrounded by a great number of islands, which are called cayos, or cays, and which the pirates make great use of, both as ports of refuge and as bases to attack the Spanish. There are fine streams and rivers and excellent ports. In the south are the towns of Santiago, Bayame, Santa Maria, Esperitu Santo, Trinidad, Xagoa, Cape de Corrientes, and others. On the north side are Havana, Puerto Mariana, Santa Cruz, Mata Ricos, Puerto del Principe, and Barracoa.

Santiago, or St. Jago, is the capital of the eastern half of the island and has its own bishop and governor. Most of its trade is with the Canary Islands, where it exports great quantities of tobacco, sugar, and hides. Although protected by a fort, it has been attacked and sacked by the pirates of Tortuga and Jamaica. The city and port of Havana lies on the north and west side of the island and is one of the most famous and strongest places in the West Indies. It has jurisdiction over the other half of the island, and the chief cities under it are Santa Cruz on the northern side and La Trinidad on the South.

An enormous quantity of tobacco is exported from Cuba to New Spain, Costa Rica, and even as far as the South Sea. In addition, ships carry the leaf and rolls of tobacco to Spain and other parts of Europe. Havana is defended by three great castles, two near the port and one on the hill that commands the town. It is estimated that 10,000 families live there, and its merchants trade with New Spain, Campeche, Honduras, and Florida.

The city and port of Havana lies on the north and west side of the island, and is one of the most famous and strongest places in the West Indies.

Above: The Castillo del Morro at Havana, in a contemporary painting and, **above right**, a modern photograph, protected the port and natural harbor from invasion. Havana was of the utmost strategic importance to the Spanish, being the principal port of all their New World colonies.

All the ships from these places and also from Caracas, Cartagena, and Costa Rica must call at Havana to take provisions for their voyage to Spain. This is the most direct route to the south of Europe and other places. The homeward-bound Silver Fleet, or flota, touches here twice a year to take onboard the rest of its cargo, such as hides, tobacco, and Campeche wood, or logwood.

The attack on Puerto del Principe, Cuba

Morgan waited two months in the cays of Cuba, assembling a fleet of 12 sail—a mix of large and small boats and 700 fighting men, who were mainly English and French. He held a council. Some wished to attack Havana at night. They argued that with the element of surprise they could plunder the city and take some priests as prisoners before the forts could be roused into action. After some discussion, this course of action was not taken. This was because some of the men had been held prisoner there, and they were of the opinion that it needed 1,500 buccaneers to take it. In that case, the ships could be anchored off the Island of Pines and the men sent upriver to Matamano, 14 leagues from Havana.

There being no possibility of gathering so great a fleet, one pirate proposed that they should assault Puerto del Principe, as he knew the place very well. It was some distance from the sea and had never been sacked by pirates. Its merchants were rich, as they traded their hides with Havana. Lying inland, they had no fear of any attack and would be unprepared. Morgan and his captains agreed and anchored the fleet in a bay near there named El Puerto de Santa Maria. However, a Spanish prisoner escaped at night and swam ashore. The pirates rushed to their canoes and gave chase, but the escapee managed to hide in the forest. He had pretended not to speak English but knew a little and had heard the words Puerto del Principe mentioned many times onboard. He then alerted the inhabitants of Puerto del Principe, who began to hide their belongings and carry off all their movable objects.

Their governor mustered 800 townspeople—freemen and slaves—and took a force to guard a position where the pirates must pass. He had trees cut down to hinder their passage and ordered ambushes to hamper their march. With the rest of his force he surrounded the town, positioning the main body on a savannah from where he could see the coming of the pirates from far away.

An ambush is prepared

The Spanish were still busy equipping their ambuscades, but the pirates escaped them. Finding the main path almost impossible to penetrate because of trees cut down by the Spaniards, Morgan led them through the woods directly to the savannah. The governor immediately sent a troop of horse to attack Morgan's men, intending to follow up their rout with his infantry. He thought the enemy would be full of fear, seeing his superior forces. However, the buccaneers advanced in good order, drums beating and with flying colors. They approached the horsemen, formed into a semicircle, and advanced into the charge of the cavalry. The buccaneers never missed their mark, and after a short time, seeing their governor fall, the Spanish retreated to the woods. Here they hoped to have a better chance to escape and reform, but most never made it that far, being instead cut down in their flight. The skirmish had lasted about four hours and resulted in minimal pirate losses. Soon after, they entered the town in high spirits. Here they met fresh resistance from men who had stayed with the women and from some who had escaped the battle. They hoped to prevent pillage and were shooting from the windows of locked houses. The pirates issued the following threat: "If you do not voluntarily surrender, you shall soon see the town in flames, and your wives and children will be torn to pieces before your faces." The townspeople then surrendered, expecting that the pirates would not stay too long, forced to leave by relieving Spanish forces.

Left: Morgan's privateers attacked with pikes, swords, daggers, muskets, and pistols to overwhelm the defenders at Puerto del Principe.

TORURE

Emglish law in pirate times allowed even a child to be hung for stealing a crust of bread. It also allowed torture if one refused to plead at a trial. In 1725, the Scottish pirate Captain Gow was ordered to be pressed to death, as he would not answer his accusers or make a plea. Upon hearing this sentence, he quickly pleaded "not guilty," but was nevertheless hung and displayed in chains at Greenwich.

Pirates of all nations were cruel to Spanish captives because of the practices of the Inquisition. A revolting account of 1604 recorded that "the Spanish in the West Indies captured two English vessels, cut off the hands, feet, noses, and ears of the crews, smeared them with honey, and tied them to trees to be tortured by flies and other insects."

Woolding (or wolding) was a nasty torture. One of Morgan's men, present at the sacking of Puerto Bello, later wrote to the Secretary of State: "It is a common thing among privateers, besides burning with matches and such-like torments, to cut a man to pieces, first some flesh, then a hand, an arm, a leg, sometimes tying a cord about his head and with a stick twisting it till the eyes shoot out, which is called woolding." It was not invented by the buccaneers, but was a recognized part of the torture the Spanish called *cordeles*, which was used in secular courts and by the Inquisition.

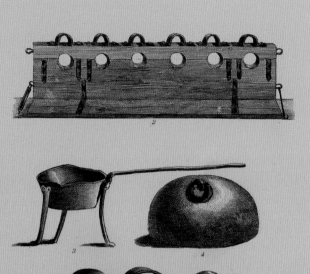

Leg irons, in the foreground; an iron pan for heating up pitch tar to pour over flesh; a stone used for pressing to death; and stocks, in the rear.

The torture of prisoners

The Spaniards were locked up, slaves as well, in several churches, and loot was collected from around the town. The privateers then searched the countryside surrounding the town, bringing in fresh booty and more prisoners daily. These privateers enjoyed eating and drinking to excess while giving little food to the prisoners locked in the churches. Every day, they tortured their prisoners to find out where they had hidden money or goods. Some unfortunate men were tortured who only made enough money to support their wives and children, but it made no difference to the pirates. Many of these prisoners perished through hanging, starvation, or torture.

Eventually, when there was no more to eat or drink or to steal, the pirates decided to leave and gave their prisoners the ultimatum of finding a ransom or being taken to Jamaica and their town burnt to ashes. Four prisoners were sent to gather the ransom, but the pirates carried on torturing prisoners. After a few days, the Spaniards returned, fatigued from the unreasonable demand, stating that they could not find any Spanish people, so had no ransom. They asked for another 15 days grace to accomplish their mission. Morgan agreed to this course of action.

However, soon afterward, seven or eight pirates came into the town with considerable booty and some more prisoners. Among them was a Negro carrying letters, which Morgan perused. He found they were from the governor of Santiago, addressed to some of the prisoners. The letters told the prisoners not to make too much haste in paying the ransom for the town or themselves but to delay the pirates with excuses, as he would relieve them in a short while. Captain Morgan immediately ordered that all their plunder should be placed on the ships. The next day he told the Spanish that he would not wait one

he other Frenchmen wanted revenge, seized their muskets and approached the English, but Captain Morgan placed himself between the two parties.

moment more for their ransom but would carry them off and reduce their town to ashes. He made no mention of the letters he had intercepted. The Spanish again answered that the task was impossible, as their people were scattered and it would take too long to collect the money. Being aware of their secret and also that the governor was on his way, Morgan ordered 500 cattle be sent to the fleet and enough salt to preserve the meat. He ordered six principal citizens taken to his ships with all the captured slaves. The next day the cattle were brought to the shore, and the Spanish asked for the return of the captives. Morgan did not trust them but knew it was pointless waiting around for a battle in which there was no booty to be won. He made the Spanish slaughter the cattle and salt the beef, so the buccaneers could speedily take it aboard the waiting ships.

The murder of the French corsair

While this was going on, a dispute arose between a French and an English pirate. I have recounted how the *boucaniers* love sucking out the warm marrow when a beast is slaughtered. The corsair had skinned an animal and the Englishman had come up and helped himself to the marrow-bones. They quarreled and agreed to a duel with muskets. On coming to the dueling-place, the English pirate had his firing-piece ready before the other and shot him from behind. The other Frenchmen wanted revenge. They seized their muskets and approached the English, but Captain Morgan placed himself between the two parties, put the Englishman in chains, and promised to have him hanged back in Jamaica. There would have been no problem if it had been a normal duel, which is often the way of settling pirate disputes, as the man would have been killed in a fair fight.

When the ships were boarded, Morgan set his prisoners free, and the fleet went to a certain safe island to divide up the loot. There was found to be only 50,000 pieces of eight in ready money, silver, and various other goods. There was resentment and grief from the pirates at such small booty, as it was insufficient to pay debts incurred in Jamaica in setting up the expedition. Morgan proposed another voyage of pillage before returning home, but the French could not agree with the English. Morgan thanked them for their company and promised to deal justice to the English criminal on the behalf of their dead comrade. This he did, hanging him in Jamaica.

Below: After a show trial, the privateer Captain William Kidd (1645–1701) was hung at the second attempt after the rope broke. He was gibbeted in an iron cage over the Thames at Execution Dock, London, where his body was left for two years as a warning to seamen who were tempted to take up piracy.

Capt. Kidd hanging in chains. p. 178.

CHAPTER III

Captain Morgan resolves to plunder and attack the city of Puerto Bello—To this effect he equips a fleet, and, with little expense and small forces, takes the said place

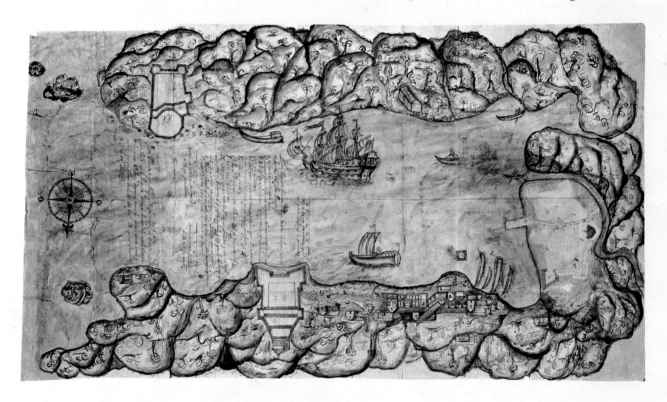

Above: This 1688 engraving from the Seville Archives dates from shortly after Morgan's attack; it shows the Bay and City of Puerto Bello.

After the French left, the English did not wish to go on another journey but were infused with courage by Captain Morgan, who said that he would make them rich if they would follow him. They were enthused sufficiently to agree, and another buccaneer ship which had been near Campeche joined Morgan. This gave him a fleet of nine vessels, including ships and great boats, and 430 men.

The assault on Puerto Bello, Panama

Henry Morgan did not tell his captains or men where he was heading, only that they would make a good fortune, unless strange circumstances altered the course of his designs. The fewer people that knew his plans before the expedition actually attacked the Spaniards, the better. The fleet approached the mainland off Costa Rica in a few days, and Morgan revealed his intentions to his captains and crews. He wished to take Puerto Bello by night and pillage the city. He told them that the raid would be easy as no-one knew that the fleet was off the coast. Some responded that they were too few in number, but Morgan replied "If our number is small, our hearts are great. And the fewer persons we are, the more union and better shares we shall have in the spoil." The buccaneers then unanimously agreed to his proposal, and I shall now give a brief description of Puerto Bello.

It is in the province of Costa Rica (now in Panama), forty leagues from the Gulf of Darien and eight leagues west of Nombre de Dios. Apart from Havana and Cartagena, it is the strongest Spanish city in all the West Indies. Two almost impregnable castles guard the entrance of the bay, protecting the town and harbor, so no boat can pass without permission. There is a garrison of 300 soldiers, and the town is constantly inhabited by around 400 families. The merchants only reside there when the galleons come to port or leave for Spain, as the place is very unhealthy because of the mountain vapors. The merchants live in Panama (on the Pacific side of the isthmus) but their warehouses are in Puerto Bello, looked after by servants. They bring silver from Panama on pack-mules ready for the arrival of the galleons belonging to the Company of Negroes, which arrive to sell slaves.

A valuable prisoner is taken

Morgan was familiar with this coastline and took his fleet to Puerto de Naos, about 10 leagues west of Puerto Bello. They arrived at dusk. The fleet then crept along the river and anchored undiscovered at Puerto del Pontin, around four leagues from their target. Here, the buccaneers manned canoes and rowing-boats, leaving only enough crew onboard to sail the ships into Puerto Bello the next day. At midnight they landed in secrecy at Estera Longa Lemos and began to march to the first outpost of the city. They were guided by an Englishman, who had been a prisoner in those parts and knew the area well. He was given the task, along with three or four others, of killing the sentry. They apprehended him with such cunning that the Spaniard was captured without being able to give a warning. Captain Morgan questioned the prisoner about the strength of the garrison and the arrangements of the town's defenses, and he told what he knew. His hands were then tied, and he was forced to march in the vanguard of the pirates, being told that if he had not been truthful he would be killed on the spot.

Having marched about a quarter of a league, the buccaneers came to a redoubt near the city, which they surrounded. Morgan commanded the captured sentry to shout to those within to surrender or they would be cut to pieces, with no quarter given. The defenders started firing, so the alarm was quickly raised within the city. The pirates soon took the redoubt, however, and confined all the officers and soldiers in one room. They then blew up the stronghold, so the Spaniards all perished.

Above left: This Howard Pyle illustration shows a gentlemanly interrogation of prisoners at Puerto Bello by Henry Morgan.

Above: The "silver mountain" at Potosi in Bolivia was the richest silver mine in the world, and its output fueled the Spanish economy and war machine. Its Indian slaves dug raw ore out of mine shafts and were later replaced by imported Africans to meet demand.

Above: This statue of San Felipe de Neri is in a church in Casco Viejo, the old quarter of Panama City. The area was built in 1673, after Morgan had destroyed the city, and is now a World Heritage Site.

Below: The Spanish governor of Puerto Bello died heroically, refusing to surrender to Morgan's men. They wanted him alive for ransom, but eventually had to shoot him.

"Fiercely and long this gallant man fought"

The taking of Puerto Bello

The pirates now fell upon the city, and its inhabitants rushed to hide their valuable goods, casting precious jewels and money into wells and cisterns and other underground places. One party of pirates was assigned to go to the cloisters and take as many religious men and women as they could. Another group was commanded to take the forts. The governor of the city was unable to rally the citizens and took refuge in one of the forts. Incessant fire was poured down upon the pirate attackers. However, the pirates took aim with great dexterity every time a gun was being loaded, managing to kill seven or eight Spaniards with their accurate fire each time. The battle lasted all morning until midday, and still the forts were not taken. The pirate ships lay just outside the harbor mouth, unable to enter because of the heavy cannon-fire from the forts on both sides of the entrance.

Being at a stalemate and having lost many men, the pirates decided to throw fireballs and hand grenades to burn down the wooden doors to the main fort. However, when they pressed home the attack, the Spaniards made them turn back, hurling down at least 50 pots of gunpowder and huge stones, causing much damage to their attackers. Morgan and his men began to despair but then saw the English flag flying from the smaller fort and a party of pirates approaching, shouting "Victory!" This gave Morgan fresh heart, especially as he knew that most of the richer citizens had taken their valuables and hidden in the castle in front of him and that most of the silver plate from the churches was also there.

Morgan ordered a dozen ladders to be made, wide enough for four men to ascend them at once. He brought out the monks and nuns he had captured and informed the governor that he would use them to set the ladders against the castle walls unless he surrendered. The governor shouted down that he would never surrender himself alive. Morgan then ordered the religious men and women to fix the ladders. The attack began, the pirates thinking that the governor would never fire on the priests and nuns, but the defenders did so. Many of the religious brethren died. One party now managed to fire the castle's gates. Other buccaneers swarmed up the ladders, carrying fireballs and stinkpots to throw at the defenders on the walls. The attack was successful, and the Spanish finally asked for quarter, throwing down their arms.

The governor takes his stand

Only the governor would not surrender, despite repeated requests from the pirates. He had killed many of them and also some of his own men who had refused to stand to arms. When asked if he would accept quarter, he replied "I had rather die as an honorable soldier than be hanged as a coward." His wife and daughter went down on their knees and begged him to accept quarter. The pirates tried by all means to take him prisoner but were forced to shoot him dead.

The final surrender was in the evening, after a day's hard fighting. Men and women were imprisoned separately and guards posted. The pirate wounded were placed in a separate house, and then the buccaneers began to celebrate. Such was the drunkenness and debauchery that just 50 stouthearted men would have been able to retake the city and wipe them all out. The next day, having searched the houses and churches and plundered all that they could find, the pirates asked the prisoners to point out the richest among them. These were asked where their wealth was hidden. If they refused to say, they

One party now managed to fire the castle's gates. Other buccaneers swarmed up the ladders, carrying fireballs and stinkpots to throw at the defenders on the walls.

Left: In this contemporary engraving, the ladders at the siege of Puerto Bello are visible, as are the firebombs and grenades being thrown by both attackers and defenders.

were put to the rack until they confessed or gave up. Many innocent souls who had nothing to hide died, and the only ones spared were those who revealed where their goods were hidden.

Soon after the president or governor of Panama received news of the sack of Puerto Bello and began gathering a force to retake the city. Some newly taken prisoners disclosed this news to the buccaneers, but they paid little attention. Their ships were in the harbor, and the enemy would have to come overland, giving them time to fire the city, embark, and escape. They had by now been at Puerto Bello for 15 days and had lost many men, either through excessive debauchery, the stench of the corpses, or from the generally unhealthy nature of the country. Most of their wounded died, and most of the prisoners died from hunger or discomfort. Instead of their customary morning cup of chocolate, they were lucky to get a raw piece of mule's flesh or a lump of stale bread.

The buccaneers now prepared for departure, taking their booty onboard their ships and acquiring and apportioning provisions to each ship. While this was going on, Morgan told the surviving prisoners that he must have a ransom for the city or he would burn it and blow up its forts. He sent two prisoners away with instructions to bring 100,000 pieces of eight back with them. Instead they went directly to the president of Panama and gave him an account of the tragedy that had befallen them. The president had finished gathering his men and set out immediately for Puerto Bello to defeat the pirates before they retreated. However, Morgan knew the president's men were coming and sent 100 men to set up an ambush at a narrow passage where the force was likely to pass. They put to flight a good proportion of the president's army, and he retired for a time to consider his options.

He sent a letter to Morgan, telling him that if he did not leave immediately with all his forces, he could expect no quarter.

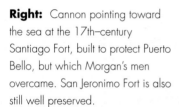

Right: Cannon pointing toward the sea at the 17th–century Santiago Fort, built to protect Puerto Bello, but which Morgan's men overcame. San Jeronimo Fort is also still well preserved.

The president sent a letter to Morgan, telling him that if he did not leave immediately with all his forces, he could expect no quarter. Morgan knew that he had a secure retreat and answered that he would not leave the forts without the ransom being paid. If it was not paid, he would kill the prisoners, blow up the castles, and burn the city. The president withdrew his forces, leaving the citizens of Puerto Bello to scrape together the monies for Morgan, which they managed to do.

Threats are exchanged

The president was astonished that only 400 men could have taken such strongly defended castles and sent another letter to Henry Morgan, asking to see a sample of the weapons which gave him such power to take the city. Morgan received the messenger with great civility and sent him back carrying a musket with a barrel four-and-a-half feet long, which fired a one ounce bullet, and a cartouche made in France, which carried 30 cartridges full of powder. The message he sent with these was that he desired him "to accept that slender pattern of arms wherewith he had taken Puerto Bello, and keep them for a twelvemonth," after which time he said he would "come to Panama and fetch them away." The governor then returned the weapons to Morgan saying that he did not need them and also sent him a ring of gold set with a rosette of emeralds, with the message that he desired him not to "give himself the labor of coming to Panama, as he had done to Puerto Bello," for the reason that he "should not fare so well here as he did there."

Morgan took the best guns from the castles, spiked any others which he could not carry away, and sailed out of Puerto Bello. On a cay south of Cuba, they divided the spoils. They had taken in ready money 215,000 pieces of eight plus linen, silks, and other goods. They then sailed to Jamaica and there began the usual scenes of debauchery after such a successful expedition. Morgan was greatly honored in Jamaica, having brought so much wealth with him.

MUSIC AND SONGS

Pirates liked musicians aboard their ships, to entertain them and to make a noise when going into battle. Singing in time also helped the efficient running of a ship. A sea shanty was a song with a definite rhythm, half sung and half chanted—a working song, to help men coordinate when pulling ropes and lines. They were also known as chanteys, so the origin is probably the word chant. Short-haul shanties were for tasks requiring numerous pulls over a short period of time, and halyard shanties were sung during heavier work, with more set-up time between pulls.

Many have been recorded, including *Mrs McGraw*:

Singing to-ri-yah, fa-la-la-la, to-ri oori oori yah,
With a to-ri-yah, fa-la-la-la, to-ri oori oori yah.

Now Mrs McGraw lived on the sea shore,
For the space of seven long years or more.
She spied a ship comin' into the bay,
"This is my son Teddy, won't you clear the way?"

(Chorus)

"Oh My dear Captain, where hae ye been?
Have ye been out sailing on the Med'ter'ean?
Have ye any news of my son, Ted?
Is the poor boy livin' or is he dead?"

(Chorus)

And up steps Ted, without any legs,
And in their place, there were two wooden pegs.
She kissed him a dozen times or two
Crying "Holy b'goes, what's become of you?"

(Chorus)

"No I wasn't drunk, nor I wasn't blind
When I left my two fine legs behind,
'Twas a big cannonball on the fifth of May
That tore my legs from my knees away!"

The title of this contemporary Flemish painting, Three Wandering Musicians, *fits in with our understanding that most musicians of the period were itinerant entertainers, carrying their pipes and fiddles with them on their travels. They were greatly prized to while away the boredom on pirate ships.*

CANNON, CANNONBALLS, AND SHOT

By 1700, cannon were available that could fairly accurately hit a target from 700 to 1,000 yards away. They used a variety of different types of ammunition. A handful of phrases, relating to cannon, that were used onboard have survived to become part of modern English. If a murderer, or swivel gun, was being fired at close range, pirates would dive to the deck, or "hit the deck," to avoid being killed or maimed. When cannon were loaded, a small amount of powder was poured into the ignition hole. To keep the powder secure before firing, a crew member pushed a finger into the hole. When the time came for ignition, he was told, "pull your finger out."

Above: *The man-of-war* Royal *in 1693, with gunports clearly visible.*

Above right: *A variety of 17th-century French cannons.*

CHASE GUNS

Chase guns were cannons in the bows of the ship, used when pursuing another ship. A stern chaser, often a nine-pounder, fitted on the stern. This type of cannon would deter chasing ships and would be aimed at their rigging and masts.

CULVERINS AND MURDERERS

A culverin was a standard 3-ton cannon, which took 18-pound cannonballs. This weapon could fire a shot a minute until it became too hot to operate. A "murderer" was a swivel gun with a long barrel and a wide mouth, which fired nails, spikes, stones, and glass. The iron pin in its stock was fitted into a socket. There were sockets for these guns at several places on a ship, so the gun could be taken quickly to wherever it was needed most.

BAR SHOT

Bar shot consisted of large iron bars. It was fired by cannon from short range, as the trajectory was unpredictable, to smash the ship's rigging and shrouds.

Below: *A shipload of barrels of gunpowder, shot, and cannon.*

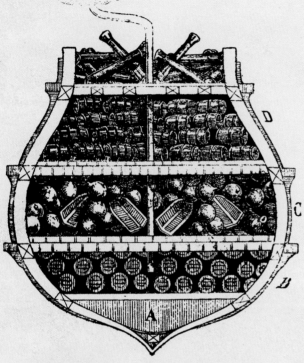

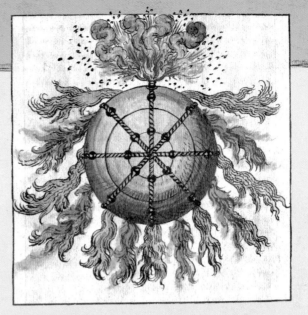

Above: *A bomb exploding—illustration by Wolff de Senftenberg, late 16th century.*

BOMBS AND FIREWORKS

As well as cast-iron shot, cannon could fire bombs, which were hollow balls filled with powder and topped with a fuse. They were intended to explode on impact—the explosion being timed by the length of the fuse. Bombs could be fired from 50 to 500 yards away, whereas a standard cannonball might travel 1,000 yards. Fireworks were devices used to set alight enemy ships. Fireballs, for instance, were cannonballs heated to red-hot in a brazier before being fired. Fire-pikes were boarding pikes with burning twine or cloth attached to them, which were thrown like javelins at the sails and decks.

CASE SHOT

Case shot, langrace, and canister shot are all names for a cylindrical can filled with small shot, stones, musket bullets, and small pieces of iron, designed to scatter destruction in as wide an area as possible on the crowded decks.

GRAPE SHOT

Grape shot was the term for a bunch of small, cast-iron balls, which were wrapped in canvas and fired by boarding parties (or used to repel them). The "grape" dispersed like buckshot, increasing the likelihood of finding a target.

CHAIN SHOT

Also called "angel shot" or "knipple shot," chain shot was created when two halves of a cannonball were joined by a short length of chain. It rotated, either cutting a swathe through a ship's rigging and sails or clearing a deck of sailors.

Right: *The cannonball at the top here is made of iron; the bottom two are from stone, which was commonly used in the New World.*

CANNONBALLS

Also known as round shot, cannonballs were used to destroy masts and rigging. Splinters of timber could incapacitate crew members, but cannonballs were not as destructive to humans as grapeshot, bar shot, or chain shot, which maximized the maiming capacity of cannon. Pirates wanted to take the ship itself, the crew, the passengers and the contents, so they did not fire at the waterline, unlike the Royal Navy, which aimed to sink enemy ships.

CHAPTER IV

Captain Morgan takes the city of Maracaibo, on the coast of New Venezuela—Piracies committed in those seas—The ruin of three Spanish ships, which were sent forth to hinder the robberies of the pirates

ↄﻉↄ

The sinking of the *Oxford*

After the pirates had squandered their money in a short time in Jamaica, Morgan gave orders for his captains to assemble at Isla de la Vaca, or Cow Island, off the south-west coast of Hispaniola. This was an excellent spot for careening, for watering, and for provisioning, as there were many wild boar on the island. Because of his successes, French and English buccaneers flocked to join Morgan's command.

A 36-gun ship from New England had recently arrived at Jamaica, and the governor sent her to join Admiral Morgan's fleet. Morgan was delighted, as she alone had the firepower to prevail against a fort if the need arose. There was also a French ship carrying 24 iron guns and 12 of brass, which Morgan wished to join his fleet. However, these French did not trust the English and would not agree. They were afraid of reprisals, as recently they had run out of food at sea and took victuals off an English ship, making no payment except worthless bills of exchange payable in Jamaica and Tortuga. Thus Morgan pretended to be friendly with the French captain, inviting him and his crew to dine on his new ship. They were then all taken prisoner, and Morgan laid claim to the ship in recompense for the victuals they had taken. This unjust action was soon followed by divine punishment, as we will perceive.

Having taken the French ship, Captain Morgan held a council with his captains on his new flagship, the *Oxford*, debating the course of their new expedition. They decided to sail for the Isle of Saona, off eastern Hispaniola, and then wait for the flota which was expected from Spain, taking any undefended

THE SPANISH FLEETS

Armada means "fleet of warships." The Armada of the Ocean Sea was organized in 1522 to protect West Indies trade, and a tax called the *averia* levied to pay it. Later, further armadas were created, to guard ships sailing from South America, to escort loot from Peru to the Pacific coast at Panama, and to attack pirates in the Caribbean. The flota, or Spanish Plate Fleet, was the treasure fleet that made its way toward Spain, generally yearly, from the gold and silver mines of South and Central America loaded with silver, gold, logwood, indigo, hides, and cacao. Captains of the Plate Fleet took an oath to burn, sink, or destroy their ships rather than let them fall into enemy hands. The *guardacosta* were privateering ships used by the Spanish to enforce their Caribbean trading monopoly.

Galleons formed the basis of the Spanish naval and merchant fleets in the 17th century, and were later adopted by other maritime nations.

GOVERNOR MODYFORD OF JAMAICA

Colonel Sir Thomas Modyford (c. 1620–1679) emigrated to become a planter in Barbados in 1647. He became Speaker of the House of Assembly in Barbados, during the reign of Charles II, and factor for the Royal Adventurers, who had a monopoly in the slave trade to the islands. His successes earned Modyford an appointment as governor of Jamaica in 1664. His arrival there, with 700 other planters, saw the establishment of a plantation economy in Jamaica, based on slave labor.

Modyford worked closely with Henry Morgan to ensure the security of Jamaica from Spanish invasion. Morgan's privateers were given letters of marque by Modyford, in effect to carry out the work of a nonexistent naval presence in the West Indies. In 1670, however, Modyford was removed as governor and returned to London with Henry Morgan to stand trial for corruption. He spent two years in the Tower of London without charge before returning to his plantations in Jamaica.

Henry Morgan always ensured he had valid letters of marque from his great friend Governor Modyford of Jamaica before he recruited for his privateering expeditions, otherwise he would have been guilty of piracy. The letter shown here is a reproduction.

stragglers in the meantime. Having come to this resolution, they had a feast on the *Oxford*, toasting health to each other and generally carousing—the officers on the poop-deck and the seamen in the forecastle. They discharged many guns, a common thing when sailors are drunk and merry. As the guns were being fired, by misfortune some sparks landed in the gunpowder in the powder room. Immediately, the ship was blown up into the air with 350 pirates and the French prisoners onboard. Only 30 survived, including the officers who had been feasting in the great cabin with Morgan, who was himself injured in the leg. Most of the living were in the stern of the ship like Morgan, the powder room being forward. More would have survived had they not been so much affected by wine.

The survivors take stock

The few survivors and the other English crews blamed the French prisoners for firing the ship. This became Morgan's new justification for seizing the French ship. The English reinforced this argument by saying that the French had been sailing with a Spanish commission to harm English shipping. They had found evidence on the French ship, a letter of marque, stating "That the said Governor (of Barracoa) did permit the French to trade in all Spanish ports, etc … And also to cruise upon the English Pirates in whatsoever place they find them, because of the multitude of hostilities which they had committed against the subjects of his Catholic Majesty, in time of peace between the two Crowns." In actuality, the French had obtained the commission to trade with the Spanish, not to attack the English. Their captain, who had survived, tried to explain this to Morgan, but was sent back with the French ship and the few surviving French prisoners to Jamaica. Here, the French tried to claim back their ship but were thrown into prison and threatened with hanging.

Morgan, meanwhile, did not lose heart and was determined to go ahead with the mission, despite the loss of his powerful flagship. Eight days after the explosion, he gave orders to search for and fish corpses out of the water, stripping their rings, clothes, and valuables. If rings could not be pulled off, the fingers were hacked off before the bodies were thrown back for the sharks. He then set sail for Saona with his 15 companion ships and 960 men to hold a council of war. His new flagship was the largest in the fleet but only carried 14 guns. A few days later the fleet arrived at Cape do Lobos, on the south of Hispaniola, midway between Cape Tiburon and Cape Punta d'Espada. Here, despite all their attempts, strong headwinds meant that the fleet could not round the cape.

Ambushed near the Bay of Ocoa

At last they were able to double the cape and seven or eight leagues further on sighted a ship. A few ships sailed toward her and, finding she was English, bought provisions. Morgan continued on, saying he would wait for the other ships at the Bay of Ocoa (on the south side of what is now the Dominican Republic), where he anchored two days later. He landed men to seek fresh water and more provisions. Every day, five or six men from each of Morgan's ships went ashore, shooting everything they could—donkeys, horses, cattle, and sheep—to take back to the fleet. However, they had been sighted by the Spanish, who saw that only a few men came ashore on each trip and resolved to lay a trap. They drove all the cattle inland and called for 300–400 soldiers from nearby Santo Domingo.

In a few days, the pirates came ashore again. Finding no beasts to slaughter, a party of about 50 ventured further inland for about three leagues, through the woods. The Spanish had seen their approach and placed a couple of cowherds and a fine herd of cattle on a plain to tempt them. The buccaneers started slaughtering beasts to carry back to their ships, all the time being watched by the Spanish soldiers. When they started back, carrying their fresh meat, the whole force of the Spaniards attacked, crying "Mata! Mata!" ("Kill! Kill!")

The pirates dropped their loads and immediately adopted a defensive stand. They retreated in good order, not fleeing, toward their ships and kept up a continuous fire until they reached the shelter of the forest. By these means many Spaniards were killed, although the pirates also suffered losses. The Spanish did not pursue them into the woods, being afraid of the deadly accuracy of their muskets and pistols. The buccaneers paused to bind their wounds and could see the Spanish carrying off their dead and wounded. Among the dead was one of their comrades, and the Spanish were moving around his body, plunging their swords into him and shouting "El cornudo ladron!" ("The cuckolded thief!") Seeing that the main Spanish force had withdrawn, the sea-rovers rushed out and killed many of this troop and recovered the body of their comrade, which had over a hundred stab wounds inflicted after his death. They buried him in the forest. They then killed a few horses left behind by the Spanish, to take back to the ships for meat, and brought their wounded back to report to Captain Morgan.

Their leader was outraged and the next day took 200 men to seek out and destroy the rest of the Spanish. As they had disappeared with all the cattle, he set fire to a few houses instead. His other ships had still not arrived, so Morgan proceeded to Saona island and waited for them there for a few days. Provisions running low, he was forced to send 150 men to land on Hispaniola to plunder the villages around Santo Domingo for food and drink. The party was unsuccessful, for the Spanish were in a state of high alert, knowing that pirates were in the vicinity.

The Isle of Aruba

The other seven ships had still not arrived, so Morgan mustered all his forces, finding that he had only 500 able men to follow him and just eight small vessels, of which his was easily the largest. His original plan had been to cruise down the coast to Caracas looting all the towns and villages, but with such a

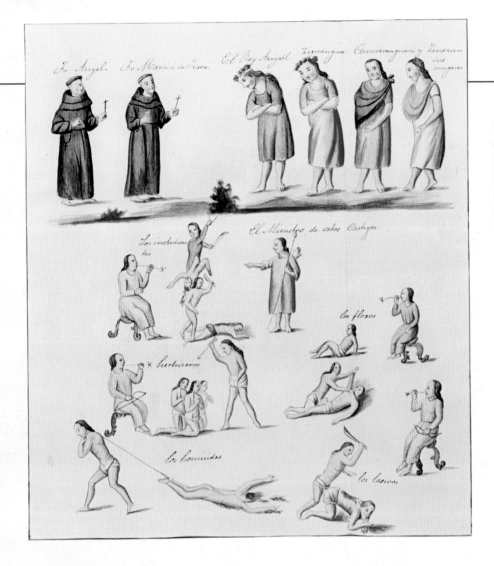

Left: An 18th-century depiction of Indians presenting themselves for conversion by Spanish friars, showing the punishments for crimes such as witchcraft, licentiousness, and murder.

small force it could not be attempted. However, one of his French captains had served with L'Olonnais at the taking of Maracaibo. He knew all of its entrances, passages, and defenses and the means by which to sack it a second time. Morgan agreed to the proposal and spoke to his men, who unanimously agreed. Thus he set sail for the island of Curaçao. When it was sighted, they landed at the isle of Aruba, 12 leagues to the west. This small island is owned by the Dutch West India Company, but it only has a small garrison of 15 soldiers. Its inhabitants are Spanish-speaking Indians, converted to the Roman Catholic faith by priests who are sent there from time to time. Every year, a priest comes from the village of Coro, on the coast of the mainland, to give them the sacrament.

The inhabitants trade with buccaneers, exchanging goats, kids, sheep, and lambs for linen, thread, and the like. The island is infertile and is covered with scrub, so only sheep and goats survive. There are also many horses, and the Indians do everything on horseback, even go just 500 paces from their homes to fetch water. There are venomous spiders, vipers, and other poisonous insects. The spider bites will make a man mad before he dies. The only treatment is to tie the victim up in a hammock for 24 hours and refuse him food or drink. The Indians believe that if he drinks he will surely die.

They then started back, carrying their fresh meat, when the whole force of the Spaniards attacked, crying "Mata! Mata!" ("Kill! Kill!")

Above: Pampatar was one of the forts built by the Spanish in response to Morgan's raids. It stands on Margarita Island (known as "The Pearl of the Caribbean"), in Venezuela, and was built between 1664 and 1684.

Captain Morgan bought sheep, goats, and wood and spent two days anchored there before he left the island. He left at night, so its inhabitants could not see in which direction he had sailed and report it to the Spanish. However, they did notice his fleet leaving.

The taking of Palomas Fort and of De La Barra and Maracaibo

The next day the small fleet arrived at the Bay of Maracaibo and anchored in eight fathoms of water in the middle of the bay, out of sight of Vigilas, or Look-out Island. That night they set sail toward land and at dawn had reached the sandbar at the entrance of the lake. However, the Spanish had built a new fort at Palomas since L'Olonnais had destroyed the last one, and it rained heavy cannon fire toward Morgan's ships, preventing their passage. Morgan began landing his men in canoes, while his ships returned fire until dusk. Around nightfall, Morgan and his men approached the fort warily and were seen by the garrison. A cannonade hurled cannonballs and shot at the advancing buccaneers. However, in the heavy smokescreen the garrison fled. Morgan was amazed—the fort was well-equipped and could have held off an attack, but then his men discovered a cellar full of gunpowder and a burning fuse about an inch away from it. Morgan hurled himself at the fuse and saved all his comrades' lives. His bravery was already the stuff of legend, and this exploit made his men even more determined to follow him anywhere. The powder was taken to the fleet, the walls were partly demolished, gun carriages burnt, and 16 cannons, capable of taking 12–24 pound cannonballs, were spiked. Eighty muskets and other military provisions were also taken aboard the fleet.

The next day the fleet passed over the bar from the Gulf of Venezuela into the great Lake of Maracaibo, to continue toward Maracaibo itself. However, they could not pass that certain sandbank, the Tablazo, which lies near the entry of the lake. Some ships went aground, but the fleet arrived at Maracaibo the next day at noon. Morgan took the ships near to the shore in order to give some light covering fire for his men to land. He was forced to put his men into canoes and small boats in front of the fort called De La Barra, but his luck was in. The Spanish defenders had fled into the woods, as

Morgan hurled himself at the fuse and saved all his comrades' lives. His bravery was already the stuff of legend, and this exploit made his men even more determined to follow him anywhere.

had all the city's inhabitants except for a few poor cripples. The pirates searched the town, expecting ambushes or to find people hiding, but found nothing. They therefore abandoned their ships and chose the best houses to live in. The church was delegated to be a guardhouse, from which a continuous watch was kept for enemy movements. The following day, a party of 100 men was sent out to bring back prisoners and plunder. They returned a day later with 30 men, women, children, and slaves and 50 mules laden with merchandise.

The torture of prisoners

All these wretched prisoners were put to the rack, to find out where the other citizens were hiding. Among other tortures they were strappadoed; that is, lifted into the air by a rope attached to their hands, which are tied behind their backs, then dropped almost to the ground before being stopped with an abrupt jerk. They were beaten with sticks, and others had their limbs stretched by cords. Some were spread-eagled with burning fuses between their fingers and toes and were thus burnt alive. Others were wolded, slender cords twisted tightly around their heads until their eyes burst out of their skulls. These maniacal tortures were carried on until the poor wretches confessed, and if they could not, they were put to death and out of torment. The tortures and racking lasted a full three weeks, in which time parties went out daily to bring in more prisoners from the forests, never returning home without booty.

The assault on Gibraltar

Now having in his hands 100 prisoners from the most important families in Maracaibo, Morgan resolved to head for Gibraltar, following in the footsteps of the infamous L'Olonnais. He equipped and reprovisioned his fleet and embarked all the prisoners. He had sent some prisoners to Gibraltar to tell its people to surrender; otherwise they should not be spared by Captain Morgan. However, the arrival of his fleet was met with continuous cannon-fire. The sea-rovers were not disheartened, encouraging each other and saying "We must make one meal of bitter things, before we come to taste the sweetness of sugar that this place affords."

Very early next morning all the pirates landed, following the French captain who had served under L'Olonnais. They marched to town through the woods rather than by the normal road, where the Spaniards were expecting them to advance from. Morgan left just a few men on the road, to make the Spanish think that they were an advance party. In the meantime, the Frenchman led the rest of Morgan's men to surprise the town from its rear. However, there was no need for such caution. The Spanish, remembering their experience under L'Olonnais, had fled, leaving only a few ambushes behind them to slow down any pursuers and defend their retreat. They had taken all of their fort's gunpowder and spiked its guns, leaving only one madman in the town.

This unfortunate man told the pirates that he knew nothing, but they nonetheless put him to the rack, whereupon he told them that he would lead them to his goods and riches. He took them to his hovel, where he had buried a few pieces of earthenware and plates and three pieces of eight. They asked him his name, and he told them he was Don Sebastian Sanchez, brother of the governor of Maracaibo. Hearing this, they tortured him again, tying him up and beating him until the blood poured from him.

At last he cried that he would take them to his sugar-mill, where they would find all his wealth and slaves. When they untied him he was unable to walk, so they tied him to a horse. In the forest, he told them that he had no mill or any possessions but lived on the charity of the hospital. This was true, as they afterward discovered. However, his tormentors were enraged. They put him again on the rack and lifted him up high with cords, tying huge weights to his feet and neck. They also burnt him alive, applying burning palm-leaves to his face, and he died after about half-an-hour of such torture. They then cut his cords and dragged him into the forest for the animals to eat him.

More of the pirates' ruthless actions

The same day, a party went out looking for prisoners and came back with a peasant and his two daughters. They threatened them with the rack in order to find other, richer citizens. The poor man said that he knew some of their hiding-places but that the Spanish had fled further into the deepest recesses of the forests, where they had built huts in which to wait for the pirates to sail away. The buccaneers thought that he was misleading them and, although he protested his innocence, they hung him.

The buccaneers now spread themselves all around Gibraltar, hiding near the plantations. They knew that the Spanish in the woods would soon run out of provisions and steal back to their country houses for food. They also found a slave, to whom they promised mountains of gold and freedom in Jamaica if he

Right: Morgan offers a slave his freedom for disclosing where the Spaniards are hiding. In the background his men are threatening captured citizens with death if they do not confess where they have hidden their goods.

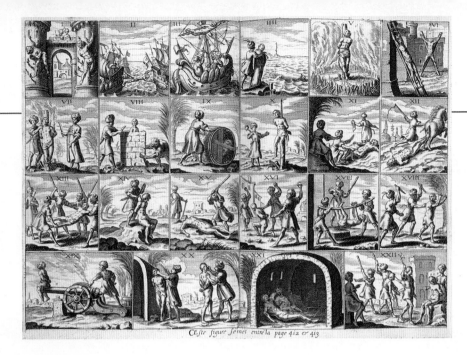

CEste figure se met entre la page 412 er 413

Left: These scenes of torture, dating from 1637, are attributed to the Barbary Corsairs of the coast of North Africa. Torture in these times was not only used to find where treasure was hidden, but also often used upon those of a different religious faith.

would show them where the citizens were living. This prospect suited the Negro very well, and he led the pirates to many of their refuges. They allowed the slave to kill some of the prisoners, which he relished. The privateers knew that the slave would never run away if he was guilty of killing Spaniards, but would have to stay with them. After eight days, the pirates returned to Gibraltar with many captives and mules laden with riches. They interrogated every one of the 250 prisoners for information about other people hiding or the location of hidden booty. Those who did not confess were tortured abominably.

The cruel fate of the poor tavern-keeper

One of the worst examples was that of an old Portuguese man in his sixties, who the Negro had falsely claimed was very rich. The Portuguese swore that the only money he had in the world was 100 pieces of eight and that a young man who lived near him had stolen it. He was not believed and thus was strappadoed so violently that his arms were pulled out of their sockets. He could not confess any more, so the pirates tied long cords to his thumbs and big toes and spread-eagled him to four stakes. The whole weight of his body was held by his thumbs and toes. Then four pirates banged great sticks up and down on each of the cords, making his body jerk and stretching his sinews. He was near death when they placed a two-hundredweight stone on his stomach, as if they intended to press him to death. Then, they kindled palm-leaves and pressed the burning leaves against his face, hair, and beard. At last, tiring of their sport, they cut the cords and took him to their guardhouse, the church, and tied him upright to a pillar. He was given just enough food and water to keep him alive and after four or five days asked for one of the prisoners to be brought to him. He asked his fellow-prisoner to promise 500 pieces of eight for his life but was beaten again by the pirates for asking for such a small sum. Eventually 1,000 pieces of eight were promised, which were raised in a few days, and the man was granted his liberty. He was only a poor tavern-keeper and so horribly maimed that it is scarcely to be believed that he would survive many more weeks following his ordeal at the hands of the pirates.

Yet even this man had not suffered the full range of tortures practised at Gibraltar. If they were minded to be merciful to the poor wretches, the pirates would lacerate them with their swords and then dispatch them by running them through. Others, however, were stabbed three or four times and then left to die in terrible pain, after lingering in agony for about four or five days. There were worse torments.

*O*thers were crucified, with kindled fuses burning between their fingers and toes. Yet others were tied up, smeared with grease, and roasted to death.

SUGAR AND SUGAR MANUFACTURE

The sugar cane plant was the main crop produced throughout the Caribbean from the 17th century onward. Most islands were covered with sugar cane for refining. Sugar was traded for use in cakes, as a sweetener in teas, and in distillation and brewing, replacing the slower-working and more labor-intensive honey. The introduction of the plantation system, slavery, and windmills for mass sugar production provided motivation for European expansion, colonization, and control in the New World. Sugar cane

was also used in large-scale rum distilleries for the first time during the mid-17th century. Originally, sugar was cured in clay pots. As it crystallized, the brown liquid, molasses, was drained out of the remaining sucrose, recycled by natural fermentation, and then distilled to form a clear liquid, which darkened in wooden casks.

This 17th-century engraving of a mill in the West Indies shows that oxen had replaced slaves in driving the wheel. Raw sugar cane, which was exported to refineries in Europe, was the most profitable crop in the world at this time.

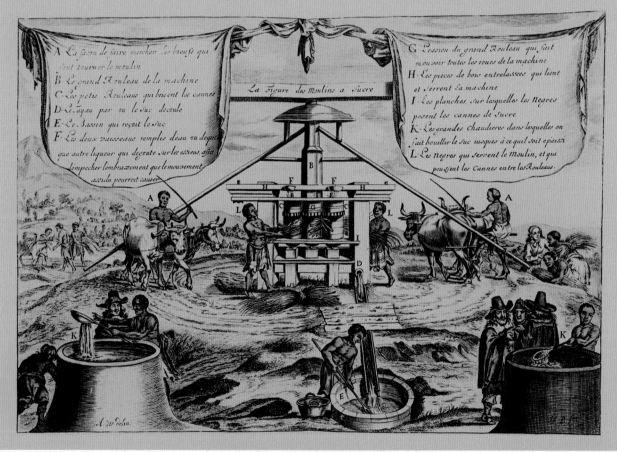

Some male prisoners were hung up by their genitals until the weight of their bodies tore them loose. Others were crucified, with burning fuses placed between their fingers and toes. Yet others were tied up, smeared with grease, and roasted to death. Having used these terrible cruelties on the white men, the pirates were no better with the slaves.

Among the slaves the pirates found one who promised to take Morgan to a certain river that flowed into the lake, where there was a ship and four barques, richly laden with the cargo of Maracaibo's citizens. One slave also informed that another slave knew the whereabouts of the governor and most of the women, but the other slave denied it. Threatened with being hung, he admitted he knew and promised to lead the buccaneers to the governor. Morgan thus split his men into two parties. A hundred were sent in saeties, or large swift boats, upriver to find the governor's ship and barques, while Morgan led 350 men to find the governor. The governor had hidden on a small island in the middle of a river, where he had built a small fort. His spies warned him of the approach of the pirates, so he retired to the top of a nearby mountain, which was only accessible in single file via a narrow passage. The defenders had also prepared fireballs to attack the pirates with if they tried to climb the mountain. Morgan traveled for two days to reach the island and then prepared to capture the governor.

However, heavy rains meant that the rivers were flooded, and men were lost trying to cross to the mountain. The pirates' powder was damp, and they had lost, in the river crossing, mules carrying all their baggage and many armaments. Also lost were some of the spoils they had taken on their way to the island, along with some female prisoners and children. The path to the mountain-top was treacherous, and a hail of gunfire meant that it was impassable. Morgan's men were in such a bad condition that just 50 well-armed lancers with pikes and spears could have killed them all. However, the Spanish were so fearful that even the sound of leaves rustling on the trees frightened them. Morgan decided that discretion was the better part of valor, his men being in no fit shape to fight, and ordered the return to Gibraltar. Sometimes they had to wade through water for half-a-mile to a mile, and more prisoners were lost on the way back from exposure or drowning. The land is very low-lying and the rivers had burst their banks and flooded the forest tracks.

Twelve days after setting out, Morgan returned to Gibraltar with a large number of prisoners but his men in a much weakened condition. Two days later, the other raiding party returned with the Spanish ship, the four barques, and more prisoners. They had been unable to take the whole cargo, because the Spanish had been warned of their coming and had unloaded the greatest part of the merchandise before they reached them. The Spaniards had intended to set the boats on fire, but the pirates arrived too quickly, so there were still some linens, silks, and other goods onboard when they got there.

The return to Maracaibo

Admiral Morgan had now been in Gibraltar for five weeks, and there was nothing further to be gained by staying. He was anxious to check if Maracaibo was still secure as an escape route to the Caribbean. He asked two prisoners to go out and ransom the town, threatening to burn it, but the Spaniards told him on their return that their people were too scattered to gather money. Morgan accepted their story and gave the prisoners a few days to gather 5,000 pieces of eight. He took hostages with him to ensure its delivery in Maracaibo and left Gibraltar. The Spanish wished to pay a ransom for his Negro guide, but Morgan refused, knowing that he would be burnt alive. Morgan arrived at Maracaibo four days later, keeping all the captured slaves to take to Jamaica.

At Maracaibo all seemed normal, but Morgan knew that there would have been time for the Spaniards to raise a relieving force while they were away. He found an old, sick man in the hospital there who was willing to tell him that there were three Spanish men-of-war at the mouth of the lake waiting for him. Fort Palomas, overlooking the lake's entry, had also been re-garrisoned and equipped with cannon. Morgan and his fleet were now trapped in Lake Maracaibo, with no prospect of escaping to the open seas. A fast sloop was sent to check the situation. It approached the Spanish ships just out of cannon range and was fired upon. The men-of-war carried 36, 26, and 16 cannon respectively, which was hugely superior to the firepower of Morgan's little ships and boats. His flagship only carried 14 guns. There was no chance of escaping overland either. They were surrounded inland by Spanish possessions. Morgan wished that the Spanish warships had sailed into the lake, where there was room for his ships to maneuver in the shallow waters.

MEDICINE AND DISEASE

Very little was known about hygiene in the 17th century. People were not aware that diseases were spread by germs that thrived on unhygienic conditions. They did not think of washing their hands before eating or dressing a wound, so diseases could spread quickly. Doctors believed in powders said to be made from unicorn horn and used live worms, fox lungs, spiders' webs, swallows' nests, and the skulls of executed criminals as ingredients. Leeches were employed to reduce blood pressure, stop clotting, and cleanse the blood. It was also discovered that the best way to treat a wound was not to put boiling oil on it, but instead to apply a cold lotion made of egg yolk, rose oil, and turpentine. In this century William Harvey discovered that blood circulates around the body, the heart acting as a pump with valves to control the flow, and Robert Boyle described how the body takes in oxygen to breathe.

SURGEONS AND THEIR MEDICINE CHESTS

John Woodall's *The Surgeon's Mate*, first published in 1617, was a manual that listed the instruments and medicines found in the ship surgeon's medicine chest and explained how to use them. Special instructions outlined emergency procedures, such as amputation, and various ailments were discussed, particularly scurvy. Among the tools and supplies found in medicine chests were "head-sawes," cauterizing irons, probes and spatulas for drawing out splinters and shot, syringes, tweezers, grippers for extracting teeth, cupping glasses, blood porringers, chafing dishes, and tinderboxes. When Blackbeard blockaded the port of Charleston, South Carolina, he demanded a chest in exchange for his hostages, who were leading citizens of the town—mainly for the mercury to treat his and his crew's syphilis.

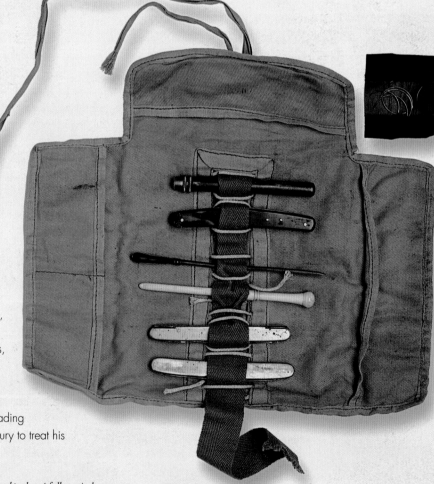

Above: *A portable naval surgical kit with knives and probes. A full surgical chest would have carried much more equipment.*

CONDITIONS ONBOARD

Aside from the rats, weevils, lice, and cockroaches on ships, livestock was kept aboard and sometimes had free reign of the deck, making for unsanitary conditions. The pirates' clothing was often wet and lice-ridden. As a result of the environment they lived in, pirates also suffered from sunburn, heat exhaustion, sun stroke, hypothermia, and exposure. Tasks such as scurrying up and down the rigging and the frequent movement of both the ship and the mast sometimes caused sailors to lose their footing and fall. Sores, cuts, and bruises were commonplace.

Above: Storms at sea caused many injuries, from broken legs to fractured skulls.

SYPHILIS

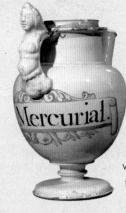

The most common and feared disease among pirates was syphilis—the first thing they looked for upon taking a ship would be the surgeon's medicine chest, where they could obtain mercury for treatment. It was understood from the beginning that syphilis is spread by sexual contact, but it was originally thought that the disease had developed from the union of a prostitute with a leper. Syphilis is very similar to leprosy and remained indistinct until the 15th century. *Lignum Vitae* wood resin caused profuse sweating and drooling, which was thought to cure syphilis. Mercury, which also caused the salivary glands to activate (due to its toxicity), was another favored treatment.

Above and right: Pharmaceutical jars for Mercury and Gayac, late 17th century or early 18th century.

SCURVY

In 1593, Captain Richard Hawkins noted that sour oranges and lemons were the best treatment for scurvy, but not until 1795 did Royal Navy vessels carry lemon juice to combat the disease, by which time it had killed an estimated 800,000 British seamen. Merchant vessels only followed the practice from 1854. Lime juice later replaced lemons on Royal Navy ships, from which practice the American slang for British people, "limeys," derived. With no fresh fruit or vegetables available, scurvy had been endemic on long voyages. It also caused shipwrecks: Crews were made so weak by lack of vitamin C that they sunk into a dull lethargy from which they could not be shaken. Symptoms began with swollen gums, loss of teeth, a weakened heart, and black blotches beneath the skin. Later, the sailor sank into a final exhausted torpor, with glazed eyes and a swollen body and legs. Wounds could not heal and spontaneous hemorrhaging into muscles and joints caused much pain. The blood vessels around the brain eventually ruptured and, gasping for breath, the seaman would die.

Right: 17th-century advertisement for "An Herculeon Antidote" for scurvy.

A Book of Directions
And Cures done by that Safe and Succesful Medicine CALLED,
AN
HERCULEON ANTIDOTE,
OR THE
GERMAN GOLDEN ELIXIR
VVhich is deservedly so called, for its Special Virtues, in Curing that
POPULAR DISEASE, the *SCURVEY*.

THIS HERCULEON ANTIDOTE, Cures by cleansing of the Blood, Purging by URINE, and gently by STOOL.

Some Diseases are Familiar to some Nations, which others are free from; the *Leprosie, Itch, Pox*, as in *Italy*, and some Parts of the *Indies*; so in the *Eastern* Parts, our *Popular* Disease is the *Scurvey*, which this Golden Elixir hath had such admirable Success far beyond any thing Extant for the *Scurvey*, and that it cures most Distempers, for there are few Diseases, but has a spice of the *Scurvey*, which corrupts the Blood.

The Symptoms and Nature of the Scurvey.
The Scurvy is the Original of most violent Distempers, which this Golden Elixir preventeth, as Stoppages, Obstructions, raising Vapours that causes Swimming and Fumes in the Head, Dimness of Sight, Deafness, an. Drowsiness which makes the Body dull and heavy, and alters the Complexion:
A

Positioned as they were, the Spanish could blast Morgan's ships as they approached the narrow inlet that led to the Gulf of Venezuela and the safety of the Caribbean. Morgan tried to calm his crews. To show them that he was not afraid, he sent a Spanish prisoner to ask ransom for the city of Maracaibo. Two days later the man returned with a letter from the Spanish admiral, which read:

Letter of Don Alonso del Campo y Espinosa, Admiral of the Spanish Fleet, unto Captain Morgan, commander of pirates.

Having understood through all our friends and neighbors the unexpected news, that you have dared to attempt and commit hostilities in the countries, cities, towns and villages belonging to his Catholic Majesty, my Sovereign Lord and Master; I let you understand, by these lines, that I have come to this place, according to my obligation, nigh unto that castle which you took out of the hands of a parcel of cowards; where I have put things in a very good posture of defense, and mounted again the artillery which you had spiked and dismounted. My intent is to dispute with you your passage out of the lake and pursue you everywhere; to the end that you may see the performance of my duty.

Notwithstanding, if you be content to surrender with humility all that you have taken, together with the slaves and all other prisoners, I will let you freely pass, without trouble or molestation; upon condition that you retire home immediately to your own country. But in case that you make any resistance or opposition to these things that I proffer unto you, I do assure you that I will command boats to come from Caracas, wherein I will put my troops, and coming to Maracaibo, will cause you utterly to perish, by putting every man to the sword.

This is my last and absolute resolution. Be prudent, therefore, and do not abuse my bounty with ingratitude. I have with me very good soldiers, who desire nothing more ardently than to revenge on you and your people all the cruelties and base infamous actions that you have committed upon the Spanish nation in America.

Dated onboard the Royal Ship named the Magdalena, *lying at anchor at the entry of the Lake of Maracaibo, this 24th day of April, 1669—Don Alonso del Campo y Espinosa.*

Morgan assembled all his men in the market-place and read out the letter, in English and in French. He did not trust the Spanish to keep their word. If he unloaded the booty and slaves, he believed that they would still be killed or, even worse, suffer at the hands of the Inquisition. He asked his men whether they would rather give up their riches or fight for their liberty. There was an unanimous agreement that they would fight to the death to keep their spoils.

Right: In Morgan's time, heretics were prosecuted by the Spanish Inquisition and executed, usually by burning at the stake, during what was known as an *Auto-da-fé* (Act of Faith)—depicted in this 1680 painting by Francisco Rizi.

Opposite page: *An American Privateer Taking A British Prize*, 1908. Howard Pyle was a noted author and artist. He painted a number of pirate scenes, many of them for his *Book of Pirates*, published in 1903.

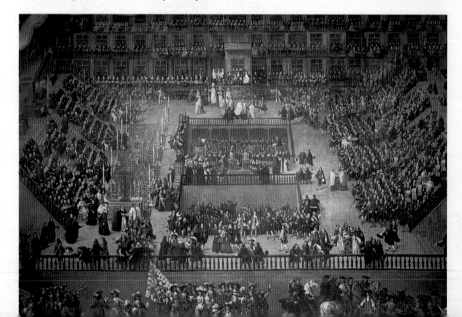

PIRATE AND BUCCANEER PRIZES

The most successful captures and raids were as follows:

Date, Captain, Ship	Prize or location	Value at time
1579, Sir Francis Drake, *Golden Hinde*	*Cacafuego*, treasure ship from Peru to Panama, taken off Ecuador	£450,000 contemporary estimate
1587, Thomas Cavendish, *Desire*	*Santa Ana*, Manila galleon, taken off California	c. £125,000
1587, Sir Francis Drake, *Golden Hinde*	*San Felipe*, East India carrack, taken off the Azores	Upward of c. £114,000
1592, Captain Crosse, *Foresight* and eight other English privateers	*Madre de Dios*, Portuguese carrack en route from India to Lisbon, taken off the Azores	c. £500,000, of which £140,000 was taken by the Crown
1607, John Ward, the *Gift*	*Reniera y Soderina*, Venetian ship, taken off Cyprus	Upward of c. £100,000
1612–13, Peter Easton, and four ships	Dutch, English, and African ships, taken in the Atlantic and Mediterranean oceans	c. 100,000 golden crowns
1613, Sir Henry Mainwaring	Spanish ships in the Mediterranean	c. 500,000 Spanish crowns
1628, Hendrick Lucifer	Spanish treasure ship off Cuba	1.2 million Dutch guilders
1628, Piet Heyn, with 31 ships	Spanish treasure fleet from Mexico, off Cuba	c. 14 million Dutch guilders
1658, Sir Christopher Myngs, *Marston Moor*	Venezuelan ports	c. £375,000
1663-65, Sir Henry Morgan, with Captains Morris and Jackman	Villa de Mosa (Honduras) and Granada (Nicaragua)	Upward of c. £100,000
1668, Sir Henry Morgan, *Oxford*, with John Morris and six cromsters	Sacked the treasure port of Puerto Bello, Panama	c. 500,000 pieces of eight, plus 300 slaves, gold, and silver

Date, Captain, Ship	Prize or location	Value at time
1669, Sir Henry Morgan, eight small ships	Sacked Maracaibo and Gibraltar; in Venezuela, took the galleon *La Marquesa*, and destroyed the *San Luis* and *Magdalena*	c. 250,000 pieces of eight, including the value of the slaves and bullion
1671, Sir Henry Morgan, *Satisfaction,* with John Morris and Bledri Morgan, and 1,400 men	Took Old Providence (1670) and Chagres Fort, and sacked Panama City	c. £30,000 claimed in ransoms at the time and 750,000 pieces of eight: The richest raid in history
1683, De Graff, van Horn and de Gammont, and five other ships	Sacked the port of San Juan de Ulua and the town of Veracruz, Mexico	c. £200,000
1695, Henry (Long Ben) Every, *Fancy,* with five other ships	*Fateh Mohamed* and *Gang-i-Sawai,* Indian treasure ships, taken in the Red Sea	c. £400,000
1698, Dirk Chivers, *Soldado,* and Robert Culliford, *Mocha*	*Great Mohamed,* Indian ship, taken in the Red Sea	c. £130,000
1717, Black Sam Bellamy, *Sulatana,* with Paulsgrave Williams	*Whydah,* slave ship, taken off Long Island, Bahamas	£25,000 from the sale of slaves; £30,000 from the sale of cargo
1719, Black Bart Roberts, *Royal Rover*	*Sagrada Familia,* and two other Portuguese treasure ships, taken in the Bay of All Saints, Brazil	40,000 moidores (Portuguese gold coins), and a fortune in diamonds and gold
1721, John Taylor, *Cassandra,* and Olivier la Bouche, *Victory*	*Nostra Senhora de Cabo,* a Portuguese ship taken at Reunion Island	c. £500,000 in diamonds and gold; £375,000 in other cargo

Opposite page: Henry Morgan watching his gunners on Lake Maracaibo. Cannon were under the command of the ship's gunner, who had to allow for the swell of the seas affecting both his ship and the target. Generally pirates tried to disable enemy ships, not sink them.

Below: Pirates often used small craft to sneak up on ships that were anchored at night. In the Caribbean, with its reefs and shoals, sailing was extremely dangerous on a dark night.

The battle of Lake Maracaibo

One of Morgan's men now came up to him and told him that he could make a brûlot, or fireship, of the ship they had captured upriver at Gibraltar. The pirate promised to destroy the flagship *Magdalena* with just a dozen men. He could fit the captured ship out like a man-of-war, with Morgan's flags flying. The decks would be filled with wooden props representing men wearing hats or montera-caps. The portholes would be filled with counterfeit cannon, big hollow logs of the type they called Negroes' drums, painted black.

The council agreed to this proposal, as they had no better options available. Morgan now tried to stall for the time they needed to effect the transformation. He sent a messenger proposing that he would leave Maracaibo alone, not claiming any ransom, and that he would give up half the slaves and set the other prisoners free without any ransom. He also said that they would give up the ransom they had asked for Gibraltar and set those hostages free. Espinosa responded to Morgan's offer by saying that the terms he had outlined in his letter were the only ones available and that Morgan had two days to surrender or be utterly destroyed by fire and sword.

Meanwhile, the prisoners and slaves were locked up and closely guarded, lest any one of them should escape and inform the Spanish of their stratagem. The jobs the slaves had been employed in, drawing up and fetching water and the like, were now taken on by buccaneers. The pirates feverishly prepared their ships for action and worked on the fireship. They collected all the tar, pitch, brimstone, and combustibles that were in the city. They mixed gunpowder and brimstone and carefully placed palm-leaves coated with tar. New portholes were made, to give the impression of a powerful ship with many cannon. Each of the wooden "cannon" was coated with tar and brimstone, and six pots of gunpowder with fuses were laid under each. The decks were filled with pieces of wood dressed like men wearing hats and armed with swords, muskets, and bandoliers. The ship was now a floating bomb.

The fireship's crew set the fuses and jumped into a boat to escape, just before she blew up. The flames from her sails and the explosion quickly took hold on the Spanish ship.

All the male prisoners were placed on one of the large barques taken at Gibraltar, and the best plunder, such as silver plate and jewels, was placed on another with the female prisoners. Each barque had 12 heavily-armed sailors onboard. Other, less valuable loot was scattered around the other small boats. The fleet headed toward the harbor entrance, the fireship leading and Morgan following in his flagship, on 30th April, 1669. The Spanish fleet was riding at anchor in the middle of the entry of the lake. It was almost dusk and Morgan ordered his ships to anchor just out of enemy range. The crews were ordered to keep vigilant in case the Spaniards tried a night attack.

At dawn the fleet starting sailing out of the lake, with the ebb tide. The Spanish cut their cables and prepared for action. The fireship approached the flagship and managed to grapple it, although the Spanish tried to fend her off. Only in the last minutes had they realized it was not a man-of-war. The fireship's crew set the fuses and jumped into a boat to escape, just before she blew up. The flames from her sails and the explosion quickly took hold on the Spanish ship, and her timber and tackle burned furiously. The great flagship was quickly abandoned. The second Spanish ship, thinking that Morgan's ship—now fast bearing down on them—was also a fireship, tried to escape toward the castle, but she grounded, and the Spanish swam for the shore after setting the ship on fire. The third ship fled but was soon captured. The pirates tried to pick up Spaniards from the sinking flagship, but many refused to be rescued, preferring to drown rather than fall into the pirates' hands.

Within a few hours the Spanish fleet had been destroyed, and Morgan's men were in high spirits. In this mood they attacked the castle, but there was heavy artillery fire. The pirates were only armed with muskets and hand grenades, and their ships' guns were too light and ineffective to breach the walls. Their accurate musket-fire did terrible damage when the Spanish were loading their guns, but any attempts to approach the walls and hurl hand grenades met with disaster. The Spanish began to throw fireballs and pots of gunpowder with lighted fuses. The pirates had lost 30 men and another 30 had been wounded before they retreated from the action at dusk, returning to their ships.

The escape still blocked

Morgan knew that the fort of Palomas now had to be taken, to allow his ships to leave the lake. The Spanish expected the pirates to bring their cannon ashore and place them near to the walls, so they had spent the night flattening any suitable positions of advantage to the pirates. They felt confident that they could hold up the buccaneers until reinforcements arrived from Caracas. The Spanish flagship broke up that evening and some of the Spanish tried to swim to it but were captured. Among them was the steersman from the smallest of the three Spanish warships. Morgan asked him what forces were on the three ships, how many more were expected, when they were coming, and from where.

The man responded that he was not Spanish but answered in the Spanish tongue. He told Morgan that six ships had been sent from Spain to cruise against the corsairs and destroy them, following the protests about the sack of Puerto Bello by Morgan. The Spanish Ambassador had complained to King Charles II, who had said that he had never given privateering commissions to attack the Spanish. Consequently, these six ships had been fitted out by orders of the Supreme Council in the State of Spain, under the command of Don Augustin de Bustos. He went on:

"He commanded the biggest ship, the Nuestra Señora de Soledad, *mounted with 48 grand guns, and 8 small ones. The Vice-Admiral was Don Alonso del Campo y Espinosa, who commanded* La Concepción, *carrying 44 great guns, and 8 small ones. There were four more vessels. The* Magdalena *was mounted with 36 great guns, and 12 small ones, and had onboard 250 men. The second was the* San Luiz, *with 26 great guns, 12 small ones, and 200 men. The third was* La Marquesa, *which carried 16 great guns, 8 small ones, and 150 men. The last was the* Nuestra Señora del Carmen *with 18 great guns, 8 small ones, and 250 men.*

We arrived at Cartagena, when the two greatest ships received orders to return to Spain, as they were judged too big to operate in these waters. With the four ships remaining, Don Alonso del Campo y Espinosa sailed to Campeche to seek out the English. We arrived at its port, but were surprised by a huge storm from the north, whereby we lost Nuestra Señora del Carmen. *We then set sail for Hispaniola, which took a few days, and headed for the port of San Domingo. Here we received intelligence that a fleet from Jamaica had passed that way, some of their men landing at Alta Gracia. One was captured and he confessed that their whole design was to pillage Caracas. Don Alonso immediately set sail for Caracas, where there were no English, but we met a boat which told us that the pirates were in Lake Maracaibo with a fleet of seven small ships and one boat.*

Below: Morgan's attack on the three men-of-war at Lake Maracaibo. The flagship nearest is exploding because of the fireship's attack; Morgan is attacking a ship in the distance; and the third ship has run aground and been set alight by its crew.

The Spanish Armada destroyed by Captaine Morgan

Upon this intelligence we arrived here; and coming nigh to the entry of the port, we shot off a gun to demand a pilot from the shore. Those on land, perceiving we were Spaniards, came willingly to us with a pilot, and told us that the English had taken Maracaibo and they were presently pillaging Gibraltar. Don Alonso, having understood the news, made a brave speech to all his soldiers and mariners, encouraging them to perform their duty, and promising to divide among them all that they should take from the English. After this, he gave orders that the guns which we had taken out of the ship that was lost should be put into the castle, and there mounted for its defense, with two 18-pound cannon out of his own ship.

The pilots conducted us into the port, and Don Alonso commanded the people that were on shore to come to his presence, to whom he gave orders to repossess the castle, reinforcing it with 100 men more than when it was taken by the English. Not long after, we heard news that you were returned from Gibraltar to Maracaibo; to which place Don Alonso wrote you a Letter, giving you an account of his arrival and design, and exhorting you to restore all that you had taken. This you refused to do; whereupon he renewed his promises and intentions to his soldiers and seamen. And having given a very good supper to all his people, he persuaded them neither to take nor give any quarter to the English that should fall into their hands.

This was the occasion of so many being drowned, who dared not to crave any quarter for their lives, as knowing their own intentions of giving none. Two days before you came against us, a certain Negro came aboard Don Alonso's ship, telling him: 'Sir, be pleased to have great care for yourself; for the English have prepared a fireship with design to burn your fleet.' But Don Alonso would not believe this intelligence, his answer being: 'How can that be? Have they, peradventure, wit enough to build a fireship? What instruments do they have to make it so?'"

The pilot's information was so useful, Morgan now being aware that there were no other Spanish warships on their way from Spain, that he offered the man shares in the expedition if he stayed with the buccaneers. The steersman accepted and told the Admiral that there were at least 30,000 to 40,000 pieces of eight on the sunken flagship, which is why the Spanish had been out in small boats trying to get to the wreck. Morgan ordered one ship to stay behind and salvage the wreck before it was stripped by the Spaniards and took the rest of the fleet to Maracaibo. Here he fitted out the captured man-of-war as his flagship and gave his own ship to another captain. A message was sent to Don Alonso in the fort, asking again for a ransom not to burn Maracaibo. He would not consent to it, but he was overruled by his advisers, and it was gathered. Morgan, promising to free his prisoners, wanted 30,000 pieces of eight and 500 cattle as provisions but settled for 20,000 and the cattle.

The next day, the cattle and part of the money was brought to Morgan. The pirates slaughtered, salted, and loaded the beef, and the next day the remaining money arrived. However, Morgan refused as yet to free his prisoners, fearing the artillery from the fort when he left the lake. He thus told the Spanish that he would free them when he was free from the danger of their cannon, hoping that they would let him freely pass through. He next sailed his fleet to the point where the burning ship had landed.

The pirates slaughtered, salted, and loaded the beef, and the next day the remaining money arrived. However, Morgan as yet refused to free his prisoners.

HENRY MORGAN'S TREASURE

Although he led six successful expeditions against the Spanish, the assets in Morgan's will only amounted to 5,263 pounds, plus his plantations in Jamaica. There have been rumors that he hid treasure when he returned from Panama ahead of the rest of his fleet. Isla de la Vache (now Île à Vache, off Haiti), was Morgan's favorite meeting place and has always been suspected as the location of any hidden treasure. Morgan sailed straight there after his

The Abacos island chain in the Bahamas is one of many locations where Henry Morgan was rumored to have buried the treasure of Panama.

internment in England and was wrecked on the *Jamaica Merchant* on its reef. His flagship, the *Oxford*, has also been found off Haiti and is being salvaged. Further rumors have placed his treasure in Jamaica, at Cayo Largo (off Havana), at Utila in Colombia, and all over the Bahamas.

The storm grew so great that he was forced to weigh anchor and run before it, fearing that they would be cast away among the Spanish on one side and the Indians on another. Neither would have shown any mercy.

His crew had salvaged 15,000 pieces of eight plus silver plate, sword-hilts, and other things of value. They had also acquired great quantities of pieces of eight which had been fused into lumps of silver by the fury of the fire. Some weighed as much as 30 pounds.

Now Morgan had to escape to the Caribbean. He told the prisoners to send messengers to Don Alonso, saying that, if he was not granted safe passage, each one of them would be strung up from his yardarms. Although there were many women and children, the governor told the messengers that they were cowards and that if they had defended their fort as strongly as he now intended to do, the pirates would not have achieved anything. His intention was to send every raider to the bottom of the sea. He would do his duty to his king and for the maintenance of his own honor. The messengers returned in great distress and reported to Morgan. Morgan told his crews that he would find a method of evading the Spanish and not to worry. To raise spirits, he decided to share out the loot they had accumulated.

There were 250,000 pieces of eight, gold, silver, jewels, pearls, other precious stones, bezoar stones (concretions that form in the stomachs of some animals, once used as an antidote for ailments), merchandise, and slaves. All his men were brought in and swore that they had concealed nothing from their comrades. Morgan's reasoning for sharing out the booty was that if it was all on one or two ships, it might be lost in a storm at sea and everyone have nothing for their efforts. After this was done, every man on each ship receiving his share, Morgan laid his plans to take the loot back to Jamaica.

The great escape

Morgan's stratagem was as follows. He waited for a favorable wind, and then embarked his men in canoes, who rowed toward the forest near the castle, landing under cover of the trees. Most of the day, parties of men were seen leaving each of the ships. The Spanish expected that Morgan was assembling his men to attack the fort that night with scaling ladders, as they saw only two or three men rowing each boat back to their ships to take on more buccaneers to land on the shore. However, Morgan's men were returning to the ships hidden on the bottom of the canoes. It seemed to the Spanish that Morgan had landed nearly all his men, but in fact they were all back on his ships. The Spaniards therefore shifted nearly all of their great cannon away from their positions covering Morgan's exit to the open seas. They were expecting a night attack from Morgan's men in the forest, on the landward side of the castle, so their men, guns, and armaments were moved to cover this new threat.

During the night, Morgan's fleet weighed anchor but did not set sail, drifting gently down the river with the ebb tide until they were near the castle. Having not alerted the Spaniards thus far, the crews suddenly crowded on full sail. The Spanish then tried to rush some of their guns around from the other side of the castle. They were still expecting an attack from the forest and thought that this was another ruse of Morgan's. However, Morgan's men were now almost out of range, helped by the strong ebb tide and the wind that Morgan had waited for. Despite a furious cannonade, the damage to the pirates' ships was fairly limited and only a few men were lost. From safely out of range, Morgan next sent a canoe to the castle carrying some prisoners, but not those taken at Gibraltar, as the ransom he had demanded for sparing that town was still unpaid. Eventually deciding to leave, he ordered a cannonade of seven great guns against the castle as his parting shot, but there was no response from the Spanish.

However, a great storm the next day meant that the fleet had to cast anchor in five or six fathoms of water. The storm grew so great that he was forced to weigh anchor and run before it, fearing that they would be cast away among the Spanish on one side or the Indians on another. Neither would have shown any mercy. Luckily, the storm subsided without any ships being lost.

The missing privateer fleet

The buccaneers who had been separated from the fleet at Cape do Lobos had arrived at the rendezvous of Saona island but missed Morgan. They did not find the letter in a jar he had left to inform them of the next meeting-place. The 400 to 500 men in this little fleet of five ships and a barque chose Captain Hansel as their new admiral, for his bravery in the taking of Puerto Bello. They headed for Cumana in the province of Caracas, 60 leagues from the west of Trinidad. They killed some Indians near the coast, but when they approached the town, a mixed force of Spanish and Indians routed the pirates. They managed to fight their way back to their ships and escape, with 100 dead and 50 wounded. On their arrival in Jamaica they met Morgan's men, who jeered them, saying "Let us see what money you brought from Cumana, and if it be as good silver as that which we bring from Maracaibo."

Below: The façade of the five-naved cathedral in Caracas, built from the 1660s onward. The contingent of Morgan's fleet that went missing after the taking of Maracaibo failed to plunder the riches on this stretch of Venezuelan coastline.

CHAPTER V

Captain Morgan goes to the Isle of Hispaniola to equip a new fleet, with intent to pillage again upon the coasts of the West Indies

Recruiting for a new expedition

Seeing that fortune was smiling on his enterprises, Henry Morgan began to set his sights even higher, trusting in the constancy of his luck. Not long after arriving in Jamaica, he found many of his former officers and men in reduced circumstances, owing to their immoderate vices and debauchery. They constantly beseeched him to lead them on fresh conquests so that they would have enough money again to spend on drink and strumpets. Thus he knew that the men of Jamaica would follow him. Morgan now told their creditors to stop harassing his men to pay their debts, as he had a new venture, which would make them more money than ever before. All over the West Indies, buccaneers heard that Morgan had a new expedition in mind and flocked to join the ever-successful admiral. He wrote to hunters

Below: Henry Morgan idling in the shade in a hammock, recruiting for his next expedition. His captains and crew were never told the target until they were at sea, to prevent Spanish spies from passing on valuable information.

in Tortuga and Hispaniola, telling them to gather on the south side of Tortuga for a venture upon which they would make their fortunes. His friend the governor of Tortuga also used his influence to communicate the message. Thus the French were again ready to join the great Morgan.

Now he arranged a new rendezvous for the assembled fleets and any others who wanted to join him—October 24th, 1670. Men trekked across the island of Hispaniola to join him at Port Couillon, near Isla de la Vaca. Others came in canoes, boats, and ships. Morgan surveyed his followers and carefully planned to provision the fleet for his expedition. He sent four ships and one boat to the mainland, to a village called Riohacha, on the River Rancheria. It was known to have the greatest supplies of maize in the region. There was also the possibility of capturing barques from Cartagena, which fished for pearls there. Another party was sent into the woods to kill and salt pigs and cattle. Others cleaned and rigged the ships, ready for the return of the maize-gatherers and hunters, so that the ships could weigh anchor immediately once they were laden with provisions.

Above: Originally fertile, the plains on the west coast of Haiti (formerly part of Hispaniola) were deforested by French settlers, leading to long-term agricultural problems. The mountainous terrain that covers the rest of the island is visible in the background.

They constantly beseeched him to lead them on fresh conquests, so that they had the money to again spend on drink and strumpets. Thus he knew that the men of Jamaica would follow him.

PIRATE TACTICS

Buccaneers were superb marksmen. Their favored method of attack was to sail in fast sloops into the musket range of heavy merchant ships. Most of the crew lay prone on the deck to avoid terrible injuries caused by grapeshot, while the musketeers picked off the helmsman and any sailors in the ship's rigging. As soon as the merchant was unable to maneuver, the pirates made for the stern, often in a pinnace (small sail or row boat) or pirogue (canoe), to jam the rudder. They then swarmed up the sides of the ship. Homebound ships were preferred targets, as they carried silver, jewels, and easily-traded loot, rather than slaves, wine, and wheat. Night attacks were also favored, especially off Tortuga: Ships usually anchored overnight in the Caribbean as the waters were so treacherous, making them sitting targets.

QUARTER

Quarter was mercy given to a surrendering or defeated crew. Pirates preferred not to fight, as did the merchant sailors who usually faced them. If the attacked ship did not accept quarter, the pirates would haul down their black flag and fly a red one, indicating that no quarter was to be given.

Below: *A Pirate Fight (1895)—a lithograph by Howard Pyle.*

BOARDING

When pirates went aboard their victim's ship, the boarding party was usually chosen by ballot. Everyone in this group had an equal share of the booty, but being on the boarding party against a ship that had not struck its colors was obviously dangerous. Sea-artists such as carpenters and surgeons were not usually risked.

Above: *The Buccaneers by Frederick Judd Waugh (1861–1940).*

Above: One ship fires a broadside in this 16th-century Dutch painting.

BROADSIDE

Firing a broadside meant that every cannon on one side of the ship was fired at once. Some might aim for the waterline, some at the men on deck, some for the gun-decks, and others for the rigging, depending upon their purpose and how they were loaded.

CUT AND RUN

To make an emergency getaway, the hemp anchor cable was cut with an axe, leaving the anchor embedded. Square-rigged ships were sometimes anchored in an open "road," with the sails furled and held by rope yarns. Another option in emergencies was to slash the rope yarns so that the sails dropped, ready for action. Other terms from this action are "cut loose," and "break out."

LONG SHOT

Cannon had no sights, could not be traversed right and left, and had only minimal vertical adjustment, which could be negated by the movement of waves. Each ball was slightly different and the gunpowder charges varied. Cannonballs were the most likely to hit and cause real damage, with a maximum effective range of 200 to 500 feet.

Below: Sailors in a Fight (1798) by Thomas Stothard.

READY TO FIRE

Pirate captains ensured that their gunners were always ready for action—they never knew when a prize might appear from around a headland, or if they might be surprised by a naval frigate. Cannon were kept loaded, with wooden plugs, or tompions, on their muzzles, to keep salt spray from spoiling the powder charge.

Left: An Attack on a Galleon (1905) by Howard Pyle.

CHAPTER VI

What happened in Riohacha

The four ships aforementioned had reached within sight of Riohacha when they were becalmed for several days. As the Spanish could see them and guessed that they were freebooters, they began to hide their goods and provisions and prepared to defend the area. In the river there was a ship from Cartagena laden with maize, which tried to escape but was captured by the buccaneers.

At dawn the next day the pirates landed and advanced. They were under heavy fire from a Spanish battery, but pressed the Spanish back toward a village. The Spanish rallied and resumed the battle until nightfall. Having lost a large number of men, although a similar number to those that the pirates had lost, the Spanish retired into the woods overnight. The next morning, the pirates found the village deserted and pursued the Spanish down the forest paths. They overtook a party of villagers and tortured them to disclose where they had hidden their goods. Those who did not confess were treated even more viciously. Parties of buccaneers were continually sent out into the woods to hunt for more Spaniards, who were also tortured. The Spanish had set up ambushes, which made the pirates even more determined to do their enemy harm.

After 15 days of this, there was no more plunder to be taken, so the buccaneers decided to return to Isla de la Vaca and told their prisoners that a ransom must be paid for not burning their village. The prisoners said that there was no more money, so the sea-rovers stated that they would accept maize, which was the real reason for their voyage anyway. Again the Spanish prevaricated but, seeing that the pirates meant what they said, agreed to bring 4,000 bushels or about 200 tons of maize. Three days later the maize was brought to the pirates and laden in their ships, so they returned to Morgan's fleet.

This force had been away for five weeks, and Morgan was beginning to worry that they had been taken, as they had ventured so near to the Spanish strongholds of Cartagena and Santa Maria. Alternatively, he thought that they might have captured a treasure ship and deserted his fleet to dissipate their earnings. Admiral Morgan had begun to contemplate other plans he might carry out with his depleted fleet. Accordingly, he was in a joyous mood when they returned, bringing plate, other types of booty, and sufficient maize to provision his entire fleet.

The fleet is prepared to sail

Immediately, Morgan's hunters were called in and all the salted meat and maize shared out between the ships. The fleet had been prepared to sail and set course for Cape Tiberon, the western point of Hispaniola. At this new rendezvous, Morgan was joined by more Jamaican freebooters, who were anxious to sail with him and had been looking for his fleet. Thus he now had a fleet of 37 ships and some smaller boats, with 2,000 well-armed men onboard, plus mariners and boys. They all had muskets, pistols, and cutlasses, along with sufficient powder and ammunition. He shared his ordnance out to ensure that each ship was properly equipped. His flagship took 22 cannon and 6 smaller brass guns. The rest of his fleet had variously 20, 18, 16, and down to 4 guns, and all had ammunition, fireballs, hand grenades, and other explosive missiles.

Because of the size of his fleet, the admiral now divided it into two squadrons, with the second squadron having its own vice-admiral, rear-admiral, officers, and commanders distinct from his

squadron. His squadron carried the English flag and the other squadron's ships flew the white flag. Every ship was given letters patent, also called letters of marque or commissions. These gave them permission for acts of violence against Spanish dominions or ships, according to the right of reprisals, as the Spanish had seized English ships which had merely landed to take on water or other necessities. The Spaniards were open and declared enemies of the King of England, according to Morgan.

Articles of agreement for the expedition

After this was done, all the captains and officers were called to a council, to sign articles of agreement to the expedition. The officers agreed that Morgan should receive a hundredth of the proceedings of the venture. This motion was put to all the crews, who agreed. Then the lieutenants and bosuns agreed that the captains should be given eight shares for their ships, in addition to their own personal shares.

Above: This late-17th-century engraving of French grenadiers shows the dangers of handling grenades and firebombs. Their duty was to get close enough to walls and trenches to throw their lit grenade, and then lead a charge through any breach in the defenses. Morgan gave a bonus to all his grenadiers for each successful throw.

CHARLES II OF ENGLAND (1630–1685)

Following his defeat at the Battle of Worcester in 1651, Prince Charles fled England and spent the next nine years in exile. In what became known as the Restoration, Charles was crowned King of England and Ireland at Westminster Abbey in 1661. He was popularly known as the Merrie Monarch, because of the liveliness and relaxed morals at his court, in contrast to a decade of rule by Oliver Cromwell and the Puritans. During his rule, England was faced with the Great Plague of London in 1665, the Great Fire of London in 1666, and surprise attack in 1667, when the Dutch sailed up the Thames. Most of English navy was sunk, except for the flagship, the HMS *Royal Charles*, which the Dutch took back to the Netherlands as a trophy. It was against this backdrop that Henry Morgan, the "Sword of England," was recalled to face trial in 1672. Morgan and his force had provided the only good news in almost the whole of Charles' reign. He was loved and feted in the populace and at court alike. Instead of giving in to Spanish pressure and imprisoning or executing Morgan, Charles gave him a knighthood and sent him back to Jamaica as lieutenant-governor.

This potrait of Charles II (c. 1675) was painted by Sir Peter Levy, who became the Principal Painter for the English monarchy in 1661.

Surgeons were to be given a personal share like every man onboard plus 200 pieces of eight for their chests of medicines. Carpenters received 100 pieces of eight plus their personal share.

Compensation and rewards are agreed

Then compensation was decided: 1,500 pieces of eight or fifteen slaves were to be granted for the loss of both legs, the choice being up to the injured man; 1,800 pieces of eight or eighteen slaves were to be given for the loss of both hands; for the loss of a leg or a hand, 600 pieces of eight or six slaves; and for the loss of an eye or a finger, 100 pieces of eight or one slave. For the pain of a body wound that needed the insertion of a pipe, compensation was 500 pieces of eight or five slaves. For a permanently stiff arm, leg, or finger, the compensation was the same as for its actual loss.

Then rewards for bravery were decided. The first to enter a castle or tear down the flag of an enemy fort and run up English colors would receive an extra 50 pieces of eight. A man who captured a prisoner when Morgan needed enemy intelligence would get 200 pieces of eight in addition to his normal share. The grenadiers would have 5 pieces of eight for every grenade they threw into a fort, as they needed to approach under enemy fire to do this.

These sums—rewards, compensations, and extra salaries, such as for the surgeons—were to be paid before the general sharing out of the booty to all of the crew. The articles were unanimously agreed and signed first by Morgan and then all the officers. The officers then held a council of war and agreed three alternative targets: Vera Cruz, Cartagena, or Panama. Panama was chosen as it was the richest city.

However, Panama had never been taken and was on the Pacific Coast, necessitating an overland expedition. As the privateers had no knowledge of its paths or defenses, they decided to take Santa

The compensation was decided: 1,500 pieces of eight or 15 slaves were to be granted for the loss of both legs, the choice being up to the injured man.

Catalina, which had previously fallen to Mansveldt but had been recaptured. They knew that either the Spanish there or their prisoners could give them the intelligence that would be vital to take Panama. Many felons were either imprisoned or forced to work on the island, so Morgan's men knew that they would find men who would be willing to help them. Another article was then agreed—that ships taken at sea or in port would form part of the booty at the end of the expedition, but that there would be a special bonus of 1,000 pieces of eight to the privateers who first boarded an enemy ship. If the captured ship was worth more than 10,000 pieces of eight, then these buccaneers would receive 10 percent. It was also agreed not to attack any except Spanish ships, to prevent news of their raid from spreading.

Below: Here we see Fort San Jose de Barachica, in Cartagena, Colombia. Morgan wanted to attack the port, but his fleet was depleted after the French left, and his captains told him that it was impregnable.

CHAPTER VII

*Captain Morgan leaves the island of Hispaniola
and goes to Santa Catalina, which he takes*

Morgan's fleet sets sail

The fleet weighed anchor at Cape Tiberon on December 16th, 1670, and four days later approached the island of Santa Catalina. It is about seven leagues in circumference, three leagues long, and one league wide. It lies about 100 leagues from Cartagena and 62 from Porto Bello, in the same longitude as Rio de Chagres. The island is bare of game except for huge flocks of pigeons at certain times of the year, and there are four rivers, but two dry up in summer. There is no trade or commerce, and the inhabitants only plant enough for their own sustenance, but they could grow tobacco for profit if they needed to.

As he approached Santa Catalina, Morgan sent a fast 14-gun ship to guard the entrance of the harbor and to prevent anyone escaping to alert the Spanish on the mainland. Before dawn on the next day, the whole fleet anchored at the bay of Aguada Grande, where the Spanish had recently installed a battery with four cannon. The admiral landed 1,000 men, who marched in order through the woods. Their only guides were some sailors who had been with the Mansveldt expedition. They came to the governor's former residence, where there was a deserted battery called Plataforma St. Jago. The Spanish had retired to the smaller island, which was joined to Santa Catalina by a bridge. This small island was so well defended by forts and batteries as to appear impregnable.

Progress was impossible because of the defensive fire, so the pirates retreated to rest for the night in some grassy fields. The hungry buccaneers were awoken around one o'clock in the morning by heavy continuous rain. They tried to pull down a few huts to make fires, but the rain was extremely cold and they were wearing only shirts and breeches, with no stockings or shoes. About a hundred men could

Right: An 18th-century view of Santa Catalina Island, off Panama. Santa Catalina was linked to Old Providence Island by a bridge.

have routed them, as their arms were wet. The rain stopped for a while, and they dried their powder and primed their muskets and began to proceed to attack again, but the heavens opened once more and they were forced to retreat for shelter, under constant fire from the Spanish.

They began to erect huts and shelters and found an old, lean horse. It had been turned loose by the Spanish and its back was full of open sores, but the starving pirates killed it and divided it into small pieces, eating it without salt or bread, more like ravenous wolves than men. The rain continued and many wanted to return to the ships, so Morgan knew that he had to do something quickly to raise their spirits and stop the expedition from falling apart. Accordingly, he sent a canoe over to the Spanish, under a white flag, informing them that unless they surrendered, no quarter would be given. Around noon, the governor sent an answer that he required two hours time to deliberate with his officers.

A plot to save the governor's face

Morgan's reputation carried the day. In two hours, the governor sent two canoes under the white flag, carrying a major and an ensign. Before they landed, they asked for two pirates as hostages for the major and ensign before they talked to Morgan, who gave them two of his captains as evidence of his serious intent. The Spanish then said that they were willing to give up the island, but the governor and his officers wished to use a stratagem so as not to lose face with their superiors. They asked that Morgan would come to the lesser island to attack the fort of San Jeronimo near the bridge. At the same time his ships would attack the castle of Santa Maria, landing more troops in canoes near the San Mateo battery. These latter troops would then intercept and capture the governor as he made his way from the fort of San Jeronimo on his way to the fort of St. Teresa. He would then lead the English troops under the pretext that they were his own men. There would be firing from both sides, but over the heads of any enemy or with blanks. Thus the English would take both forts. The Spanish prisoners would be landed unharmed on the mainland.

Above: A remarkable array of Spanish colonial architecture survives in the Americas. Churches such as this one, in Guatemala, would have contained great quantities of gold and silver ornaments, making them targets for pirates.

153

MORGAN'S FLEET FOR PANAMA

The *Calendar of State Papers* records the following captains on the 28 English and 8 French ships that sailed under Henry Morgan to Panama. Certain names for ships, such as *Fortune* and *Endeavour*, were particularly popular:

Ship	Captain	Tons	Guns	Crew
Satisfaction, frigate	Henry Morgan	120	22	140
Mary, frigate	Thomas Harris	50	12	70
May-Flower	Joseph Bradley	70	14	100
Pearle	Lawrence Prince	50	12	70
Civillian	John Erasmus	80	12	75
Dolphin, frigate	John Morris	60	10	60
Lily	Richard Norman	50	10	50
Port Royal	James Delliatt	50	12	55
Gift	Thomas Rogers	40	12	60
John of Vaughall	John Pyne	70	6	60
Thomas	Humphrey Thurston	50	8	45
Fortune (1)	Richard Ludbury	40	6	40
Constant Thomas	Coone Leloramell	60	6	40
Fortune (2)	Richard Dobson	25	6	35
Prosperous	Richard Wills	16	4	35
Abraham Oferenda	Richard Taylor	60	4	30
Virgin Queen	John Barnett	50	-	30
Recovery	John Shepherd	18	3	30
William, sloop	Thomas Woodriffe	12	-	30
Betty, sloop	William Curson	12	-	25
Fortune, ketch (3)	Clement Symons	40	4	40
Endeavour (1)	John Harmanson	23	4	35
Bonadventure	Roger Taylor	20	-	23
Prosperous	Patrick Dunbar	10	-	16
Endeavour (2)	Charles Swan	16	2	30
Lambe, sloop	Richard Powell	30	4	30
Fortune (4)	John Reekes	16	3	30
Free Gift	Roger Kelly	15	4	40
Ste. Catherine (French)	Tribetor	100	14	110
Galliardena (French)	Gascoine	80	10	80
Ste. John (French)	Diego	80	10	80
Ste. Peter (French)	Pearse Hantol	80	10	90
Le Diable Volante (French)	Desnangla	40	6	50
Le Serfe, sloop (French)	Joseph	25	2	40
Le Lyon, sloop (French)	Charles	30	3	40
Le Ste. Marie (French)	John Linaux	30	4	30
		1,585	239	1,846

H̲e had convinced the other two men, both Indians, that they would be burnt alive if they did not act as Morgan's guides. He needed them, as they knew the region better than he did.

All this was effected with no casualties on either side. For the next few days, the privateers waged war on every chicken, pig, or beast they came across, such was their hunger. On the morning after the surrender, Morgan counted 450 prisoners, including 190 from the garrison, 40 married couples with 43 children, 31 slaves of the king with 8 children, 8 convicts, 39 Negroes belonging to private owners, and 27 female Negroes with 34 children. The men were sent to the plantations to acquire food for Morgan's men and ships and the women and children locked in the church.

Weighing up the defenses

Morgan next reviewed the island's fortifications. There were 10 fortresses, or batteries. San Jeronimo had eight great guns, firing cannonballs of 12, 8, and 6 pounds, and also 6 pipes (each containing 10 muskets), another 60 muskets, and plenty of gunpowder and other ammunition. Plataforma San Mateo had three 8-pound cannon. The third fort, St. Teresa, had twenty great guns of 18, 12, 8, and 6-pound carriage, with 10 pipes (of 10 muskets each), and another 90 muskets. It was built of stone and mortar, had thick walls, and was surrounded by a 20 foot ditch, which was difficult to cross. There was a drawbridge to the fortress, and in its middle was another walled mound, mounting four cannon and commanding the harbor and countryside. The sea pounded the seaward side, making it inaccessible. On the landward side, there was only one path 3 to 4 feet broad, with precipitous drops on either side. The fourth battery, the Plataforma de San Augustin, had three cannon of 8 and 6-pound carriage. La Plataforma de la Concepción had two 8-pound guns, and the Plataforma de Nuestra Señora de Guadeloupe had two 12-pounders. San Salvador had two 8-pounders, the Plataforma de los Artilleros had two 6-pounder cannon, and Santa Cruz had three guns of 8 and 6 pounds. The last defensive position, the Fort of San José, had six guns of 8 and 12-pound carriage, plus 2 pipes of muskets, 20 other muskets, and plenty of munitions.

In the storehouse 30,000 pounds of gunpowder was recovered. This stock, along with the other armaments described, was taken aboard Morgan's fleet. The fort and batteries of San José were partially destroyed, the guns spiked, and the gun-carriages burnt. St. Teresa and San Jeronimo were left with a pirate garrison. Morgan asked to see any convicts from Panama or Puerto Bello. Three were discovered who knew these areas. They offered to be Morgan's guides when he offered them freedom and full shares of his booty. One of them was a great criminal, with the most to gain. He convinced the other two, both Indians, that they would be burnt alive if they did not act as guides. He needed these two, as they knew the region better than he did.

Morgan now decided to send a small force to attack the fortress on the mouth of the River Chagres, which his fleet had to pass to progress to Panama. He sent just 400 men in four ships and a barque, as the appearance of his whole fleet would have caused a warning that would reach the Spanish all along the coast and inland. He and his fleet remained at Santa Catalina, waiting for news of the latest attack.

Above: The bridge that links the islands of Old Providence and Santa Catalina today. The first bridge between the two islands was built by privateers.

CHAPTER VIII

*Captain Morgan takes the Castle of Chagres with 400
men sent for this purpose from the Isle of Santa Catalina*

Bradley's assault on Castillo San Lorenzo

Command of the expedition was given to Captain Joseph Bradley, a man with long experience of raiding this coast, who had been at Santa Catalina under Admiral Mansveldt. He was known as a brave man by privateers and Spaniards alike. Within three days his flotilla arrived at the Castle of Chagres, called Castillo San Lorenzo by the Spanish, at the mouth of the River Chagres. The castle stood at the summit of a mountain and was surrounded by a 30-foot deep moat, so was accessible only by its drawbridge. Its walls consisted of two palisades infilled with earth—the equivalent of the best walls built of stone or brick. To the south it was impossible to approach it because of the incline of the mountain, and to its north was a broad river. On the seaward side it had two bastions and on the landward there were four.

At the foot of the castle there was a great tower, with eight cannon defending the river from entry. It was supported by a further two batteries lower down the slope, each with six cannon, guarding the river banks. At one side of the castle were two great warehouses full of munitions and merchandise, and near them a stairway had been constructed up the mountainside to the castle. West of these fortifications was a small and useful harbor for small vessels, where the water varies from three to eight fathoms only. In front of the castle was a reasonable anchorage of seven to eight fathoms, but also a reef, which could only be seen at low tide.

Right: This photograph shows thatched huts in the Chagres River Valley, c. 1900. The materials used to build them and the method of construction had not changed much since the 17th century.

Opposite page: This rusting cannon at San Lorenzo fort still stands guard over the mouth of the River Chagres.

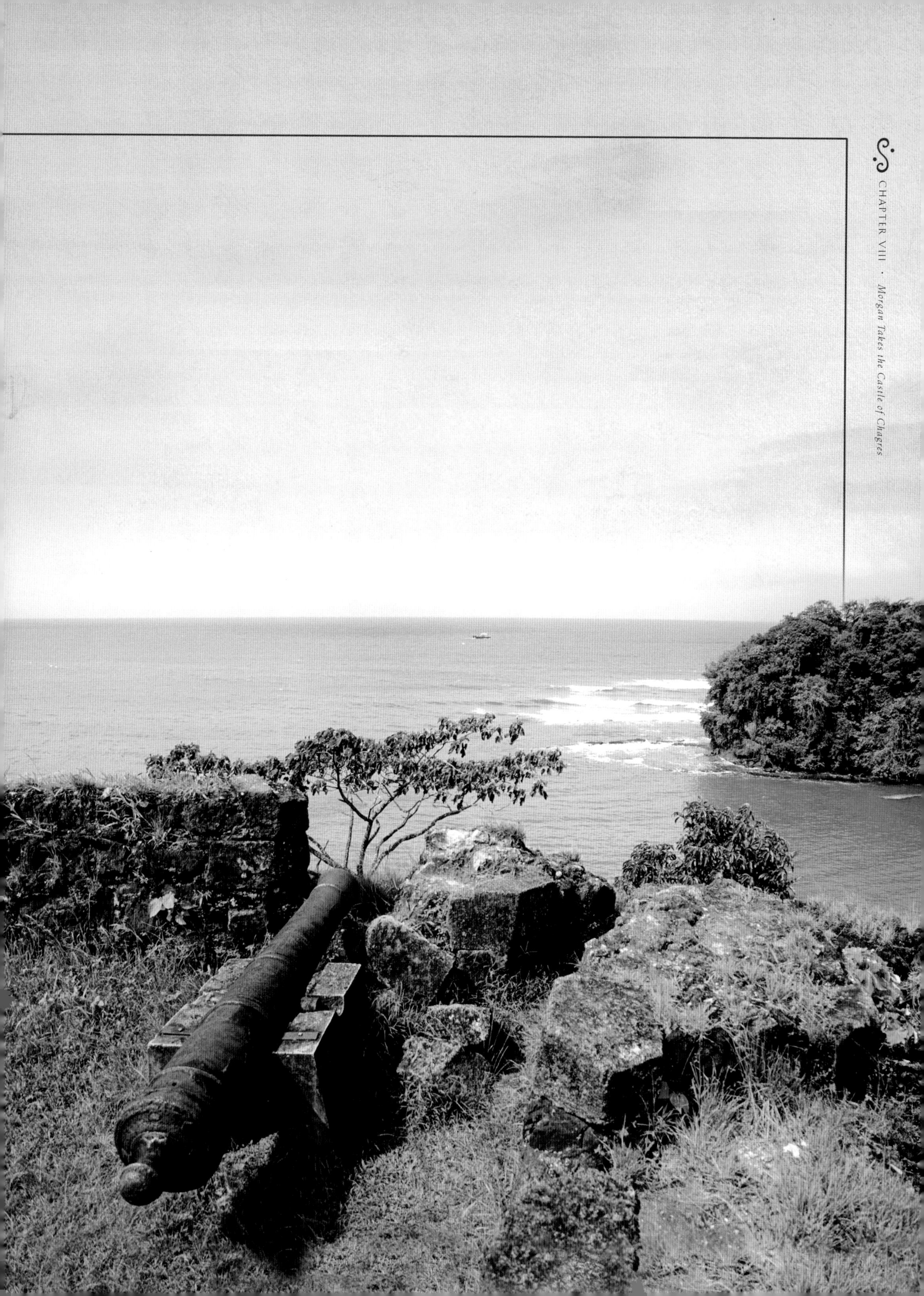

On seeing Captain Bradley's approach, the Spanish cannon began continuous fire, so he cast anchor in a small port about a league away. At dawn the next day the privateers disembarked, wishing to cut thorough the forests, take the fortress, and then bring their ships upriver. However, the tracks were almost impassable with mud and boulders. They had to hack their way through the lianas and undergrowth and did not approach San Lorenzo until two o'clock. The guides had led them to an open plain near the castle with no cover, and they suffered severe losses. There was no cover for their attacks, and they had no clear view of its defenders. Nevertheless, they were determined not to go home to Jamaica in shame like those luckless souls who had failed at Cumana.

Time and time again they attacked with muskets and grenades but were repulsed and began to fear for the success of their venture. The Spanish, knowing that they were virtually impregnable and seeing the constant pirate casualties, shouted down at them, "Let the others come, too, English dogs, enemies of God and the King! You shall not go to Panama!" The buccaneers regrouped for an attack in the evening, under cover of darkness, hoping to throw their grenades and fireballs and scale the palisades

SIR FRANCIS DRAKE

Sir Francis Drake (1540–96) was seen as a bold adventurer by his countrymen. On his Central American campaign he took Venta Cruz in Panama, after gleaning information from Indians and Cimaroons (Maroons, African slaves who had escaped the Spanish).

The most celebrated of his adventures along the Spanish Main, however, was his capture of the Spanish Silver Train at Nombre de Dios in March 1573. With a crew including many French privateers and Maroons, Drake raided the waters around Darien and tracked the Silver Train to the nearby port of Nombre de Dios. He made off with a fortune in gold, but had to leave behind another fortune in silver, because it was too heavy to carry back to England. It was during this

expedition that, in the central mountains of the Isthmus of Panama, he became the first Englishman to see the Pacific Ocean. He remarked as he saw it that he hoped that one day an Englishman would be able to sail it, which he would years later as part of his circumnavigation of the world. Drake also led an English fleet to "singe the beard of the King of Spain," when he destroyed the Spanish fleet at Cadiz in 1587. He also fought against the Spanish Armada in 1588, and died in the Caribbean on another expedition to find treasure. The Spanish called him *El Draque*—the Dragon.

These romanticized pictures show Sir Francis Drake: Left, wounded at Nombre de Dios, middle, receiving information about the location of Panama's treasure; and right, being knighted by Queen Elizabeth I in 1581.

Cowley & his Men taking in Provisions at the Island of Juan Fernandez.

somehow. They were yet again repulsed, but one of their men was shot in his shoulder by an arrow. Maddened, he pulled it out, wound some cotton wadding around the arrowhead, set it alight, and fired it back into the castle. The cotton ignited palm leaves used to thatch houses within the castle walls and smoke soon arose. His comrades began to copy his example, and one arrow indirectly ignited a quantity of gunpowder as a burning roof came crashing down.

The buccaneers renewed their attack while the Spanish were trying to put out the fires, but the flames spread rapidly through the dry wooden houses and their thatched roofs, fanned by a fierce wind. The defenders also had too little water to keep the fire at bay. The privateers took advantage of the confusion to concentrate on setting light to the wooden palisades. Many men were lost, however, as the Spanish threw down pots of gunpowder with lighted fuses. By midnight the fires were so great that the pirates were able to creep close to the fort and fire through the flames at the men trying to extinguish them. By daybreak the palisades had burnt down in one place, causing men, cannon, and huge heaps of earth to fall into the dry moat. The governor saw the danger that the buccaneers might cross the earth spoil to fight their way into the castle and positioned more guns in the gap, but their gunners were easily picked off by the sharpshooters. Throughout the morning the Spanish casualties mounted alarmingly, both from the effects of the conflagration and the deadly musket-fire.

About midday, the pirates managed to fight their way across the breach, which was now only defended by the governor and 25 men, who fought with pikes, muskets, swords, and even stones.

Above: William Ambrosia Cowley was an English buccaneer who published the first chart of the Galápagos Islands in the 17th century. Here he is shown gathering provisions for his fleet.

He refused quarter and was dispatched with a musket ball to the head, whereupon the remaining soldiers in the guardhouse surrendered.

Eventually, their ammunition ran out. The privateers gained the castle, but its remaining defenders refused quarter and threw themselves over its walls to certain death on the rocks below. The governor managed to retreat to a guardhouse that had two cannon, intending to sell himself dearly. He refused quarter and was dispatched with a musket-ball to the head, whereupon the remaining soldiers in the guardhouse surrendered. Of the 314 defenders, all the officers had died, and of the 30 survivors there were less than 10 who were not wounded. The privateers now managed to quell the fires.

The president is forewarned

The prisoners were interrogated and it was found that the president of Panama had received intelligence about Morgan's intended mission. He had received this information from Cartagena, three weeks previously, from an Irishman who had deserted the privateers at Riohacha. He told the Spanish that Morgan was assembling his fleet off Hispaniola to attack Panama. Thus the president had sent another 164 men to bolster the garrison at the fortress at Chagres, with extra food and armaments. He had also arranged several ambushes along the River Chagres and had deployed his army on the plain outside Panama. His forces included 2,400 Spaniards, 600 half-breeds, and 600 Indians, and he intended to use 2,000 wild cattle to stampede through the buccaneers.

Bradley had not tried to take the lower tower and batteries, as he would have been fired upon both from the forts and by the castle from above. The next day, his forces discovered that the Spaniards from the lower forts had vanished in the night. The battle had cost the privateers 100 men dead and 70 badly wounded out of a force of less than 400, as some men had been left to guard the ships. They made the Spanish survivors bury the English dead, but the Spanish corpses were hurled off the walls into the sea. The wounded were tended in the church. Captain Bradley's legs had been shot off and he lingered for another few days in agony before dying.

Morgan sets sail for the Castle of Chagres

On hearing the news, Morgan sailed immediately. He had all Santa Catalina's cannon thrown into the sea but in a place where he could recover them, as he wished to return and take the island as a permanent possession. All its buildings were burnt except the castle of St. Teresa, where he intended to return after Panama. Morgan took his prisoners with him, arriving at the River Chagres eight days after the fortress had been taken, although his flagship and three other ships were grounded on the reef. No men or supplies were lost, but a strong northerly wind meant that the ships were wrecked.

Morgan repaired the fortress, making the prisoners repair the palisades of the castle and erect new ones around the lower outworks. He provisioned the castle with maize and cassava. He took several chatas, which are flat-bottomed boats used for carrying goods in the river trade, and poled along like Dutch barges. They each carried two cannon and four smaller brass guns. Four rowing boats were used along with the ships' canoes to take his force upriver. Five hundred men, including the wounded, were left to garrison the fort. Morgan remembered his mistake when trapped at Maracaibo and also left 150 men to man the ships that remained at anchorage. There were now 1,200 men packed into the small boats to sail, pole, and row their way upriver toward Panama. No food supplies were laden because of lack of space and the need to carry munitions and powder. Morgan expected to find supplies where the Spanish were laying their ambushes, which became a major problem.

Opposite page: A French drawing dating from 1688 of a manioc (cassava) plant. The roots are an essential source of carbohydrates and a staple food across the Americas. They can be processed into flour to make a type of bread.

Le Manyoc

Le Manyoc est la plante dont on fait le pain ___
jls font aussi une boisson quils nomment Oüycou,___
endroits dou les feuilles sont tombées, car il ne se depouille
d'enbas, tombent, jl croist d'autres en haut qui le rendent
a celles de Lagnus castus, et qui sont mal designées dans
ou quatre coudées de haut, plus ou moins, selon la diuersité
ses branches; jl porte de la graine qui produit du bois qui est
qui vient directement de la graine ne uaut rien parce qu'elle
habitans distinguent par la couleur des queües, des costes dans
de l'epaisseur d'un quart d'escu d'un violet fort brun, mais
d'auantage en terre que les autres. Le gris a l'escorce du
beaucoup, et quelques fois fort peu, le pain n'en est pas
jl n'est que dix mois en terre, jl raporte beaucoup et fait
dans la terre. Le blanc a l'escorce du bois blanchastre,
et raporte beaucoup de racines, mais elles se resoluent
et de tres bon goust, on ny trouue pas son compte, et peu
plante, qui plantent de celuy cy pour en auoir bien tost
blanc qu'on ne le sçauroit distinguer qu'auec peine. on le
son suc, et sans qu'il face aucun mal comme feroient ___
l'instant ceux qui en auroient mangé. Un arpent de terre
terres semées en bled n'en nourriroient en Europe, et lors
est pour le moins aussi bonne, et aussy nourrissante que
tout le suc qui est un poison, mais qui ne laisse aucun
toute crue sans la conuertir en cassaue.

que les habitans des Isles Antilles apellent Cassaue, et dont ___
C'est un arbrisseau fort fortu, remply de noeuds qui viennent aux ___
pas de ses feuilles tout a la fois, mais a mesure qu'il croist, et que les feuilles
tousiours uert; jl jette plusieurs branches chargées de feuilles qui ressemblent
Alechamps, et dans les autres Autheurs. Il croist ordinairement de trois
du terroir, ou des saisons, Il est fort tendre, et d'un coup de baston on brise
tres bon pour estre planté et qui pousse de belles racines, mais la plante
ne produit que de foibles racines, jl y en a de six, ou de sept sortes que les
feuilles, ou de l'escorce de la racine. Le violet a une escorce sur sa racine
le dedans est blanc comme neige, Il fait le pain de meilleur goust, et dure
bois et de la racine grise et est fort inegal, car quelques fois jl raporte
mauuais. Le vert a les feuilles plus vertes et plus dures que les autres,
d'excellent pain, mais lors qu'il est mur, jl ne se conserue pas long temps
mais celle de la racine, et le dedans est jaune, jl vient en six ou sept mois,
toutes en eau de sorte que quoy que le pain en soit jaune comme de l'or,
de gens en font, jl ny que ceux qui sont pressés et qui n'ont point de Manyoc
jl y en a d'une autre sorte qu'on apele Kamanyoc qui ressemble si fort au
fait cuire tout entier comme des patates et on le mange sans exprimer
indubitablement tous les autres Manyoes qui seroient mourir dans
planté en Manyoc nourrit plus de gens que six arpens des meilleures
que la cassaue est fraische et bien faite et qu'on y est accoustumé elle
le pain. Pour faire de la Cassaue auec la racine de Manyoc on en tire
mauuaise qualité a la farine que les Negres mangent souuent
sans qu'elle leur face aucun mal.

CHAPTER IX

Captain Morgan departs from the Castle of Chagres at the head of 1,200 men, with the design of taking the city of Panama

The pirates' journey upstream

On August 18th, 1670, the sea-rovers began paddling up the Chagres river in 5 small boats with guns and 32 canoes. They only covered 6 leagues that day and rested at a deserted village named Rio de los Brazos. His men stretched out to sleep, their limbs aching from being cramped into crowded boats. No food could be found as the plantation owners and house owners had fled and taken all their provisions with them. The buccaneers had only tobacco to smoke or chew upon after a hard day rowing upstream.

They set off again at dawn and reached La Cruz de San Juan Gallego (near Gatun) by midday. The river was so low because of lack of rain that they had to leave their 5 boats there. Several trees had also been felled across the river, stopping the passage of any large vessels. Morgan was informed by his guides that in another 2 leagues the country would be suitable for some of the party to traverse by land, so Morgan left 160 men to protect his boats. They could cover Morgan's retreat with their cannon if things went wrong. The crews were ordered never to go ashore in case any were captured and told the Spanish that Morgan's force was now down to only 1,040 starving men.

Below: A view over the River Chagres near the fort of San Lorenzo. Morgan's route across the Isthmus to Panama would have been plotted from such positions.

Left: The remains of the Camino de Cruces, the original Spanish trail across the Isthmus, can still be seen today.

On the third day, men were sent with a guide to try to find a way overland through the rainforest and to assess Spanish ambuscades but found only impenetrable swamps. Morgan now had to split his force, sending some in canoes to Cedro Bueno. With great difficulty they made it, and the canoes were sent back to bring the remaining men upriver that evening. The men were now faint with hunger and wanted desperately to encounter Spanish or Indian enemies in order to get at their food.

No food to be had

The fourth day saw most of the privateers cutting their way through the jungle with a guide. Another guide went with two canoes about three musket-shots in advance of the other canoes, in case there were any ambushes along the riverbanks. However, the Spanish had spies watching all along their routes, able to warn any defenders in good time or to tell citizens and natives to vanish, taking all their provisions with them. Morgan's men were now famished and in a weakened state for any battle. The men in canoes and the land force met at Torno Caballos. The guide in the advance canoes had warned the land party that an ambush was not far along their march. The buccaneers had rejoiced at the news—they would have food after four days of eating nothing. But there were no provisions at Torno Caballos except 150 leather bags, which had once held meat and bread. Its 500 defenders had left nothing there. The pirates ate the bags, fighting for the scraps of leather.

After resting, the party moved on to Torno Muni, which was supposed to be the site of another ambuscade. This was also cleared of provisions, so the privateers fanned out to search for food in the jungle. Nothing was found. Those with bits of leather left from Torno Caballos ate them for supper.

The men were now faint with hunger and wanted desperately to encounter Spanish or Indian enemies, in order to get at their food.

THE PIRATE DIET

Wooden ships "were damp, dark, cheerless places, reeking with the stench of bilge water and rotten meat." They leaked and were difficult to dry, so pirates often suffered from illnesses brought on by wet conditions. A pirate ship might need twice the personnel of a merchant ship, so men were often packed together in overcrowded conditions.

As well as carrying loot, the ship needed more guns and munitions than the average boat and more people for fighting. Pirates kept the decks clean by washing them down with brandy, and fumigated below deck by burning pitch and brimstone. Despite these measures, the ships were full of cockroaches, fleas, and rats. Rats were often used to supplement the diet of salt beef or pork. Neither flour nor dried beans would keep for long in the damp hulls of ships, and only salted meat and fish would last. Water went off quickly in the wooden casks, so alcohol was preferred. Men ate off square wooden platters, using both sides, and used no knives or forks, "cleaning" their plates with bread instead.

Meat was preserved in brine in wooden casks. A chemical reaction during this process caused salt-hardened fat to became attached to the walls of the barrel. The ship's cook might scrape this and give it to the crew while they were waiting to eat—they would "chew the fat" and make small talk before their meal—but he would generally try to keep some for his "slush fund." This fat was used for greasing masts, preserving leather, cooking, and making candles, so it could be sold in port.

Carcass of Beef *(1655) by Rembrandt van Rijn (1606–69). Freshly slaughtered meat was a real luxury for mariners. They would have had to eat it quickly, before it was attacked by flies and rats or rotted in the tropical heat.*

To eat leather, they first cut it into thin slices then beat it between two stones, often dipping it into river water to make it soft and supple. Then they scraped off the hair and roasted or broiled it on a fire. They ate small morsels, helping it down with copious drinks of water and thus fought off the pangs of hunger for a short time.

On the fifth day at noon they found the traces of another ambush at Barbacoa, with the same sad results as before. Again, nearby plantations and houses had all been subject to the Spanish strategy of starving the attackers. By fortune a newly-dug pit was discovered and opened up to find two sacks of meal, some wheat, two large jars of wine, and some plantains. Morgan at once commandeered the find, as some of his men were extremely weak by now. Those worst-affected were supplied with provisions. Those unable to march were placed in canoes, and those in canoes were moved to the land party. All day they progressed slowly, at dusk coming to another plantation which had been stripped. The men could not sleep, they were so ravenous.

The sixth day came, and progress was painfully slow through the jungle. Apart from the difficulties of carrying all their weaponry while slashing their way forward and being constantly attacked by insects, they had to rest more and more in the tropical heat as they were exhausted through lack of food. They

Two or three buccaneers were killed by arrows, and the Indians taunted them from the depths of the jungle, shouting "Ha! Perros!—A la savana! A la savana!" ("Ha! Dogs! To the plain, to the plain!")

ate leaves, seeds, berries, and grasses as they kept trudging forward. However, at noon they found a plantation with a barn full of maize. They were so overjoyed that they battered down its doors and stuffed their mouths full of the dry corn.

Taunted by the enemy

Each man was provisioned with his share. The privateers had carried on for another hour when they sighted some Indians and expected an ambush. Rushing to combat, they threw away the maize they were carrying to lighten their load, in the expectation that they could take provisions from the Indians. However, all they found were 100 Indians, who were watching them from the other side of the river. Some pirates jumped into the water to try and get across to them. They were determined that if there was no food they would eat the enemy, but the natives melted away into the woods. Two or three buccaneers were killed by arrows and the Indians taunted them from the depths of the jungle, shouting "Ha! Perros!—A la savana! A la savana!" ("Ha! Dogs!—To the plain! To the plain!")

That night they were forced to sleep where they were, as the way to Panama meant crossing the river toward the Indians. Some of the men fell to complaining about Morgan's luck having run out. Others countered that they would rather die than return to poverty. The more courageous laughed and joked at these conversations. One of their guides brought comfort, telling them that they were near a village. He said it would certainly be defended, but would have many provisions for the starving men.

Thus they spent most of the night sleepless, preparing their arms for battle. Each man discharged his pistols and muskets with a bullet, to check that they had not been damaged. They then crossed the river in the canoes, leaving Santa Cruz on the seventh day. The privateers marched until noon, when from a distance they saw smoke rising from the chimneys of the village of Venta de Cruz (Cruces). Hope sprang in their chests—there were people there, so there must be supplies. The people must be roasting or boiling their dinners for them! When they arrived, in great expectation, they found that the fires had been started by the Spanish. All the houses were burning except one, the royal storehouse and stables.

Left: This contemporary engraving shows a Spanish cavalryman in "New Spain." Most of the European colonies in the Americas fell under Spanish rule.

ll at once a hail of 3,000 or 4,000 arrows rained down on them, but they could not discern who their enemy was or where they were hiding.

All the animals had vanished except a few stray dogs and cats, which the buccaneers shot, roasted, and ate. Perhaps the royal property had been left untouched because it was a crime to fire it or because there was not enough time. In the king's stables they found 15 or 16 jars of Peru wine and a leather sack containing bread. They started drinking the wine and almost every man fell sick, because their contracted stomachs were full of grass and seeds from the march. Morgan understood this but told them that the wine was poisoned, knowing that it could do the weakened men no good at all. They spent another discontented night in the charred ruins of Venta Cruz, 26 leagues from the River Chagres but only 8 from Panama. Venta Cruz was the highest point on the river that would accept boats or canoes. From there provisions were taken by mule train to Panama and silver brought from Panama to Venta Cruz to be loaded on boats. Morgan was forced to leave his canoes and sent them back to where his boats were stationed. Only one was kept hidden on the river, since it might be needed for intelligence work on the return journey from Panama.

The men are confined to camp

Morgan's men had seen Spaniards and Indians in nearby plantations, so Morgan gave orders that no one was to leave camp and that any foraging party had to be at least 100 strong. He wanted no prisoners taken who could tell the president that his force was now less than 1,000 men in a feeble state. However, hunger overcame the privateers and some went off in parties of 5 or 6 to search desperately for food. One party of marauders was surprised by a mixed force of Spaniards and Indians, and a privateer was taken prisoner, much to Morgan's disappointment. He charged the men involved to keep this news secret, otherwise morale in his troops would have sunk even lower, if that was possible.

On the next day, the eighth day of their trek, Morgan sent a vanguard of 200 men to see if there were any ambuscades on the last eight leagues to Panama. It was a better road, and at times 12 men could march abreast, but it narrowed now and again into traps for the defenders. After marching for 10 hours, the vanguard approached Quebrada Obscura having seen no enemies. All at once a hail of 3,000 or 4,000 arrows rained down on them, but they could not discern who their enemy was or where they were hiding. They fired at shadows in the woods, glimpsing through the trees in front of them Indians moving to higher ground. The privateers raced forward into the forest, and the Indians fled before them.

One band of Indians stayed to fight their ground, to allow their brothers to escape and reform. Eventually, their chief fell to the ground badly wounded among 3 or 4 of his dead tribesmen. The buccaneers were anxious to take a prisoner, but he would not accept quarter and tried to raise himself, thrusting his azagaya and wounding a pirate. As he tried to make the fatal blow, he was shot dead by a pistol. The Indians were so fleet of foot in their woods that not one was caught. All the survivors escaped and carried on firing arrows at the chasing pirates, many being deflected by trees. The vanguard had lost 8 men and 10 had been wounded. Morgan now had well under 1,000 fighting fit men for the last push against the treasure city of Panama.

Coming to a wide savannah, the pirates saw some of the Indians on a mountain which overlooked their way forward. Fifty of Morgan's fittest and fastest men were sent to try and capture a prisoner, but the Indians were too nimble and afterward showed themselves in another place, calling out "A la savana! A la savana, cornudos, perros Ingleses!" ("To the plain! To the plain, you cuckolds, you

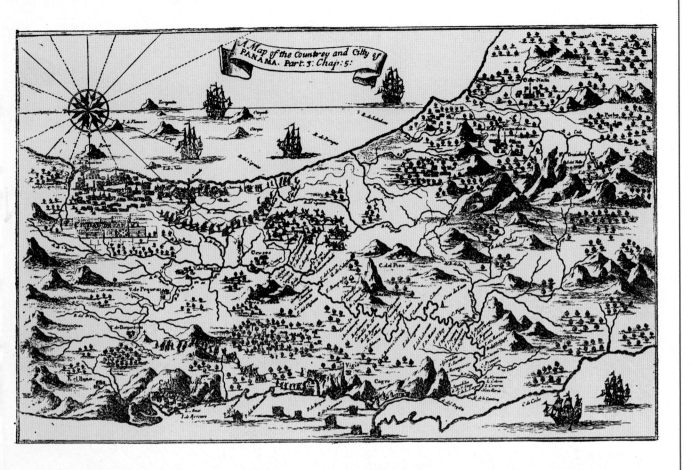

you English dogs!") While the wounded privateers were being treated, Morgan noticed that there was a wooded valley between the hill his men were stationed on and the hill that the Indians and Spanish possessed. He expected another ambush and once again sent a vanguard of 200 of his best men. As they moved down the hill toward the forest so did the enemy, as if to fight in the woods. Instead, however, they vanished, leaving the path open.

That night there was torrential rain, causing the pirates to march quickly seeking shelter, but all the homes and villages of the Indians had been burned and their animals and provisions removed. The privateers needed refuge to prevent their arms and powder from becoming wet and useless. At last a few small shepherd's huts were found. Morgan placed in each a small number of men, with all the arms from the rest of their companies. The guns were stacked so that each man could quickly grab one if there was a night attack. Guards had been placed on the perimeter of their camp, every night of their journey, to alert the men of such an attack. The majority of the men spent a miserable night in the open fields, under pouring rain which fell until morning.

At last their goal is in sight!

At dawn on the ninth day, Morgan set off again under cloud cover, trying to make ground before the searing heat of the noon sun but being badly slowed by the muddy terrain. After an hour or so, around 20 Spaniards were seen ahead, observing the pirates' movements. Morgan tried to take prisoners, but they hid in caves that were unknown to the pirates or their guides. Eventually, the weary men trudged to the top of another mountain and saw the South Sea—the Pacific Ocean!

Above: To reach the treasure city of Panama, Morgan's men had to tramp through rainforest across the "Isthmus of Darien," illustrated in this 1668 map.

167

Right: An angel looks out over Casco Viejo, the old quarter of Panama City, which was rebuilt on a new site after Morgan's raid.

At last they were in sight of their goal. They could see a galleon and six coastal craft en route from Panama City to Taboga and Taboquilla. Descending the mountain, they came to a great plain where hundreds of cattle grazed. Delighted, they took to killing and flaying cows, bulls, horses, and asses, while others lit fires to cook the meat. The animals were hacked to pieces and thrown into the fires. The men hardly waited for it to get hot before they grabbed the meat and stuffed it in their mouths, blood running down their cheeks and chests. They more resembled cannibals than Europeans at banquet.

Morgan interrupted their feasting with the order to stand to. The men quickly came into line, each clutching a piece of meat. The march to Panama restarted, and 50 men were sent in front to try and take prisoners. Morgan was in the dreadful situation of having no idea of the strength and disposition of his enemies or whether their numbers and disposition had altered since he had been told, a fortnight previously, that there were 3,600 men waiting. Near evening, this vanguard came upon 200 Spanish cavalry, who shouted at them and then rode off, but they did not understand what was being said.

Soon after this, the highest steeple of Panama City could be seen clearly. The buccaneers threw their hats in the air, jumped, shouted for joy, and sounded their trumpets and drums. They had achieved what was thought impossible, crossing the Panama Isthmus against superior forces. In their minds, with Morgan leading them and meat in their bellies, the battle was as good as won. Morgan pitched camp for the evening, and a troop of 50 Spanish cavalry approached from the city, possibly alerted by

The animals were quickly hacked to pieces and thrown into the fires. The men hardly waited for it to get hot before they grabbed the meat and stuffed it into their mouths, blood running down their cheeks and chests. They more resembled cannibals than Europeans at banquet.

the trumpets and drums. They sounded their own trumpet, keeping out of musket-shot of the jubilant privateers and shouting, "Perros! Nos veremos!" ("Dogs! We will meet thee!") Then most returned to the city, leaving seven or eight, who were deputed to watch and report the pirates' movements. Soon after, the city started firing its greatest guns, which continued all through the night, but Morgan's men were unperturbed, being out of range as they were. They collected straw to make palliasses to sleep on before the morrow's battle. The 200 cavalrymen seen earlier in the evening reappeared behind the pirates cutting off their exit, so they were in effect besieged. The pirates placed sentries before opening their satchels and pulling out their pieces of bull or horse flesh for their supper, then slept in their new beds, impatient for the great day.

The pirates march on Panama City

At sunrise on the tenth day, Morgan drew up his men in battle order and began the march to Panama City, flags flying and drums beating. One of the guides approached Morgan and suggested that there could be strong ambuscades on the normal highway, suggesting a new path through the woods. Morgan instantly agreed, although the new path was extremely difficult to force a way through. However, the Spaniards were taken by surprise, never expecting such a treacherous route to be taken. They were forced to move from their ambuscades and batteries and draw up in the plain outside the city, to meet the pirates when they emerged from the forests. The president arranged his battle formation, which consisted of two squadrons of cavalry, four regiments on foot, and a huge number of wild bulls, driven by Indians with a few Negroes to help them.

Below: Morgan's bold attack on Panama City, featured here in an undated illustration, became the stuff of legend.

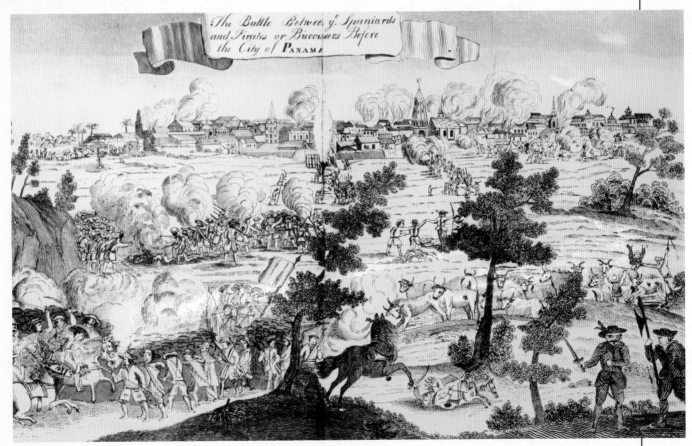

169

PIECES OF EIGHT

Pieces of eight, or dollars, were silver Spanish coins, which were worth four pesetas or eight reales. In the 17th and 18th centuries, there were so many of these coins in circulation that they were accepted almost anywhere in the world. The American dollar sign ($) was derived from the numeral eight (8) that was stamped on the side. The modern American term, "not worth two bits," is from the days when Spanish-milled dollars were cut into eight equal pieces. Two "bits" was two eighths, which was a quarter dollar. Pieces of eight were produced for about 300 years, in Mexico, Peru, and Colombia, and became the standard unit of trade between Europe and China. They were common currency in all of England's colonies, valued at four shillings and sixpence, and were legal tender in the United States up until 1857. Gold was used for escudos, which were the same value as pieces of eight. Gold doubloons were worth eight escudos. Before the Spanish started exploiting Potosi (today in Bolivia), silver was almost as valuable as gold in the Old World. Such were the quantities taken from the New World—the Spanish took four billion pesos of silver and gold between 1492 and 1830—that silver dropped to about one fifteenth of the value of gold.

Gold doubloons and escudos and silver pesos and dollars were always subject to "clipping," whereby portions of the precious metals were shaved off for profit. This practice was halted by the introduction of milled edges on machine-made coins.

The buccaneers surmounted a small hill, from where Morgan could see the city, the president's forces, and Spanish battle groupings on the plains below them. He could see that they were outnumbered about four to one and was uncertain of the outcome. However, there was no choice but to fight, with the expectation of very heavy casualties. The privateers would fight to the death, as they could expect no quarter. They encouraged each other with talk of vast riches and the good life back in Jamaica and Tortuga.

Morgan had less than 1,000 fit men and used what he called his "lozenge" formation of two wings, a rear battalion, and a vanguard of 200 French sharpshooters with the finest muskets. Thus they marched down the hill and approached the enemy on the savannah. As they neared, the Spanish shouted "Viva el Rey!" ("God save the King!"), and their cavalry began to move toward Morgan's men. It was January 20th and they had been struggling through the rainforest for ten days.

The charge begins

The field had been much softened by the previous heavy rains, and the squadrons of cavalry were bogged down in quagmire. As the Spanish horsemen slowly progressed, the French marksmen primed their muskets and fired. One rank knelt and fired while the one behind primed and then fired, allowing the first rank to reload and fire. This meant that the cavalry were faced with a steady fusillade, with no intermission in the firing. The Spanish fired a volley from horseback and tried to press home the attack.

Meanwhile, the Spanish infantry was trying to come to the support of their horsemen but were coming under attack on each side, from the wings of Morgan's forces. The wild bulls were driven at the rear battalion of the privateers, in the hope that they would break up their formation. However, the marksmen on the exposed last rank of the rear turned to face the bulls. They waved flags and shot the leading bulls, causing most of the herd to turn and stampede through its drovers. Meanwhile, Morgan's vanguard and wings carried on picking off the Spanish cavalry and infantry with their fast and accurate firing.

After two hours of hard fighting, many of the Spanish lay dead on the field of battle. Most of the cavalrymen and their horses were among the fallen, and the few remaining survivors fled. The infantry, seeing their superiors retreating, knew they had no chance of victory. They fired one last shot, threw down their weapons, and ran in all directions to try to escape. The privateers, exhausted after their journey and the exertions of the battle, did not generally follow them. When they did come across a number of the retreating enemy, in the reeds of a stream nearby, they were immediately shot. A group of gray friars (Franciscans) was also captured. They were taken to Morgan. He ordered them to be shot with pistols despite their pleas for mercy.

Below: The Spanish cavalry proved to be no match for Morgan's sharpshooters, as portrayed in this engraving.

They had expected the Spanish to flee after their severe losses. Instead there was strong cannon fire, sending pieces of iron shot, or grapeshot, into their midst, and a fusillade of musket-fire.

Below: An unattributed engraving shows Morgan's men with the Franciscan friars.

Opposite page: Valuable silks and tapestries were often taken as booty. This silk, depicting Christopher Columbus, was embroidered in 16th-century Spain.

Morgan interviewed a captured cavalry captain, who had been found wounded on the battlefield. He was informed that the Spanish had 400 cavalry, 24 companies of 100 foot-soldiers, 600 Indians, and a number of Negros and half-breeds, who were in charge of the 2,000 bulls. In addition, Morgan was told that there were gun emplacements in the city, surrounded by trenches and reinforced with meal-sacks. There was also a fort with eight brass cannon and 50 soldiers, past which Morgan's men must march. Morgan changed his line of march to avoid it but first reviewed his forces. He had lost some men but found that they had killed and wounded more Spaniards than had been thought. There were 600 dead plus the wounded and prisoners, so the buccaneers were heartened that the opposing forces had been hurt so much. They viewed the next battle, if there were to be one, as likely to be easier than the one they had survived. After a rest, they again pledged their allegiance to one another and restarted their march, taking their prisoners with them.

They were surprised by the strength of the city's defenses. They had expected the Spanish to flee after their severe losses. Instead there was strong cannon fire, sending pieces of iron shot, or grapeshot, into their midst and a fusillade of musket-fire. The main streets had breastworks composed of full sacks of meal and each was defended by batteries of cannon. Fighting was difficult, street by street, and the privateers suffered far more losses than they had on the plain. However, they were so determined that they slowly pushed the defenders back, and after three hours of violent fighting the Spaniards left the city.

The buccaneers searched for booty, but the long warning of their approach had allowed the town's citizens to take their goods away and hide them. Despite the forewarning, there were several warehouses well-stocked with silks, cloths, linen, and other items of value. Morgan issued a command that no one should drink any wine, saying he had intelligence that it had been poisoned. Many believed that he said this to keep his men sober, in case of an unexpected attack from the Spanish.

DRINK AND CAROUSING

Pirates were often drunk because there was little alternative liquid. Barrels of water quickly became slimy and water carried all types of illnesses. Cider, beer, and wine were preferred to water, both on land and at sea. From the 17th century onward, Caribbean rum became more popular at sea than beer, which turned sour quickly. When wearing damp clothing at sea day and night and subsisting on small portions of awful food, alcohol provided much-needed calories to keep the body temperature up. Wine was stored in lead "pipes" in the West Indies, giving the seasoned alcoholic illnesses such as the "dry gripes." Glass was too fragile for use onboard, so instead the crew drank from leather jugs, which were treated with tar pitch to help them hold their shape.

DRINKING TO EXCESS

When it came to alcohol, the language was colorful. "Sucky" meant drunk. A "suck-bottle" was a drunkard. "Suck" was strong alcohol, and "rum suck" was very good quality rum. To "suck one's face" was to drink heavily. There were many pirate terms for being sick from over-consumption, perhaps the most evocative being "the cat has kittened in my mouth."

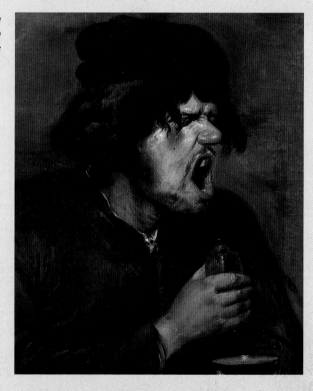

Right: Drinking was the privateer's delight. This Flemish painting, The Bitter Draught, *dates from the early 17th century.*

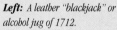

Left: A leather "blackjack" or alcohol jug of 1712.

RUMFUSTIAN AND PUNCH

Rumfustian was a popular hot pirate drink blended from raw eggs, sugar, sherry, beer, and gin. "Rumbullion" was stronger—"the demon offspring of rumfustian." To make punch, distilled alcohol or wine was mixed with tea, fruit juice, sugar, spices, and lime juice. Pirates often drank it from a ladle out of the bowl. Taverns were often referred to as punch-houses.

Above: *The windmill at the Trois-Rivières rum distillery in Martinique.*

RUM

Rum was called variously "grog," "the pirates' drink," "kill-devil," "Barbados water," "demon water," and "Nelson's blood." It was plentiful in the Caribbean as it was easily made from sugar cane. It was distilled from the 1640s onward, so is considered to be the world's oldest distilled spirit.

"SODOM OF THE NEW WORLD"

Port Royal was the largest English or French settlement in the New World outside Boston. In 1680, there were over 100 licensed taverns for a population of 3,000. By 1690, 1 in 4 of its buildings were "brothels, gaming houses, taverns and grog shops." A 17th-century clergyman returned to England straight away, on the same ship as he sailed out on, writing, "This town is the Sodom of the new World and since the majority of its population consists of pirates, cut-throats, whores, and some of the vilest persons in the whole of the world. I felt my permanence there was of no use."

Above: *An American engraving of pirates in a tavern. While they were on land, sea-rovers spent most of their time and money in such places.*

THREE SHEETS TO THE WIND

A "sheet" is a line used for trimming a sail to the wind. There is only one sheet on fore-and aft sails, and there are just two on a square sail set on a yardarm. On a Bermuda-rigged vessel there are two sheets for the jib-foresail and one for the main sail. Thus, a drunken man, even if he had three sheets to trim his sails and steer his course, would still be too unsteady to steer a straight course. When all three sheets were allowed to run free, they were said to be "in the wind," and the ship would lurch and stagger. If the boat is "three sheets to the wind," the sails are not drawing wind and the ship will not make progress, but drift downwind.

Left: *Colored engraving from the 19th century of Henry Morgan celebrating.*

CHAPTER X

Captain Morgan sends several canoes and boats to the south sea—He sets fire to the city of Panama—Robberies and cruelties are committed there by the pirates until their return to the Castle of Chagres

c✢✧

Below: Catedral Metropolitana, in Panama's Casco Viejo (Old Quarter), took more than 100 years to build. It was finally consecrated in 1798.

Bottom: This cathedral tower, where Morgan held prisoners, is almost the only relic remaining of Old Panama.

Opposite Page: A portrait of Henry Morgan at the sacking of Old Panama, 1671.

The firing of the city

Admiral Morgan moved quickly to secure Panama, placing guards at key points both within and outside the city. After that his first command was for 25 men to seize a barque that had been grounded in mud at low tide and trapped in the port. At high tide a galleon could enter, but at low tide the sea retreated a mile, leaving only mud in the harbor. Around noon, he sent men to set fire to several great buildings but circulated a rumor that the Spaniards had started the fires. By nightfall most of the city was ablaze. The pirates tried to check the fires by blowing up houses in the path of the flames but were unsuccessful. Most houses were made of lumber, usually of cedar, and many of the finest contained embroideries and magnificent paintings that had not been sent away.

There were 7 monasteries, a convent, a hospital, a cathedral, and a parish church, all burnt. These churches would normally have contained precious altar-pieces, jewels, silver, and gold, but the monks had taken all the valuables. Some 2,000 houses belonged to wealthy merchants and another 3,000 to tradesmen and other people. Many stables were also destroyed, as they were used to house the horses and mules of the king and others and were necessary to transport the silver plate to the flota in the Caribbean. In Panama's suburbs were fertile plantations, orchards, and gardens.

The Genoese had a stately and magnificent house in Panama for the trade and commerce of Negroes. This building was burnt to the ground on Morgan's command. More than 5,000 buildings were consumed by the fires, and a further 200 warehouses met the same fate. Some contained meal, and many were full of slaves hiding from the pirates, but all were destroyed. The fires persisted for 4 weeks, during which time the pirates were encamped outside the city, expecting that the Spanish would regroup and attack again.

Morgan had lost many men. His wounded were kept in the only church left standing. Despite the reduced state of his forces and the threat of a Spanish attack, he now sent 150 men to Chagres Castle to report the news of victory. The main body of the buccaneers escorted the party out of and away from the city, watched by several parties of Spaniards. Several times Morgan's men tried to attack them, but they moved away at the first sign of aggression. That afternoon Morgan moved his men into the city, but there was hardly any building left inhabitable. They raked through the ashes for melted gold or silver and found many precious articles hidden in wells and cisterns.

The escape of the treasure galleon

Still under surveillance from the Spanish, on the next day Morgan equipped 2 troops of pirates, 150 men in each, under the command of John Davis. They were instructed to discover where the inhabitants were hiding and after 2 days of searching brought back more than 200 prisoners—men, women, and slaves. The same day the captured barque returned with 3 boats taken off Taboga and Taboquilla. The

pirates had just missed capturing a treasure galleon laden with the king's plate and gold, silver, and jewels belonging to Panama's richest merchants. There were also nuns onboard, keeping watch over the treasures of Panama's churches. The ship would have been easy to capture—she was armed with only 7 cannon and 12 muskets. She had left port so quickly that she had only mainmast topsails and not enough water for her long voyage to Spain.

The pirates learnt of it by taking 7 men in the ship's boat, who had been sent ashore to fetch precious water. Unfortunately, Davis was too preoccupied drinking and entertaining some Spanish female prisoners, and the galleon managed to limp away. The next day, he realized his mistake and set off in chase, but the Spaniards had assumed that their boat had been taken by the buccaneers, since it could not be found. When he heard of the blunder, Morgan was furious and immediately fitted out and sent all 4 barques in port along with 120 men, to search for the galleon. Prisoners had told him that they thought they knew where the ship would go for shelter. After 8 fruitless days, they returned to Taboga and Taboquilla. They found there a good ship from Payta, laden with sugar, biscuits, cloth and soap, and carrying 20,000 pieces of eight. There was no resistance. Another ship carrying prisoners from the islands was also taken back to Panama.

The convoy sent to Chagres returned, bearing good news for their admiral. Two of the ships he had left there were at sea, cruising the estuary in readiness, should the fort be attacked. This could hopefully

JOHN DAVIS AND THE TREASURE GALLEON

It seems that the real identity of John Davis was Robert Searle, who was based at Port Royal, Jamaica. He captained the eight-gun *Cagway* under Christopher Myngs in attacks on Santa Marta, in Colombia, and Santiago de Cuba, and he was involved in a number of expeditions and raids in the Caribbean thereafter.

In Morgan's expedition to Panama, Davis was given the task of preventing any Spanish ships from escaping the port. Davis discovered and repaired a barque, which the Spaniards had tried to burn, and used her to capture three other ships. He and his crew carried on searching coastal areas for hidden ships, taking prisoners from the islands where they stopped.

On Taboga, his men discovered a hidden store of Peruvian wine. By that evening, most were too drunk to move or even post lookouts, so no one saw a Spanish galleon coming from seaward to anchor. This ship lowered a boat full of empty casks to fetch fresh water. By luck, the privateers surprised and captured the

Spanish boat's seven-man crew. Davis threatened them with torture and found out that the ship had been the 400-ton *Santissima Trinidad*, laden with Spanish silver plate and huge quantities of gold, pearls, jewels, and other precious goods belonging to the richest merchants of Panama.

Davis ordered his men to seize the galleon, but they were too inebriated to obey. The captain of the treasure ship, alarmed when his men failed to return and suspicious of the barque moored nearby, weighed anchor and fled. He was out of sight by dawn. Following this incident Davis was reprimanded by Morgan and never regained his favor. Years later, the Spanish captain of the *Santissima Trinidad* was captured in the Pacific by the English privateer, William Dampier, and told the story of his narrow escape.

An example of Spanish treasure, this silver goblet was produced in South America during the 17th century. Captain Morgan and his contemporaries battled ferociously for such booty.

give time for the other ships to reach the open seas. They came across a Spanish ship in sight of the castle and began the chase. The pirates in the castle immediately ran up Spanish flags, and the Spanish captain sailed into the harbor at Chagres, hoping to be saved from the chasing pirates. However, he and all his men were taken prisoner. The ship was found to be carrying mainly provisions. The men Morgan had left were running out of food, so the ship's cargo was worth more to them than silver plate.

More torture at the hands of the pirates

With this news, Morgan decided that he could spend more time in the province of Panama ensuring that he had looted anything worth taking back with him. Bands of 200 pirates were sent out daily on expeditions, and when they returned, another band was equipped and sent out. Before long they were accumulating more riches and capturing prisoners, who were tortured for information about where they had hidden their valuables. In the meantime, Morgan's ships at Chagres resumed their pirating activities. They were safer in the open seas or the estuary, prepared for action, than they would be anchored in the port or in the harbor roads.

One of the prisoners taken outside Panama was a servant from a rich gentleman's house. He himself was a poor man, but he had stolen a fine shirt and silk breeches to replace his rags. There was a silver key in the pocket of the trousers, and he was tortured to discover which cabinet or chest the key fitted.

Above: Howard Pyle's painting shows Morgan's men returning to Panama after searching for loot. The pirate on the right has brought a bloody souvenir back with him.

Still with no confession, they wolded him, that is twisted a cord around his forehead until his eyes appeared as big as eggs, ready to fall out of his skull.

Right: The merchant's wife who enamored Morgan would have been dressed in a similar style to the sitter in this painting, *The Countess of Valencia* (1690–1692), painted by Claudio Coello (1642–93).

He told his torturers that he had found the key in a rich man's house, but they did not believe him and put him on the rack. Still with no confession, they wolded him, that is twisted a cord around his forehead until his eyes appeared as big as eggs, ready to fall out of his skull. As he had no answer for them, they strung him up by his genitals, beat him, and then cut off his nose and ears, before singeing his face with burning straw so that he could no longer speak or scream. As he was close to death and could tell them nothing, they ordered a Negro to put a lance through his body.

The beautiful prisoner

No persons were spared from the cruelty of the pirates, and members of the religious community were given less quarter than others, unless they had large sums of money available for ransom. Women were also badly used, as in the case of Captain Morgan. As soon as any beautiful woman was brought into his presence, he used every means available to bend her to his will. For instance, there was a gentleman's wife from the islands of Taboga and Taboquilla, who was young and unsurpassed in beauty amongst European women. Her husband, a rich merchant, was on business in Peru. Morgan commanded that she should have her own apartment and a Negro woman to wait on her and that she should be treated with the greatest respect. The lady begged to be placed among her relations, fearing the admiral's designs on her chastity, but Morgan told her she would be safer under his protection, and she received victuals from his own table.

The enraged Morgan had her locked up in solitary confinement. Her clothes were taken away, and she was fed on a starvation diet.

The woman now came to believe that Morgan was indeed a gentleman and that the pirates were not as evil as had been supposed. She had even heard that they did not believe in Jesus Christ or the Holy Trinity. When the Spanish army had left the city to fight the buccaneers, the soldiers' wives had asked them to bring back souvenirs from the ladrones, or robbers, and some had wanted to go out and watch the pirates being slaughtered. However, their husbands had refused, saying that the pirates were all deformed beasts. When these women saw the pirates, they exclaimed, "Jesus, los ladrones son como los españoles!" ("Jesus, the robbers are like the Spanish!") The merchant's wife, misunderstanding Morgan's false civility, said "Los ladrones son tan corteses, como si fueron Espanoles." ("The robbers are as courteous as if they were Spanish.")

Morgan's advances are rebuffed

Every day Morgan visited the church where his prisoners were held and especially the room where the gentlewoman was kept. He looked in on her through the lattice screen, made conversation with her in Spanish, and allowed her friends to visit her. After three days of this treatment, he sent the lady a note asking her to consent to his will. After receiving no response, on the fourth day he asked her in person, giving her gifts of jewels and gold. The lady refused his advances, at which point Morgan became threatening, promising her a thousand tortures and cruelties at his hands. She remained resolute in her defiance, telling him "Sir, my life is in your hands; but as to my body, in relation to that which you would persuade me to do, my soul shall sooner be separated from it, through the violence of your arms, than I shall condescend to your request."

Below: This map shows Morgan's route to Panama. The Spanish never expected a land attack from the Atlantic.

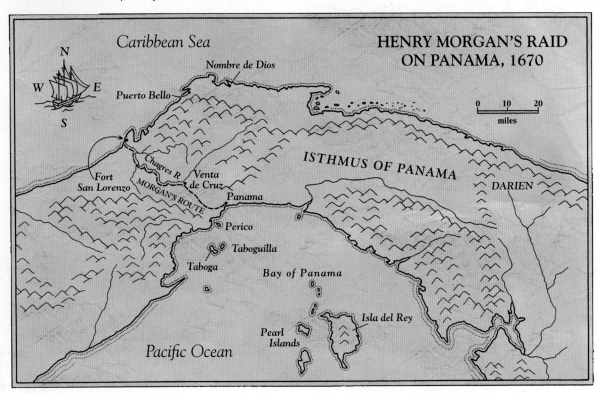

Right: These Franciscan martyrs were painted by Don Juan Carreno de Miranda (1614–1685). Pirates in the Caribbean, including Morgan, were suspicious of Spanish priests: This was the era of the Inquisition.

The enraged Morgan had her locked up in solitary confinement. Her clothes were taken away, and she was fed on a starvation diet. Her resolve did not weaken, and she prayed to God to give her the strength to resist Morgan's violence. Morgan's excuse for his treatment of her was that she had been in contact with the Spanish by sending out her Negro slave with several letters. I could not believe how steadfast and courageous this woman was. Once or twice I helped by smuggling food to her.

Departure from Panama

Having stayed in Panama for three weeks, Morgan prepared to leave the burnt city. His companies were ordered to find mules to haul the spoils of the city to the river eight leagues away, where the canoes were moored. At this time, 100 pirates colluded to take the largest ship from Panama port, rove the South Sea, and return to Europe via the East Indies. They began to gather previously hidden provisions—muskets, powder, and cannon—but Morgan was alerted to their plan. He commanded that the mainmast of the ship was to be cut down and burnt, along with those of all the other boats in the port.

All the guns in the castle, batteries, and ships, were spiked. Morgan sent prisoners to try to ransom men, women, and slaves, and also some monks to ransom their brethren. Intelligence had been received from prisoners that the president of Panama had laid ambuscades for when the privateers left Panama,

*T*he defenders he had left there had sometimes to kill the buzzards, which were feeding off the dead Spaniards, to stave off their own hunger pangs.

so scouts were also sent out. They returned with new prisoners, who said that the president had wanted to effect these plans but could find no troops willing to carry out his orders, and his men had deserted.

On February 14th, 1671, Morgan left Panama with 175 mules laden with silver, gold, and other precious items, plus 600 prisoners. After traveling a league outside the city, they encamped in a circle by a river, with the prisoners in the centre. All night long the prisoners called out, not wanting to leave their city. The women were crying for their starving children and pleaded on their knees with Morgan to let them go. Morgan coldly replied that he did not have any interest in their moaning, just their money. If ransoms were paid, they would be released. He had kept them on short rations, almost starving, because that way their pleas for ransom would be all the stronger.

The march moved on the next day, made up of a vanguard of privateers, prisoners in the middle, and pirates as a rearguard, constantly prodding, punching, and pushing their prisoners to march more quickly. The sun came high ahead, and the path was tortuous. The beautiful woman who Morgan had tried to seduce was led between two pirates, crying. She told them that she had asked two monks to fetch money she had hidden, so she could pay her ransom, but they had used it to free some of their brothers instead. The privateers did not believe her, but a slave brought her a letter confirming this, and Morgan let her go, seizing the monks in her place. They were released three days later, their ransoms paid by their brothers. The party next arrived at Venta de Cruz on the River Chagres, and Morgan gave the prisoners three days to bring in their ransoms or be transported to Jamaica. Rice and maize was collected to provision his ships. Some ransoms were paid and prisoners released. The buccaneers left Venta de Cruz by canoe and on foot, taking all the booty they could carry.

The privateers are searched

About halfway to Chagres Castle, Morgan made all his men line up in their companies. Every man was made to swear that he had not concealed any booty, gold, silver, pearls, ambergris, or diamonds—not even a sixpence. Telling his men that he had known some false fellows to lie, he commanded that every man should be searched and their satchels all inspected, having previously agreed this plan with each of his captains and confidantes. One man from each company searched all the others before suffering the same indignity. Morgan and his captains were also searched before the march carried on.

The boats, canoes, mule-train, and marchers arrived at the Castle of Chagres on March 19th. All was well, except that most of the wounded who had been left there had died of their wounds, hunger, or fever. The defenders sometimes had to kill the buzzards, which fed off the dead Spaniards, to stave off their own hunger pangs. These birds are the size of turkeys. The first time I saw them, I mistakenly shot two, thinking they were so. Great devourers of flesh, four will eat an ox or a horse in just a day. As quickly as they eat, they get rid of it at the other end. Being timid birds, they will not attack any living animal, even a small one, if it is still able to move.

Below: These Turkey Vultures (also known as buzzards) feed on carrion. They soar to great heights, but have a well-developed sense of smell that allows them to focus quickly on dead or dying animals.

he pirates who stayed at Chagres Castle said that when the buzzards first flew down to pick at the corpses, they were so thin that there was not more than two ounces of flesh on their whole bodies. After a fortnight's feasting, however, they were as fat as turkeys.

Their beaks cannot pierce an animal's skin, so they peck out the eyes to make a hole and laboriously creep into the belly of the animal and eat it from the inside, leaving only its skin and bones.

They do terrible damage to herds in the fields. When a cow, mare, or sheep gives birth, they will swoop down and peck out the eyes of the newborn calf, foal, or lamb. Whole flocks of them followed the hunters just as they now follow buccaneers, for no expedition exists without rich pickings for these birds, of either men or animals. Their presence warned the Spanish of the privateers' presence. When they saw a flock, they would say "The corsairs are coming." Buzzards are found on the American continent and on some of the islands, such as Cuba or Jamaica. Some say there were many on Hispaniola but that they were driven out by witchcraft. They are found in and around towns, where they scavenge on any refuse that is thrown out. You can always see them on the tops of churches and houses, on the alert. As soon as any meat or anything else is thrown out of a house, instantly 10 or 20 of them swoop down for it. They can fast for a long time—the experts say that they can live for a whole month without food. The pirates who stayed at Chagres Castle said that when the buzzards first flew down to pick at the corpses, they were so thin that there was not more than two ounces of flesh on their whole bodies. After a fortnight's feasting, however, they were as fat as turkeys. I include these facts as we have no such birds in Europe.

The sharing of the booty and Morgan's betrayal

On arriving at Chagres, Morgan recommended that the booty be shared out as soon as possible, as food was so scarce. The pirates agreed to this and also to his proposal that a sloop should be sent to Puerto Bello to set the prisoners from Santa Catalina free and to demand a ransom for the Castle of Chagres.

Right: The booty is shared out at Chagres before embarkation, in this Howard Pyle painting. Many pirates objected to what they considered to be their unfair allocation.

The ship returned just two days later, with a curt Spanish refusal to treat with Morgan, informing him that the English could do what they pleased to the castle. Immediately Morgan began sharing out the proceeds of the expedition, but there were many complaints, as each man only received 200 pieces of eight. The silver plate was reckoned as being worth only 10 pieces of eight per pound, various jewels were dirt cheap, and many jewels also seemed to be missing, for which Morgan was blamed. However, he would hear no complaints or accusations. Seeing the opinion of his followers swing against their leader, he demolished the castle's walls, burnt its buildings, and placed its brass guns on his ship.

Without calling a privateer council, he then immediately set sail with no warning, followed out by only three or four ships commanded by his closest captains. Some of the French ships gave chase, as they believed that these ships had concealed most of the dividend of the expedition. However, they had to return, being neither victualled nor provisioned for a voyage to Jamaica. Admiral Morgan had left nothing for his luckless pursuers, and the vast majority of the members of the expedition were stuck in their ships at Chagres, beside a burning fort and without food.

Above: Morgan and his favorite captains set sail unexpectedly for Port Royal, in this unattributed engraving.

GLOSSARY

acajou apple – the edible fruit of the cashew tree (*Anacardium occidentale*).

ambergris – a waxlike substance originating as a secretion in the intestines of the sperm whale. It can be found floating in tropical seas and is used in perfume manufacture.

asiento (or assiento) – Spanish for "agreement." Refers specifically to the permission granted by the Spanish government to other countries to sell slaves to the Spanish colonies, 1543–1834.

azagaya (also assegai or assagai) – a spear-like weapon with an iron point, used for throwing.

bandolier – a shoulder belt with loops or pockets to hold cartridges.

barbacoa (or barbecu) – the Taíno Indian fire-pit used for cooking, from which "barbecue" comes.

barque – a three-masted sailing ship, in which the foremast and mainmast are square-rigged, and the mizzenmast rigged fore-and-aft.

bezoar stone – stony concretions found in the intestines of mostly ruminant animals, sought after because they were believed to be an antidote against any poison, or as precious gems like pearls.

bondservant (or bondsman) – a person bound into service without wages.

boucan – a French term for the framework of green wood used by *boucaniers* as a grill for cooking meat (see buccaneer).

buccaneer – from the French *boucanier*, which referred to the hunters of wild bulls and cows, who cooked their meat on a *boucan*. This term later came to refer to pirates.

brûlot (also fireship) – a ship loaded with burning material and explosives and set adrift, to ignite and blow up an enemy's ships.

cacique – a native chief, in Latin America and the Spanish-speaking Caribbean.

caltrop – a spiked metal ball thrown on the ground to impede cavalry horses.

careen – to turn a ship on its side for cleaning, caulking, or repair.

carrack – a large merchant ship operating in European waters from the 14th to the 17th century.

chata – a flat-bottomed boat.

copal – the resin obtained from various tropical trees, used to make varnish.

corsair – a pirate operating along the southern coast of the Mediterranean in the 17th century; also used to describe a pirate ship.

cromster – a small ship used for work inshore during the 16th and 17th centuries.

derroterro (or derrotero) – a set of sailing directions used by the Spanish in the 16th and 17th centuries, which showed views of the coast drawn from seaward; the equivalent Portuguese word, *roteiro*, became the French *routier*, and the English *rutter*.

doubloon – a Spanish gold coin, from *doblón*, meaning double, referred to as such because it was worth twice the value of the pistole, a coin used throughout Europe in the 17th and 18th centuries.

dropsy – a condition characterized by an excess of watery fluid collecting in the tissues of the body, now called edema.

fathom – a unit of length equal to six feet, used chiefly in reference to the depth of water.

flota (also Silver Fleet and Plate Fleet) – the Spanish convoy of ships transporting European goods to the Spanish colonies in the Americas and gold and silver back to Spain from the 16th to the 18th century.

flyboat (also saetia) – any of various small, swift boats.

freebooter – a pirate or lawless adventurer.

furstic (or fustic) – a tropical American tree with heartwood that yields dyes.

gabion – a container of wickerwork, filled with earth or stone and used in fortifications.

galliot – a small, fast galley widely used in the Mediterranean.

grog – spirits, typically rum, diluted with water; reputedly from "Old Grog," the nickname of Admiral Vernon (1684–1757), who first ordered diluted rum to be served to sailors.

hoy – a small, single-masted coastal sailing vessel, typically rigged fore-and-aft.

hundredweight (or short hundredweight) – a unit of weight equal to 100 pounds; a twentieth of a ton. A long hundredweight (used in the United Kingdom) was equal to 112 pounds.

ladrone – robber or brigand.

landlubber – a person unfamiliar with the sea or sailing.

league – the former measure of distance on land; equivalent to about three miles.

letter of marque – a license to equip an armed vessel and use it in the capture of enemy merchant shipping and to commit acts that would otherwise be deemed piracy.

liana – a woody climbing plant that hangs from trees in tropical rainforests.

maiz – the Spanish term for maize or corn.

mal d'estomac – French for "bad stomach."

mammee apple – the edible fruit of the *Mammea americana* tree, similar to the mangosteen.

man-of-war – an armed naval sailing ship.

matate – Indian slaves used by the Spaniards.

mattock – a digging and grubbing tool with features of an axe or pick

moidore – a Portuguese gold coin that was widely used in England in the 18th century, with a value equivalent to 27 English shillings.

montera cap – headgear similar to that worn by Spanish bullfighters.

nopal – a cactus; the edible, fleshy pads are widely used in Mexican cuisine.

palliasse – a straw mattress.

parley – a conference held between opposing sides in a dispute.

pateraras – a device that fired stones or a mortar piece.

pieces of eight – silver Spanish coins or dollars worth four pesetas or eight reales. In the 17th and 18th centuries there were so many in circulation that they were accepted almost anywhere in the world.

pipe – a device used for firing several muskets at once.

piragua (or pirogue) – a small, flat-bottomed boat used by West African fishermen and the Cajuns of the Louisiana marsh; not intended for overnight travel but light enough to be taken onto land.

press gang – a force who conscripted people to serve in the military or navy by force and without notice, used by the British Royal Navy from 1664 until the early 19th century.

privateer – an armed ship, privately owned, which held a government commission and was authorized for use in war and in capturing enemy ships; also used to describe a pirate.

quarter – an act of mercy or pity afforded to an enemy or opponent.

roadstead – a sheltered stretch of water near the shore where ships can ride at anchor.

seadog – an old or experienced sailor.

shanty (or chanty) – a song with alternating solo and chorus, sung by sailors while performing physical labor.

stinkpot – small clay pot filled with burning sulfur and sometimes rotten fish, which was thrown onto the deck during a fight as a crude form of tear gas.

strappado – a form of torture in which a victim is suspended in the air by a rope attached to his hands, which are tied behind his back.

teredos worms – ship worms that bore into wood and weaken the structure.

veycou – an alcoholic drink similar to beer, made from the fermented meal of the cassava root.

yardarm – the outer extremity of a ship's yard; the horizontal spar from which the sails hang.

FURTHER READING

Books

Breverton, Terry. *Admiral Sir Henry Morgan: The Greatest Buccaneer of Them All*. Louisiana: Pelican Publishing, 2005.

Breverton, Terry, *The Pirate Dictionary*. Louisiana: Pelican Publishing, 2004.

Cordingley, David. *Under The Black Flag*. New York: Random House, 2006.

Earle, Peter. *The Sack of Panama: Captain Morgan and the Battle for the Caribbean*. New York: St. Martin's Press, 2007.

Galvin, Peter R. *Patterns of Pillage : A Geography of Caribbean-Based Piracy in Spanish America 1536–1718*. New York: Peter Lang Publishing, 1999.

Gerhard, Peter. *Pirates of the Pacific: 1575–1742*. Lincoln: University of Nebraska Press, 1990.

Kemp, P. H. and Lloyd, Christopher. *The Brethren of the Coast: British and French Buccaneers in the South Seas*. New York: St. Martin's Press, 1961.

Lane, Kris. *Pillaging the Empire*. New York: M.E. Sharpe, 1998.

Little, Benerson. *The Sea Rover's Practice: Pirate Tactics and Techniques 1630–1730*. Washington D.C.: Potomac Books, 2005

Little, Benerson. *The Buccaneer's Realm: Pirate Life on the Spanish Main 1674–1688*. Washington D.C.: Potomac Books, 2007.

Linebaugh, Peter and Rediker, Markus. *The Many-Headed Hydra: Sailors, Slaves, Commoners and the History of the Revolutionary Atlantic*. Boston: Beacon Press, 2000.

Rediker, Markus and Flinn, Kathleen, *The Slave Ship: A Human History,* New York: Penguin, 2007.

Talty, Stephan. *Empire of Blue Water: Captain Morgan's Great Pirate Army, the Epic Battle for the Americas, and the Catastrophe That Ended the Outlaws' Bloody Reign*. New York: Crown Publishing Group, 2007.

Winston, Alexander. *No Man Knows My Grave*. Houghton Mifflin: Boston, 1969.

Websites

www.thepirateking.com
An extensive array of information on pirates, buccaneers, and privateers, in a site run by Rob Ossian.

www.freenet.homepage.de/hawkeyepike.index
Swashbuckler's Cove is a well-organized site with timelines, biographies, pirate havens, and more.

www.inkyfingers.com/pyrates
The Pyrates' Cove includes coverage of pirates' weapons, crime and punishment, ships, and flags, which will stimulate readers to widen their research.

www.piratesoul.com
Pirate Soul is a simple, informative, and expanding site.

www.en.wikipedia.org/wiki/List_of_pirates
Wikipedia provides excellent background and links to facts on dozens of pirates and privateers.

www.gutenberg.org/etext/19564
Project Gutenberg has the complete *Pirates' Who's Who* by Philip Gosse.

www.nationalgeographic.com/pirates/
Pirate fun for children from National Geographic.

www.piratesinfo.com/main.php
Handy, quick-fire material on famous pirates and how they lived.

INDEX

ACKNOWLEDGMENTS

Sources: AKG = akg-images, London BAL = Bridgeman Art Library AA = The Art Archive   MEPL = Mary Evans Picture Library Scala = Scala, Florence

b = bottom c = centre t= top l = left r= right

Pages: 1 Getty Images/Hulton; 4-5 BAL/Royal Geographical Society; 8 Topfoto; 9 Corbis/Blue Lantern Studio; 10-12 Esquemeling, J, *The Buccaneers of America 1684-1685,* Routledge, 1928; 14-15 & 16 BAL; 17t Corbis; 17b Topfoto; 18tl Alamy; 18b MEPL; 19t Marshall Editions, London; 20 Topfoto/Roger Viollet; 21 MEPL; 22bl Scala/DeAgostini Collection; 22br AA/General Archive of the Indies Seville; 23 & 24t Corbis/Owen Franken; 24b Photo Library/Oxford Scientific Films; 25 Corbis/Stapleton Collection; 26 Scala/The Pierpont Morgan Library; 27 MEPL 28 Alamy; 30 BAL/Bibliotheque Nationale, Paris, France, Archives Charmet; 31 MEPL; 32 BAL/Historique de la Marine, Vincennes, France; 35 BAL/Private Collection; 36 DK Images; 38-39 AKG; 40 MPL; 41BAL/Fitzwilliam Museum, University of Cambridge; 42 Library of Congress/ Manuscript Division; 43 BAL/The Stapleton Collection; 44tl AA/ Eileen Tweedy; 44bl AA/Biblioteca Nacional Madrid / Gianni Dagli Orti; 44br Art Directors/Trip; 45t Corbis/Macduff Everton; 45cr Oronoz; 45b AA; 46 BAL/Library/Delaware Art Museum, Wilmington, USA, Gift of Dr James Stillman; 48 BAL/Private Collection; 49 AKG/Rabatti-Domingie; 50 BAL/Private Collection; 51l Image from Exquemelin, A.O., *Los Piratas de America.* Editora de Santo Domingo, Spain 1979; 51r AKG/Staatliche Kunstslgen, Ruestkammer; 54 DK Images; 55 Pierre_ LeGrand; 56 MEPL; 57 The British Library, London; 58t Scala/HIP; 58b AA; 58-59 Corbis/Bohemian Nomad Picturemakers; 60tScala/HIP; 60b AA/Musee Conde Chantilly/Dagli Orti; 61 BAL/Prado, Madrid; 62 Esquemeling, John, *The History of the Buccaneers of America,* Sanborn, Carter and Bazin: Boston, 1856; 63 BAL/British Library, London; 64 BAL/Private Collection/Peter Newark American Pictures; 66t BAL/Musee Carnavalet, Paris/Giraudon; 66b Corbis/James L. Amos; 66bl Getty Images; 66l, 67trl, 67tc, 67bl, 67br Images courtesy of DK Images; 69 DeAgostini/The Indies Archives; 70t Scala/HIP; 70b Image courtesy of Terry Breverton; 71Corbis/Stapleton Collection; 72 Topfoto/HIP; 73AKG; 74 Corbis/Bettmann; 75 Exquemelin, A.O., *The Buccaneers of America,* Editora Taller, 1992; 76 BAL/Library of Congress, Washington D.C; 77 South American Pictures; 78 Corbis/Jonathan Blair; 79 National Maritime Museum; 80 DeAgostini; 82 Corbis/Jonathan Blair; 83 Jupiter Images; 84bl The Lordprice Collection; 84br National Maritime Museum; 85tr Corbis/Joel W. Rogers; 85cl & 85br *A Concise Guide to Ships,* Hamlyn, 1973; 87 Topfoto/Fotomas; 88 Corbis/David Muench; 89 AA/Galleria Estense, Modena/Dagli Orti; 90 AA/Biblioteca Nazionale Marciana Venice/Dagli Orti; 93 BAL/Library of Congress, Washington D.C; 95 AA/Navy Historical Service Vincennes France/ Dagli Orti; 96-97 BAL/Service Historique de la Marine, Vincennes, France; 98 BAL /Peter Newark Pictures; 100 National Archives/Public Records Office, London; 101 MEPL; 102 Corbis 103 Corbis/Danny Lehman; 104 MEPL; 105 AKG; 106 National Maritime Museum; 107 Photos12.com/Oronoz; 108tl AKG; 108tr AA; 109 BAL; 110 MEPL; 111 AA; 112 Photos12.com/Oronoz; 113tl BAL/Aisa;113tr Hispanic Society; 114t Alamy; 114b MEPL; 115 Exquemelin, A.O., *De Americaenesche Zee-Rovers,* Amsterdam, 1678; 116 BAL/Aisa; 117 AA/Museo del Prado Madrid;118t Eye Ubiquitous; 118bl Scala/British Library/HIP; 118br MEPL; 119tr BAL; 119c & 119b Courtesy of DK Images; 120 Photos12.com/Oronoz; 121t Courtesy of Piratedocuments.com; 123 BAL; 125 Corbis/Richard Cummins; 126 Exquemelin, A.O., *De Americaenesche Zee-Rovers,* Amsterdam, 1678; 127 Scala/HIP; 128 BAL/Private Collection; 130 Courtesy of DK Images; 131tl BAL/Art Museum, Mass; 131tr BAL/Archives Charmet; 131b Wellcome Images; 132b AKG; 133 BAL/Private Collection' 136 & 137 Getty Images/Hulton;139 BAL; 141 AGE Fotostock; 143 BAL; 144 Scala/New York Public Library; 145 Eye Ubiquitous; 146l Superstock/Frederick Judd Waugh; 146r BAL/Private Collection; 147t BAL; 147c National Maritime Museum; 147b BAL; 149 MEPL; 150 BAL/Philip Mould Ltd, London; 151 Corbis/Jeremy Horner; 153t MEPL; 153b South American Pictures; 155 Corbis/Richard Bickel; 156 Corbis; 157 AGE Fotostock; 158bl, 158bc & 158br MEPL; 159 DK Images; 161AKG; 162 Corbis/Blaine Harrington; 163 Corbis/Richard Hamilton Smith; 164 AA; 165 Photos12.com/Oronoz; 167 Lord Price Collection; 168 AGE Fotostock/Ken Welsh; 169 Corbis/Bettman; 170 AGE Fotostock/Richard T. Nowitz; 171 Getty Images/Hulton; 172 MEPL; 173 BAL/Giraudon; 174l BAL/Ashmolean Museum, University of Oxford; 174r AA/Musee des Beaux Arts Dijon/Dagli Orti; 175t Alamy/Banana Pancake; 75cr BAL/Peter Newark's Pictures; 175b AKG; 176t Alamy/Humberto Olarte Cupas; 177 Getty Images/Hulton; BAL/Thomas Lumley Antiques, London; 179 MEPL; 180 BAL/Instituto de Valencia de Don Juan, Madrid; 181 Marshall Editions, image from Esquemeling, J., *The Buccaneers of America,* William Swan Stallybrass (ed.), George Routledge & Sons, 1924; 182 BAL/Museo de Santa Cruz, Toledo; 183 Corbis/Academy of Natural Sciences of Philadelphia; 184 & 185 MEPL.